KT-370-516

My England Years

Sir Bobby
Charlton

My England Years

THE AUTOBIOGRAPHY

with James Lawton

headline

Copyright © 2008 Sir Bobby Charlton

The right of Sir Bobby Charlton to be identified as the Author of
the Work has been asserted by him in accordance with the
Copyright, Designs and Patents Act 1988.

First published in 2008 by
HEADLINE PUBLISHING GROUP

2

Apart from any use permitted under UK copyright law, this publication may
only be reproduced, stored, or transmitted, in any form, or by any means,
with prior permission in writing of the publishers or, in the case of
reprographic production, in accordance with the terms of licences issued
by the Copyright Licensing Agency.

Every effort has been made to fulfil requirements with regard to reproducing
copyright material. The author and publisher will be glad to rectify any
omissions at the earliest opportunity.

Cataloguing in Publication Data is available from the British Library

Hardback ISBN 978 0 7553 1621 2
Trade paperback ISBN 978 0 7553 1781 3

Typeset in Baskerville MT by
Palimpsest Book Production Limited, Grangemouth, Stirlingshire

Printed and bound in Great Britain by
Clays Ltd, St Ives plc

Headline's policy is to use papers that are natural, renewable and
recyclable products and made from wood grown in sustainable forests.
The logging and manufacturing processes are expected to conform to
the environmental regulations of the country of origin.

HEADLINE PUBLISHING GROUP
An Hachette Livre UK Company
338 Euston Road
London NW1 3BH

www.headline.co.uk
www.hachettelivre.co.uk

For Sir Alf Ramsey, Bobby Moore, Alan Ball and the rest of the lads without whom I would not have this story to tell

CONTENTS

Acknowledgements

As I attempted to do before, in the first volume of my memoirs, *My Manchester United Years*, I hope that in the following pages I have given credit to all those to whom I owe a debt of gratitude for helping me so generously on my way. The cast list of helpers, and great opponents, is vast and I have tried to mention them all. Above everything, is my thanks to the game which has allowed me to see and enjoy so much of the world that shares my love for football – the greatest game of them all.

In the production of *My England Years* I am grateful, again, for the enthusiasm and support and skill of my editor David Wilson, and my friend and collaborator James Lawton. Thanks also go to Rhea Halford and Louise Rothwell for all their hard work, skill and enthusiasm.

I would also like to thank Kerr MacRae, who has been a huge support from the very outset of the writing of my story, and also Georgina Moore and her team who have organised my signing events and publicity activities with great professionalism and understanding.

PROLOGUE

THE RAREST, AND the greatest, feeling I have ever known as a footballer is that on at least one day I had everything I needed to produce the very best of myself. Almost every run, every pass, every decoy move was fuelled by certainty.

I felt I could run forever in any company, including the one in which I seemed to be sharing every stride and every heartbeat, that of the great young Franz Beckenbauer, who had been thrown against me, as I had been set upon him.

This did not result in one of those spectacular goals that helped build my reputation down the years, but it gave me a deeper sense than ever before that I had done everything expected of me for the good of the team.

That summed up the ethos of this group of players – the team. There were no stars, no egos, no possibility of anyone failing to understand what precisely he had to do, or believing that he had a role somehow separate from all those around him. The tacklers tackled and the runners ran, and it was clear that they would keep doing it until the job was done. Then if it was undone, as it was so late in the game, well, it had to be done again. There could only be this time, this game. There was nothing beyond it. Nothing, at least, worth thinking about until the matter was settled.

That day locked into my heart and my consciousness so strongly that I knew, as it was happening, that it would never dim. Whenever there is the need, I can reach for it as easily as I turn the page of my morning newspaper. It is the diamond of my days – 30 July 1966.

Of all my time in football it was the day that brought the deepest satisfaction, the cleanest, least complicated sense of achievement. I knew immediately it would always be shared with the nation, and yet I could also keep it as the most treasured football possession. I know my fellow professionals, with whom I lived it most intimately, felt the same.

On that day, when I helped England win the World Cup, I also learned that a perfect team performance was possible. I found out that if you gave enough of yourself, in the company of team-mates who were of the same mind and spirit and who trusted the leadership they had been given as deeply as you did, you could master anything that was put before you. You could come off the field without a single regret. You could get to the very heart of the game that had for so long dominated your existence.

This is the reason, above all others, that makes that summer's day in old Wembley unique in my memory, and so uplifting whenever I recall it, as I do of my own accord or by request almost every day of my life.

First, though, I should explain why the joy that came with England's victory and my own contribution was so heightened beyond anything else I had, or would, experience on a football field. Much was coloured by the still vivid memory of my first days with the England team, eight years earlier. Those moments in turn, long imagined and fondly dreamt of, were coloured by the tragedy of Munich in which I had been caught only months earlier.

No, being called by England was certainly not as I thought it would be when, as a boy, I went with my brother Jack to the cinema in Ashington to watch the grainy Pathé News film of our great relative, Jackie Milburn, making his debut against Northern Ireland. Then, no ambition could have been less clouded by doubt, not with 'Wor Jackie' already at the peak of football and the picture house billing the snippet of newsreel alongside the main feature.

The idea of wearing my nation's shirt was both possible, because of my early progress in football, and thrilling. I had set myself a series of targets – and they had all been met. I played for my school, my district, my county and then my country at schoolboy level. Professional football followed quite naturally but when the invitation from England came, it was not so simple. I had to respond to it in the time of pain that followed in the wake of Munich and seemed to change every-thing in my life.

This was made all the harder when, still mourning beloved team-mates and friends, I saw headlines announcing me as a new star who could both rally my stricken club, Manchester United, and make a major impact in the national team.

For a little while it was too much. Roger Byrne, Duncan Edwards and Tommy Taylor were key components of an England team heading for the 1958 World Cup as serious contenders, but when they fell in Munich, I became United's sole representative in the national side. It seemed as though everything was moving too fast, too chaotically. I looked at the newspapers and saw those flattering headlines, but when I looked in the mirror I saw just a boy, and one who feared he might be stretched beyond his limits.

So much was expected of me so suddenly. For a long time I had been in a deep learning process. Jimmy Murphy, Sir Matt Busby's tough assistant manager, was my mentor and he would seize on every mistake, hold up a hundred examples of where I was going wrong. On our first meeting, he had built up Duncan almost as a mythic figure, a young god of the game.

Now it seemed I was expected to take on at least something of that mantle – and those expectations. The newspapers painted a picture of a boy who had become a man overnight, and one whose future for both United and England was completely assured. Headlines such as 'Bobby Dazzler' filled me with more apprehension than pleasure.

There were so many matches to play, and numerous emotional ordeals to be borne, often provoked by people who wanted to talk about Munich, to offer sympathy, when so much of my world had been lost, maybe beyond recovery, on the snowy airfield in Germany. All of a sudden, playing alongside idols such as Tom Finney and Billy Wright was no longer the ultimate bonus, but another burden.

Yet, step by step, and with much good luck that accumulated down the years, I had been brought to that day at Wembley, one to which I can return so completely it might be yesterday, and never with the fear that I will find any of the shadows or the doubts that sooner or later are part of everyone's experience.

Now, perhaps more than ever, I can put the proper value on a perfect day and on the England years that took me to every corner of the world and made rivals and friends of such great men as Pelé and Franz Beckenbauer, Lev Yashin and Alfredo di Stefano.

The day England won the World Cup is where I have to start – and probably end – my account, because the lessons of it have grown stronger, more vital, each time I think of what was achieved, and how it happened. I feel this so powerfully, so unchangeably, it means that when I am asked about the future of our national game and the chances of it ever again scoring such a triumph, I invariably go back to the time when it seemed the nation had never been so united outside of days of war.

I go back to ninety minutes, and then half an hour of extra time, when everything was as it should have been; when no one neglected to run or cover for each other, or forgot for a second that the job had still to be done. I return there not as some ageing conqueror spinning out the years, but as a pilgrim who was once shown the light – a light that seemed so accessible to anyone who had their eyes even half open but, unfortunately, shone only briefly before being obscured for so many years.

It was the greatest of my days, not just because of the glory that I knew I would have with my team-mates forever, and the emotion released in the tears that streamed down my cheeks for all the world to see when I embraced Jack, and agreed that no siblings who played football could ever have shared such a moment. There was all that certainly, but something more was built into that special day.

Perhaps the most powerful sense was that we had taken ourselves beyond even our highest ambitions and found something that was somehow bigger than anything we could have imagined when we first set off. Suddenly, it wasn't about a trophy, however prestigious, or a place in the record books, and still less about a bonus of £1,000 from the Football Association. It was about how we could look at ourselves when each of us had played our last games.

We had seen what could be done when you gave everything because you knew it was right. Everything we had been asked to do, however hard it appeared to be at times, however many sacrifices of personal life it involved, and however many weeks we had to go without seeing our wives or young children, had a point and a reward that became more obvious with every success.

There was a beautiful simplicity to what happened on 30 July 1966, more so than at any point earlier or later in my career. Certainly, if we are talking about the weight of emotional baggage, there is no doubt I carried far more of it, and of much greater complexity, into the same Wembley stadium two years later.

When Manchester United beat Benfica to win the European Cup a decade after the Munich tragedy and my deepest embraces were with Sir Matt Busby and Bill Foulkes, fellow survivors of the pain that for so long we feared was beyond any kind of redemption, I was both overwhelmed by the past and liberated from it – or at least I thought so. That was something of an illusion, a comforting one no doubt as Nobby Stiles and I left our celebrating team-mates to join up with an England tour, but an illusion nonetheless. I learned quickly enough that not all the guilt of surviving Munich, when so many team-mates had died, could be banished by one night of great triumph. There were simply too many feelings, too many regrets, to parcel up neatly, even on an extraordinary night when our nerves and our skills held against one of the best teams in Europe.

When England won the World Cup, there were no such warring emotions. We had our wounded, of body and spirit, on the way to the final. The great Jimmy Greaves, one of the best players of his or any other generation of English football, would always be haunted by the day he was required to be just another spectator. But none of this took us beyond the boundaries of the game we played. They were the hurts and the disappointments that are commonplace in football. You have to understand they can happen any time, even when you are the youngest, most wide-eyed trainee professional.

My tears were untouched by any doubts or questions – and, I have to say, were entirely in keeping with my belief that it is only in victory that a competitor is entitled to cry without any fear of regret. The tears were my most natural expression of a satisfaction that filled me completely.

The keenest edge of my pleasure came from the fact that this was an effort of the purest football kind. There had been no diversions, no confusions of roles or purpose. Each man had been told what he had to do and was happy to do it because he could see the sense of it. Perhaps our play did not match that of Brazil four years earlier in Chile, or four years later in Mexico, maybe it did not light up the sky with flights of fantasy and unfathomable skill, but it was good, intelligent, honest football, built on the very best values of our English game. Above all, it rested on faith in a manager who built us up, brick by brick, man by man, into an unbreakable unit and gave us a wonderful sense of ourselves and our potential to beat the world.

Yes, there were tactical adjustments to make against an excellent German team and their young superstar Beckenbauer. Nobby had to make his tackles, Jack had to take anything high, and Bobby Moore had to read every point of defensive weakness with his unerring eye and uncanny responses, but essentially we would play to strengths developed down the years.

Most crucially, we never lost our focus, and if we had the advantage of playing all our games at Wembley, it was one that we refused to squander. This, I believe, was an ill-considered achievement in itself because along with the familiarity of the ground on which we fought, there was also the expectation and pressure that is peculiar to playing in front of your own people. This is especially so when they have been told, in the most emphatic way, that they could confidently look forward to the moment of victory and are quick to display their displeasure at the first hints of serious doubt.

Many of the following pages will inevitably centre on the work of, and the inspiration provided by, Sir Alf Ramsey. His approach was filled with so many fundamental lessons about how to make a football team, and it is very sad they have laid fallow for so long. But for the moment it is maybe enough to say that his gift to his players, and the football nation he was so desperate to make proud, was the ability to make everybody believe that if we did the right things, made enough sacrifices, the World Cup could indeed be ours.

Many of the images that are rooted in my memory are, I am sure, as familiar to all those who saw them in the stadium or on black-and-white television as they are to me. I think now to the abandoned pleasure of my friend and team-mate Nobby, whose jig of triumph is perhaps the most enduring symbol of that happiest of afternoons. I see the shudder that ran through George Cohen, our fierce and always correct full back, when

Nobby planted a kiss, wet and toothless, on his mouth. Like so many other proud Englishmen and women, I smile with pride at our captain Bobby Moore, who always looked the part, and always was the part, wiping the moisture from his hands before receiving the trophy from the Queen.

I hear the piping tones of the baby, and perhaps in some ways the hero of our team that day, Alan Ball – if we can put aside for just a moment the decisive value of Geoff Hurst's hat-trick – saying that he never wanted this day to end. I see the look of satisfaction in the eyes of some of the quieter ones, Martin Peters, Roger Hunt, Ray Wilson and Gordon Banks, and I will never forget it as long as I live.

I had never known such a unity of hope on the terraces and action on the field. We all felt the vigorous, even ecstatic, pleasure that radiated from the field of play across the whole nation, perhaps even to a degree that could almost bear comparison to Victory in Europe Day, twenty-one years earlier.

I will never put aside the rush of feeling I had for a lad whom I knew for just a short while before the tournament began and never saw again because, to me, he will always stand out as England's Everyman in that long-ago summer – the representative of the nation we had striven so hard to please.

Naturally, at such a moment of triumph you think of those closest to you and, of course, the great privilege, among so many others, was to stand shoulder to shoulder with my brother. Brothers can have their arguments and their fights, and heaven knows Jack and I have had a few that have become public property and required us to work through with some pain and embarrassment. If they are very lucky, though, they can have moments that will unite them forever in a way that goes beyond the coincidence of sharing the same womb. Jack and I had such a time, on a gilded day that would be with us for a lifetime, and we would be strange men indeed if we ever lost sight of the value of that.

Among my first thoughts were my wife Norma, who had so

transformed my life, my little daughters Suzanne and Andrea, my mother Cissie, who had been so intent on Jack and me becoming successful footballers, and my father Robert, who in his quiet and dogged way had made me both sad and proud when he said he couldn't attend the semi-final game with Portugal because he was due on shift at the colliery. That was his duty, just as mine and Jack's was to play as well as we could for England.

Yet among all those closest to me whom I had been most anxious to make proud when I woke that morning, there was another, that lad. I'd met him just a few weeks before the tournament began, and I remember his face well because it was filled with the most intense hope. In the lead-up to the World Cup he seemed to have become, forever, part of my life and, for those vital days, even my professional conscience.

His name was Trevor Atkinson and day after day on a secluded little beach in Majorca his close-cropped head popped up from behind a deckchair, a pedalo stand or a beach-side bar. I had taken Norma and the girls there for what was supposed to be a relaxing break between the stresses of a long season and the challenge that lay ahead that summer. There could be no break from football, though, when Trevor Atkinson appeared, as he did unfailingly each day. I developed a sixth sense. It told me that in the next second he would be at my side, questioning, exhorting, almost, it seemed, speaking for the nation before whom my team-mates and I would so soon have to perform.

He was not a pest because I could no more get football out of my head, immerse myself in the buckets and spades, than I could go without breath, and it was as though Trevor gave some of my tensions their point. With him at my side, I didn't have to imagine the importance of what lay ahead. He confirmed it in each of our conversations. I too was consumed by the question of whether England could win the World Cup and if this lad was passionate in his interest, and had his beliefs about how the triumph could be achieved, he also knew something of the game. He knew its quirks, its injustices, and what it required if you were to deal with all of these and still win.

He had started with Spennymoor United in my own North East country and now he was playing with Darlington. He accepted that he had gone as far as he ever would in professional football, but then he said it would always be his life.

He died some years ago and it is one of my regrets that I never had the chance, or maybe made the chance, to tell him how deeply he had entered my thinking by the time I went into the tournament, and how, in the good days and the bad ones, he was always present.

It seemed to me that if I wanted to isolate the best feelings in the country about football, and the deepest hopes, and have some idea of quite how many dreams I carried along with my team-mates when I went out on the field wearing my nation's shirt, I could do no better than choose Trevor Atkinson as my silent companion through the coming weeks.

When we struggled against Uruguay in the first match, and there was a sudden fear of anticlimax among the fans if not the team, and the boos rolled down from the terraces, I hoped that Trevor would understand that there was so much more football to be played. Even though we hadn't won, hadn't even scored, we had averted a disaster and were still well set to qualify for the quarter-finals.

I thought of Trevor when I scored the goal against Mexico in the next match, a goal that was spectacular enough to re-ignite some of the belief that had been challenged by the frustrating resistance of Uruguay. I fancied I saw him punching the air, as I did, when the shot that was so vital to our momentum swirled beyond the Mexican goalkeeper. Trevor was the point of contact, beyond my family and my fellow players, with a nation who realised their team would probably never have a better chance of winning the greatest prize in the game.

Even today, he comes into my thoughts when someone says, 'Bobby, when are we going to win the World Cup again?'

I think of the intensity and longing on his face when we sat on the sand of the little beach of Campo del Mar and discussed the threat of the Argentines, a most dangerous team, the Germans and the defending champions Brazil. Norma was never irritated by the fact that I could be so easily distracted by this stranger who came into our lives each day. I suspect that deep down she too understood that until the issue was settled, I was, like him, a prisoner of a challenge that had been embraced by so many people.

When the emotion of the field drained away, when the banqueting was done, I finally asked myself, how did we win it?

We won it because we never lost our concentration on a single aim. We won it because we had been given leadership and because we were never in any doubt about how much the people cared.

That's the reason I will never forget Trevor Atkinson, someone who did not play beyond the Third Division but who, even if he never knew it, had a role in the greatest day of English football. In a strange but compelling way, he became for me a presence as tangible as my brother Jack or Nobby in moments of success or crisis. Just like Sir Alf Ramsey, he made the call to duty.

The time is now due for another group of Englishmen to do the same. I refuse to believe that it will not happen, that the emotions that burst into life all those years ago are dead forever.

When the latest England coach, Fabio Capello, spoke to me on one of his first scouting missions in England, I was indeed heartened. Like Ramsey, he spoke in short, blunt sentences. Like Ramsey, he was immaculately dressed. He seemed to be a man who cared for detail and performance rather than reputation, and he was quite specific about his ambition. 'Charlton,' he said, 'I wish to take England to the World Cup final in South Africa.'

I was lifted by a promise of the future that might, who knew, just one day take me back to the best of England's – and my own – past. It was, I thought, time enough.

1

THE WRIGHT EXAMPLE

MUNICH HAD BEEN so cold and so cruel in February 1958. The warmth and kindness, and the thrill, I found in Glasgow just two months later might have belonged not just to a different city but to another world.

It was because of this contrast I kept up my guard for some time after the first landmark of my England career – that and a little of the feelings that had permeated through to me from a few of those who worked at the pithead when I was a boy, people who had been so wounded by life that they would always be reluctant to trust happiness.

So I scored my first goal for England. It was, if I am entirely honest, what I had always believed I was born to do. Such confidence grew from the confirmation that indeed I was among the most talented youngsters in the land. This came with my selection for England Schoolboys at the age of fifteen and my two goals against Wales in a packed and yelling Wembley. That was a day that set almost all the First Division club scouts running to my house, telling me that I was destined to play at the highest level. These soothsayers were proved correct when I read in the *Manchester Evening News* seven years later that I would be playing for England against Scotland. But what did it mean any longer? How easily could I throw up my arms in celebration at my goal without feeling that somehow it was wrong to do so?

I believe now this questioning – at a time when those who

didn't know me so well might have seen nothing more than triumph written in the blaze of headlines greeting my arrival in the England team – was my defence against the worst that life can bring. Certainly, and despite all the good things that have happened to me since, I have to admit it is an attitude, a caution maybe, I have never been able to put aside easily, at least not completely.

Whenever I try to make sense of my feelings back then, one fact remains quite clear. As hard as I tried, I couldn't stop doubting the optimism that had always been so much a part of me. It is difficult, after all, to be jubilant when so often, any time of day or night, and especially night, your strongest urge is to cry, for what has been taken away and, you fear, might never be replaced.

The problem was that deep down I didn't think it was right to feel so good again, so quickly after the air crash. I had been granted survival – was it not too much to expect success as well? And, even more questionably in my own mind, should I hope to enjoy it? Could I feel as free and as whole as I always had on a football field, whether in the mud or the frost of the North East or some great stadium in Europe?

As I look back, maybe all I really know for sure is that if anybody had told me that so quickly after the ruin and grief of Munich I would be playing for England, I would have withdrawn, in still more disbelief, a little further into my hospital bed. After all those funerals I couldn't face, the idea that men with great names in the game would be able to persuade me that there would again be life and football without shadows and fear and uncertainty was inconceivable. All that belonged in another lifetime, with another set of hopes that had left me now and could not be recovered, at least not in the way I had always imagined, and if by some miracle of healing, those things became possible, it could not happen so soon.

Before Munich, everything had seemed so simple. I would

play for Manchester United and then England, by way of an extra treat, and that would be my life. My mother might warn me against the perils of my chosen trade, she might talk about the need for education and ask me where I would be if I suffered some serious injury, but even when I saw team-mates cut down and agonising about what would become of them, none of it touched me because I knew what was going to happen. I was untouchable. I was going to play forever.

Then suddenly that made no sense. The new reality dawned in the hospital in Germany – the only certainty was that no one, and least of all a kid who had up to that moment experienced so little of life, could ever again tell what was going to happen tomorrow, let alone in a future that no longer had any borders to protect the old confidence. The new reality was the lost lives of friends and team-mates and the abandoned hopes that had been so strong in the days before.

So when I arrived in the Marine Hotel in Troon, where the England captain Billy Wright welcomed me and announced that we would be sharing a room, I felt I had to try to explain quite how jumbled and confused my feelings were, and how this day that I had fantasised about for so long could not now, whatever happened, be anything like I had once anticipated.

I was anxious not to appear disrespectful and I hoped the captain of England understood what I was trying to say, but then I also thought I knew well enough what playing for my country could mean. I had done it at Wembley in the Schoolboy game against Wales in front of a vast, young, yelling crowd of 93,000. That experience had taken me to a place far from the rough fields on which I first kicked a ball, where you always felt cold and the wind was always in your face.

When the scouts filled our house in Ashington after the Welsh game, I thought to myself, 'This is wonderful. I can do this. I can play for England.' These were the best lads in the country and I could measure myself against them and feel that I was equal to the tests that lay ahead. We beat Wales comfortably in the return match in Cardiff and scored eight against the Republic of Ireland and this gave me so much confidence when I reported to Old Trafford to start my professional career.

So, of course, it should have been the most natural progression, settling into the Marine Hotel, hobnobbing with the great international footballers, as my late friend and hero Duncan Edwards had done, as though it was not a privilege but a right. I should have been looking forward to Hampden Park as a rite of passage rather than any kind of trial.

I did say to Billy that if Munich hadn't happened, these now would be the proudest and most exciting days of my life. All the messages of congratulation would have been read and savoured and re-read a hundred times until the paper they were written on wore away in my hands. I would have been thinking of nothing else, and planning every moment of my performance, listening and looking, desperate to make the right impression as I went to the big stadium in the company of such men as Billy, Tom Finney and Johnny Haynes.

I would also have travelled back more than eighteen months to the night in my digs in Manchester when I couldn't sleep because it was the eve of my first game for Manchester United, against Charlton Athletic. Before the first streaks of dawn flecked the sky, I wanted to get out of bed, run into the street and shout that I was playing for United, and make the dead, waiting hours of that seemingly endless night fly by.

As I tried to explain all this to the England captain, he was patient, perhaps at first thinking I was merely nervous, and went out of his way to reassure me. I was a talented young player, he said, and should relax, and feel that I was in the right place with the right people who would do all they could to make the challenge facing me easier. He told me I would not lack opportunities to make a good impression. However gloomy or emotional I became, he refused to let go of the possibility that, at some point in the next few days, all the pain and pressure, and even the doubts that I could carry on, would be placed in a new and much more encouraging light.

This, he said, was a time that I should not fear but take hold of and enjoy, because it would never come again in so fresh and exciting a way. If I responded in the right way, it could bring a whole new dimension to my career and my life. I could look back, not on another ordeal, but on an uplifting experience that had filled me with new ambition and – something I maybe needed more than anything else – a belief that my life could be renewed.

Billy was right, of course, but that would be proved only by action and time. Conversation, however encouraging and kind, in a hotel room with a man I admired so much for what he did on the field and the modest way he conducted himself off it, was not enough.

In the end, in a passage of football that still seems magical, the captain's argument was taken up, and won, out on the field of Hampden Park by the brilliance of Tom Finney. If the great player had taken me by the hand – and never let it go – he could have done no more to make me understand Billy's point of view, that this was something to be enjoyed for its own sake. Tomorrow I could continue to agonise as much as I liked, but today I must play, I must do the thing that I had always believed would be the core of my life.

When I was a boy, I watched Finney and saw that he was a fine, creative player. I saw his speed and his touch and his tremendous appetite. I saw his dribbling skills and the absolute control he exerted over his talent. There was nothing showy, or irrelevant, about Tom Finney. However, it was also true that, back then, no footballer stood higher in my admiration than Stanley Matthews. No one made my blood run so quickly.

There was a beautiful mystery to his game that haunts me

still. Standing on the terraces of St James' Park, I told Jack that Matthews was unique and we would never see anyone to compare with him as long as we lived. That spindly, stooping figure became my great hero almost from the first moment I saw him. No one could so beguile a crowd or bewilder an opponent as Matthews.

But when I said that to Jack, I had not yet played with Finney, or been given, at the dawn of my international career, quite such a perfectly honed example of the game at its most brilliant – and most simple. I had never known at first hand – not even in the company of my late United colleague, the emerging but not yet fully mature Duncan Edwards – quite what it was to have a team-mate who saw everything, could do everything, and never once exploited either his vision or his talent on behalf of himself rather than his team-mates.

This, in my eyes, will always be the mark of the greatest footballers – it was the supreme quality of Pelé – as opposed to the most gifted ones. I still go to the football museum in Preston to watch with awe the carefully edited, and freshly coloured, film of 'The Matthews Final' of 1953, but nothing I see surpasses something Finney did at Hampden Park on a spring day five years later, which was so directly to my benefit.

Anyone who was in the huge, packed stadium all those years ago, and whose memory holds, will understand easily enough the depth of my gratitude.

Finney made my first goal for England in my first match. He made anything seem possible. He made the game look ridiculously easy, not only for himself but for all those lucky enough to be on his side.

By the time I played for England at the age of twenty, some harsh realities had indeed intruded into, and overshadowed, some of my boyish dreams. But when Finney set off on the run I would never forget, and I realised that I had to make sure not a stride of it was wasted, I was a little in love with the game again, and all the possibilities that it offered me.

My mood, and my view of the world, had not been transformed, so instantly, into a permanent condition; I knew that
well enough, despite all my excitement and exhilaration. A door
had not been slammed shut on grief that was still bone-deep –
how could it be? – but it had been half-closed, as Billy Wright
said it would be. Stirrings of those feelings I'd had when I first
thought of playing for England rose to the surface, and what it
might mean, sooner or later, to walk in the steps of my great
relative, Jackie Milburn. I was taken back, at least some of the
way, to a time when nothing in our lives would ever be as uncom-
plicated or as pleasurable as playing or watching football.

Tom Finney gave me something to carry into the future, a
burst of hope that one day football would again be as completely
satisfying and as beautiful as before. No troubled lad could ever
have been told more eloquently about the wonders of life that
can come so unexpectedly in even the most unpromising circumstances – or that the most magical of these wonders could
be the kindness of a tough and proud opponent.

This was Tommy Younger, goalkeeper for Liverpool and
Scotland, and what he said to me when he ran to the centre
circle to have a word before the restart after I'd scored is as
warming today as it was fifty years ago. The big man was at
my shoulder, shaking my hand and saying, 'Congratulations on
your first game – and your first goal. There will be many more,
laddie.'

Perhaps there was something on my face, which I know can
be mournful from time to time, that drew such concern and,
when I think about it, compassion. Like Billy Wright, Younger
went out of his way to be encouraging. Old pros are supposed
to be resentful of new blood, envying their youth and all the
days that lay ahead of them, but in Glasgow I found quite the
opposite.

It was amazing to me that Billy Wright would be sharing a
room with me. Of all my opponents in my brief career in club

football up until then, with the exception of Alfredo di Stefano and his Real Madrid, it was Wright and the Wolves team who had loomed largest.

Once, when we beat them, and I saw desperation on the face of their captain, I took it as the supreme evidence that there was no limit to the potential of my own team, because to beat Wolves, their big, strong defenders and quick and skilful forwards dressed in gold, you had to do so much more than merely play well. You had to function completely as a team.

Billy was saying nothing but the truth when he told me that I should have no fear going into my first international because I was surrounded by good professionals. Even though they were stripped of my fallen team-mates, Duncan Edwards, Roger Byrne and Tommy Taylor, England were still formidably strong. Derek Kevan, West Bromwich Albion's big forward, was not so quick or polished as Taylor, and although they were fine players, Bill Slater of Wolves and Jim Langley of Fulham could not hope to match the power and authority of Edwards and Byrne, but England were far from bereft of the highest talent.

We had, above all others, Finney, so quiet and calm but also so confident in himself before he burst into life on the field. We had the great Johnny Haynes, who passed the ball so exquisitely and with such bite, who was already the model for so many aspiring midfield playmakers. We had the wonderfully clever little Blackburn Rovers winger Bryan Douglas, who later developed his craft superbly when he moved inside. They all welcomed me and tried to take away the tension.

So I listened to what Wright had to say and that was when I tried to explain to him that my fear was not so much of being overwhelmed by the Scots and their passionate support at Hampden Park, but was instead rooted in another layer of the pressure that had been building on me since I first regained consciousness in Munich.

For evidence, I showed him a bundle of mail that required

replies. From the odd tax notice, my post had swollen to more than forty letters a day. Wright said that a hard but vital lesson for every professional was that if you made something of a name for yourself, whatever the circumstances, your duties did not stop when you walked off the field. The public believed that you were their property, and to a certain extent you were. They filled the grounds, paid your wages and, if you were lucky, appointed you among their heroes. They also gave you responsibilities, which could be shirked only at the risk of their anger.

Wright also had to deal with some personal mail but as he did so, he outlined, very gently, some of what I could expect at Hampden. Even though he had known me for just a short time, he must have realised that a lot of what weighed on my mind went beyond the touchlines of a football field, but that was no reason, he felt, not to say that I was still about to enjoy one of the most momentous experiences of my career.

'Bobby,' he said, 'however you feel now, I tell you that once you're involved in the game you're going to love every minute of it. If you get a chance, just take a look at the great terrace behind the right-hand goal. There must be nearly fifty thousand fans squeezed in so tightly they can hardly move. From the pitch, they look just like little birds waiting to be fed.'

Billy's description was perfect. The Scots didn't score but after one close call I looked up at the great fluttering crowd and they might have been a throng of starlings on a telephone wire. He was right, too, about the enjoyment that would take hold a little more each time I had the ball at my feet and the vast crowd responded to the play.

As well as so many other discoveries, I had my love of Scotland confirmed that day. Tommy Younger's gesture no doubt helped, but it was an old attachment that was strengthened. While growing up in the North East, the odds were that when you talked about going to a cup final you meant the one at Hampden not Wembley, unless Newcastle might be involved. It was too expensive to go to London as a neutral, even if you could get a ticket, and in Glasgow you were guaranteed the most extraordinary theatre. As my first international game wore on, and all the little birds chirped their way to a frenzy of frustration as we took control, the more I said to myself, 'This is good, I want more of this' – and the bigger and louder Hampden became.

I had sat enthralled at the Bernabeu in Madrid when di Stefano unveiled some of his most devastating work, but I had never known a crowd quite like this. They had been brought to a pitch of excitement by the Powderhall sprinters, who raced on the track before we went out on to the field, and reminded me of those bewitching days when I accompanied my beloved grandfather Tanner and his stable of runners to miners' galas around the North East. Maybe it was the sight of those runners that took me back so quickly to so many of the certainties of my boyhood. Tanner was with me again, coaxing the best out of me, telling me that if I did my work, and kept my concentration, nothing was beyond me. I might even play for my country, and just imagine the pride in that. Tanner was dying, and could no longer watch me play. I would sit at his bedside and read him the football reports in the Saturday evening sports pink edition, but right to the end he kept telling me that everything was in my hands. I had been given all the talent any lad who wanted to play football would ever need.

The day in Glasgow lingers so strongly in my mind that I felt a strong surge of anger when the Football Association decided the most fitting opponents for England when the new Wembley was unveiled in 2007 would be Germany. Given my experiences in a World Cup final and quarter-final, I doubt that too many people understand more deeply the football rivalry with Germany that was created in 1966, but I thought the case for Scotland was overwhelming when it came to mark a new phase in the history of the traditional home of the England game.

I thought it was a time to rekindle some old priorities, to go back to our strongest and oldest roots as a football nation. England versus Scotland is surely a game that runs in our blood – mine, certainly. I lived in a place where the border was insignificant. Working people on both sides of it had so much in common, and if we had fought wars against each other down the centuries, more recently we had stood together, with terrible loss of life.

As my first game for England unfolded, Billy Wright's assurances, as against my own fears, were proving accurate. The blast of the crowd, the excitement of the journey along the Clyde and all the people coming into the streets, had set my blood flowing. Tommy Docherty conceded a free kick, which I took quickly to find Douglas, who, with typically neat skill, put it past Younger. Kevan made it 2–0 from Douglas, and twenty minutes into the second half I scored the first of my 49 international goals. Kevan scored another goal late in the second half, but by then it felt to me as though I was no longer involved in a contest. Against all my worries and reservations, and the treadmill so much of my football had become, I had been given the chance to shine – and I had taken it.

It helped greatly that I had been so fiercely tutored in one of the basic duties of an attacking midfielder by my mentor at Old Trafford, United assistant manager Jimmy Murphy. Whenever a winger launched himself towards the dead-ball line, the obligation was quite basic, Murphy always insisted. You ran hard for the expected cross, however speculative the winger's foray. But then Finney didn't speculate. He executed whatever chore he settled upon, and almost as often as a cross it might be a direct attack on goal. On this occasion Finney's intentions were as transparent as the distress of the man who was trying to close him down, right back Alex Parker.

Parker, with more courage than hope, attempted to jockey Finney and win a little time for his fellow defenders. It was futile. Finney dropped his shoulder, Parker went the wrong way, and I thought, 'Right foot or left, I know what Tom's going to do now . . . he's thinking, how easy can I make it for the man tearing down the middle?' He looked up, for half a stride, to measure my run and then floated the ball perfectly into my path.

The ball came to my right side and, since we enjoyed a comfortable lead, I gave no thought to safety. I volleyed the ball home from around sixteen yards, yelling with a pleasure that no longer had to be questioned. In the morning, the newspapers announced that I was the author of a wonder goal and that I was heading for stardom in the coming World Cup in Sweden.

I knew that I had struck a powerful shot, as I had so many times before, sometimes with success, sometimes not. The wonder had come in Finney's absolute mastery of the winger's art.

For me, that was a decisive moment in deciding between Finney and Matthews. Today, controversy surrounds the relative merits of Cristiano Ronaldo and George Best, but the question of Finney or Matthews was always going to be easier to resolve because they played at the same time against the same defenders and the same tactics.

Initially, I leaned towards Matthews because I saw more of him at St James' Park and a boy is always going to be more susceptible to star quality than is a fellow professional. But in the end, the sheer range and depth of Finney's talent became overwhelmingly apparent. Finney, apart from sharing Matthews' deadly pace over ten yards, did two things that were never part of the latter's make-up – he headed the ball and he tackled, sometimes quite ferociously.

It is not a case of deserting Stanley's cause. He had a talent that would have glowed in any circumstances, but if you ask who would have made more impression on today's game of heightened speed and strength, I would have to say Finney, but even as I say this I am haunted all over again by the ability of Matthews to move and thrill, unforgettably, all those people who made a pilgrimage to wherever he was playing, or where it was hoped he would be playing.

Stoke City and then Blackpool, when he moved to Bloomfield Road, were the names that leapt out of each new season's fixture list. At St James' Park, Jack and I were often surrounded by people who had travelled across the country to see Matthews, convinced that if they never saw him in the flesh, they would regret it for the rest of their lives. He was every young foot-baller's dream. He was helped, of course, by the naivety of the tactics that allowed him to persecute a full back throughout the game. Today he would be double marked, there would always be somebody backing up the first defender, but then a full back was on his own, and against Matthews on his best days he was the loneliest man in the world.

It was as though the ball was tied to Matthews' feet and, when he was on his toes, you knew the full back was beaten the moment he rested on his wrong foot. Matthews was gone, either right side or left, and then his options were to play to the feet of a team-mate who had worked himself free, or put the ball on Stanley Mortensen's head. Soon after playing with Finney for the first time, and seeing him strike the most brilliant form in Moscow a month later, I was reminded most strongly of Matthews' particular talent by Brazil's Garrincha in the World Cup finals in Sweden. He had the same, burning ten-yard pace, the same ability to make a goal a formality.

Many years later, I told Stan Mortensen of my fascination with Matthews, and about all the times I had compared him with Finney. I recalled how I sat with Jack in the shale near the corner flag at Newcastle and saw Matthews for the first time, and how I was a little surprised that I found myself thinking, 'Well, he's just a man who wears an overcoat like everybody else, he doesn't have wings or a halo.' I also told Stan that I had often wondered about his own feelings on the subject, because once, when Matthews sent in a perfect corner for a headed goal at Newcastle, he had immediately run over to shout, 'Great cross.' But then when I was taken to Hampden Park to watch England against Scotland, and Finney supplied a similar service, I noted that Stan did not make a similar acknowledgement. He just ran back to the centre circle. I asked why it was so. 'Well,' said Mortensen, 'you know Stanley always made sure the lace on the ball was pointing away from me. I always thought that was very considerate because the lace hurt.'

I competed against Finney at club level several times, and saw him play at Deepdale for Preston, once brilliantly when my Uncle Stan's team, Leicester City, were the visitors. Compelling evidence was also provided by his club team-mates. They swore that no one could be more committed or resilient. While Matthews was the despair of huge crowds all over the country when he was announced as a non-starter because of a relatively minor injury, Finney was relentless. Talking to some Preston players after a match at Deepdale, telling them how well their team-mate had played, I was told, 'No, lad, that was normal. You should watch Tom play match after match, in any conditions against any opponents, against full backs who, by the end of the games, want to kill him, and then you see that he really is unbelievable.'

At Hampden Park I saw why it was that Tom Finney's team-mates were so unanimous and so deep in their praise. I saw the range and the depth and the willingness to do everything that was required of him to help the team. I also saw the generosity that is common to great players, who are so sure of their ability they do not need to parade it at every opportunity. When people talk of the extraordinary talent of Pelé, they sometimes forget that so much of his genius was expressed in the simplest but also deadliest of passes to a better placed team-mate. Some describe this as peripheral vision but that is a gift that grows with experience and awareness of the rhythm of a game. What Finney showed me against Scotland was something more. It was the brain and the accomplishment of a great player but the heart of a humble one.

It was something to take from Scotland and, like my first cap, always care for as a rare gift. Another memorable present was two fine haggis from the head waiter at the Marine Hotel. He was thanking me for my compliment to the chef who had produced this dish. Some visitors push haggis aside on the grounds that it must be an acquired taste, but I said how much I enjoyed it, and whenever I returned with England, the head waiter gave me the same present – two cannonballs of lamb's liver, oatmeal and spices wrapped in a sheep's stomach – and I always accepted with unbroken enthusiasm.

I loved haggis from my first bite. It was a taste I did not have to work to acquire, no more than my first love for football, and today it remains as appealing as when I first tried it at the table of heroes who did so much to make me feel whole again.

Billy Wright became a friend as well as a hero, and an example of how a famous sportsman should behave. Long after his death, his widow, Joy, of the famous Beverley Sisters singing trio, occasionally wrote to me, telling me how much she still missed the gentle man who had brought so much into her life that she never found elsewhere, even in all the glamour of her show-business career.

I told her I remembered so vividly how he helped me through the most difficult time of my life, how he told me what I would see and feel at Hampden Park would persuade me that, far from being over, my football life had scarcely begun. I also told her that with the help of Tom Finney, he was proved right beyond my most optimistic dreams.

2

A TOURIST IN SWEDEN

ALL THE AGONISING over how to deal with the new pressure of being an international star did not occupy me for long. It was halted abruptly under a steely Moscow sky by Walter Winterbottom, the first of only two England managers I would ever play for, almost exactly a month after the hurrahs of Hampden Park.

I cannot say I was shattered because, despite the care shown by Billy Wright in Glasgow and the success I found there and, just over a couple of weeks later, at Wembley when I scored twice against Portugal, I was still uncertain of my feelings about playing for England. But whatever thoughts I might have been entertaining off the pitch, I felt my form on it had been unaffected, and that I had the goals and the headlines to prove it. Yet maybe Walter, and possibly Billy Wright, had a view that my concentration was less than a hundred per cent, that maybe part of my head was somewhere else. It was also possible, I speculated, that the manager was looking for more defensive qualities in midfield than I provided. Whatever the reasons were for my exclusion from the team to meet the USSR, I still didn't believe it was my emotional state that had impaired my performance in the 5–0 thrashing by Yugoslavia that followed the game against Portugal. As a player I was what I was, young and instinctive and those other thoughts were pushed back, for a little while, when I was playing the game. Elsewhere, what was occupying my mind was the question of whether my international career could grow into anything more than a luxury that I might not be able to maintain comfortably on top of my duties for Manchester United, who were fighting so desperately, and with maybe too many raw and overstretched young players, to re-make themselves.

So if I was a little surprised – and a part of me a little saddened too – it had to be much less so than anyone who had been following the sports pages. Some of the leading Fleet Street football writers, including my friend of the future, Geoffrey Green of *The Times*, had convinced themselves, rather more than me, that I had become an instant fixture in the national team. They were talking of a natural-born international, someone who had just walked on to the stage so easily he might have owned it.

We had arrived in Moscow in some disarray after our meeting with Yugsoslavia and Winterbottom was quick to separate me from the presumptions of the writers and fans – and some of my own. He was a gentleman with a kindly manner but he did not soften his message when he took me aside to say that the England selectors, of which he was only one, had decided to drop me after my third game, which I had gone into with the encouraging record of three goals in two matches.

He also chastised me, which made for a rather reflective and sombre visit to Lenin's tomb in Red Square. The manager said I had to think more deeply about my contribution to the team. I had to study, particularly, the one made by Johnny Haynes, a great midfielder, who, he said, was willing to do things that apparently I wasn't. Haynes, who a few years later would become English football's first £100-a-week player, had a wider game, Winterbottom pointed out.

'Bobby,' he said, 'you have to do a lot more running. The next time you see Haynes, study every move he makes. He always wants the ball and when he's passed it, he's always looking to receive it again. It's not enough to do everything positive, you also have to think negative at times; you have to think of denying the other team the ball. It's always going to be a vital part of the game. If Haynes loses the ball, look at his anger as he fights to get it back.'

I had to progress in that direction if I wanted to win back my place. Walter painted a picture of me that depicted, most of all, a rather dreamy kid, talented but somehow off the pace and well short of a proper understanding of what lay before him.

This verdict was something of a jolt, although I was aware that Haynes had for some years been declaring himself, on the field that is, a master player. He had acquired almost a cult following among up-and-coming midfielders, and not least my younger club-mate at Old Trafford, Johnny Giles. Long after Giles had proved himself to be one of the most influential players in the game with Leeds United – Alf Ramsey had expressed his regret that Giles hadn't been born an Englishman, and Matt Busby had said his biggest mistake was allowing him to leave Old Trafford – he said that Haynes had been his main inspiration.

No, I wasn't ignorant of Haynes's quality, especially after playing alongside him in a few matches and noting that he oozed an authority I had rarely seen. Nor was I surprised that Winterbottom wanted more from me. He was, after all, speaking from the gospel of Jimmy Murphy. Since I'd known him, Murphy had been drilling into me the message that one of the dividing lines between a true professional and a merely talented amateur was his willingness to work off the ball, to be constantly involved in both the rhythm and the reading of a game.

It was not enough to score goals, however spectacular. They grabbed headlines from time to time but they didn't necessarily guarantee you a permanent place in a national team, especially if you went a game without scoring, which I realised was the serious mistake I had made in Belgrade. There, according to Winterbottom, and also to some degree in my own mind, I had fallen from the level I had set for myself against Scotland and Portugal.

Winterbottom said that so soon before a World Cup he had to be looking for rather more in a player of true international status, and that for me and any other contender for a place alongside him in England's midfield, Haynes had almost everything that was needed.

In other circumstances, I might have been upset but I understood that Walter had a difficult job to do, and it wasn't as though I couldn't put being dropped into some kind of sharp perspective. I was able to comfort myself a little that the bad news came as a result of a performance surrounded by special circumstances and pressures in Belgrade, where three months earlier I could still count England regulars Duncan Edwards, Roger Byrne and Tommy Taylor among my Manchester United team-mates.

In effect, the manager told me I had lost my place because I wasn't getting stuck in sufficiently for his satisfaction. It wasn't just a matter of doing well on the ball. Yes, I had looked good in that situation and had scored some goals, but I was also required to run and work at a much higher rate. In this respect, he said he had been particularly disappointed by my last performance. I had shown a lot of promise in my opening games but what he had seen in Belgrade just wasn't good enough. Promise had to be built upon.

In some respects, the only oddity was in hearing those words in the cultured tones of my England manager because I had indeed heard many variations of them in the more basic language and the Rhondda Valley accent of Jimmy Murphy.

Although I didn't say it to Winterbottom, by the time I reached Moscow I realised I might be vulnerable to paying the price of not only my own sub-par performance but for being part of one of England's heaviest defeats on foreign soil. In fact, it was our worst loss since the ones administered by Hungary half a decade earlier, losses so harmful to the pride of the football nation that everyone agreed England had to find a new and more sophisticated way of playing the game we had given to the world. If the gift was now being repaid, Belgrade proved it was with no gratitude and not a penny of interest.

The confidence of the whole team had been high before the game, but on the pitch we were seriously off colour, with the result that we were not so much beaten as torn apart. For me, the defeat still stands out as one of my first serious lessons in the folly of taking anything for granted in football. As it turned out, I was not the only victim of a defeat that drew shocking headlines back home. Our goalkeeper, Eddie Hopkinson, lost his place and Jim Langley of Fulham gave way to Tommy Banks, the Bolton Wanderers full back, who tackled like a tank and would later be a significant figure in the push by the Professional Footballers' Association to raise the £20-per-week wage limit.

In a meeting in Manchester, Banks replied to a member of the Association who said that footballers should remember they didn't have to go down a pit or to a factory bench to earn their living. Banks said, 'I would like to see how the average miner dealt with Stanley Matthews.'

My place went to fellow north-easterner Bobby Robson, who had drawn a lot of attention to himself with a strong presence and fine passing for West Bromwich Albion. In addition, Ronnie Clayton of Blackburn, who had struggled at least as much as I had, gave way to Eddie Clamp of Wolves, who, like Banks, would be winning his first cap.

The fact that the four heads rolled was not a surprise, given the scale of the defeat. The panel of Football Association councillors who 'assisted' Walter in the picking of the team – amazingly, it was only when Alf Ramsey was appointed five years later that this absurd system was abandoned – could not, after all, be seen to be doing nothing in the face of national disgrace. Terrible stories about the selection process circulated in the dressing rooms of the English game and were seized upon by players who believed they were not being treated fairly. You heard of selectors, club chairmen, saying such things as, 'Fair's fair, lads, it's time for our boy to get a run.'

I do not say this in any fit of fifty-year-old pique. Nobody needed to tell me I had played poorly in Belgrade, and I'm not suggesting, even at this distance, that my demotion had anything to do with conspiracies of special interests in the selection room. But there was no doubt Winterbottom had a minefield of a job, which, looking back, he ultimately could not win.

I was certainly not going to give him any more grief than he was already experiencing on the back pages of the newspapers and, no doubt, in the committee room. No player distinguished himself in Belgrade and I was prepared to believe that my performance was indeed one of the worst.

The fact is, and maybe this was significant in how I played, that I didn't like the place those few months earlier when I went there with United for the European Cup quarter-final against Red Star. I never felt completely at ease and this was in spite of the fact that, after playing quite brilliantly in the first half, we earned a 3–3 draw, which took us through to the next stage, a feat over which we were still congratulating ourselves on the following day when we flew down through snow-filled skies to re-fuel in Munich.

And returning to Belgrade so quickly inevitably did bring back some of those emotions I had carried into my first meeting with Billy Wright in Troon. Although I had denied it to myself, maybe on reflection such thoughts did gnaw at me a little too much as the Yugoslavs launched themselves at us powerfully after the minute's silence for my fallen team-mates.

On that first visit, I was shocked by the overwhelming military presence, the sense that one false step could land you in trouble. That and the huge pictures of President Tito gazing sternly down on streets full of ruts and potholes and women workers dressed in drab uniforms and men's boots made for a feeling of foreboding. Then, perhaps understandably, when I returned to the grey city beside the Danube, the faces I saw most vividly in my mind's eye did not include Tito's but were those of my Manchester United team-mates who, but for the tragedy in Munich, would have been on the England team bus, bumping and rattling into the city through the flat fields and apartment buildings that separated it from the airport. No doubt I would have been sitting beside one of them, most likely the peerless Duncan, or my Saturday night pal Tommy Taylor, chatting about all that had become familiar and exciting in my life as a member of a team that seemed to have been directed towards the stars.

A few days earlier, the second of my two goals against Portugal was a left-footed blockbuster that attracted still more headlines and the idea that I was indeed the new golden boy of England. But there was no gold and scarcely a scrap of silver at my feet in the big grey army stadium where not long ago I had felt confident that United were on the way to dominating a European game that for so long had been under the shadow of di Stefano and his Real Madrid team-mates.

Before the game, Billy Wright recounted how four years earlier, when England lost by a single goal, the crowd had lit newspapers and made a great bowl of fire and smoke in anticipation of their victory. This time, though, the heat was created entirely on the field by a quick, hard and skilful Yugoslav team. Even the talent, and rampant form, of Tom Finney was briefly lost in the tide that flowed strongly against us and which produced a hat-trick for their right winger Aleksandar Petakovic. When we came off the field, we didn't know where to look. Our performance was something that was hard to dwell upon as we travelled on to the next stage of a tour that had turned into an ordeal.

As we flew into Moscow for the game against the USSR – the last one before the World Cup squad was to be announced back in London – I realised my place was in jeopardy and kept reassuring myself that there would be other opportunities in better times and that maybe, with the great tournament so close, I had been pitched into a little bit too much pressure. Maybe things would settle down. Perhaps Belgrade was just a necessary reminder that in football you will always only be as good as your last performance.

Sometimes, I told myself, you just have to accept that everything can't go your way all the time. I held no resentment towards Walter Winterbottom, not then or later, when my continued absence from the team became a major issue in the press.

To be perfectly honest, though, there was a time after the World Cup, for which I was selected with no great promise of forcing myself into the action, when I did reflect, 'Well, maybe I could have got at least one game. Maybe I could have done something. Perhaps I could have knocked in a goal.' In that way, I was touched by a feeling that it was possible some of the noise being made by the press on my behalf had at least a little foundation.

Winterbottom was a tremendous thinker on the theory of the game, and you could not but be impressed by his presence, but I never really saw him as a football professional, not like Busby or Murphy – and not like the great contemporary managers, such as Stan Cullis at Wolves, or Bill Nicholson, who was working so well to build on the push-and-run days of his predecessor at Spurs, Arthur Rowe, and was recruited by Winterbottom as an adviser for the challenge in Sweden.

Perhaps because of his background, Walter could command respect but he was not someone who could mix easily with the lads, and he would certainly not invite any of them to his hotel room, as Murphy did, for a bottle of beer or a glass of Mateus Rosé and some long and intense discussion on the game and its characters.

It was, I suppose, the difference between a tough army drill instructor and the wing commander Walter became when he served in the RAF during the Second World War. Above all, he had the bearing of the schoolmaster he was before entering the game, and although he had been on Manchester United's books, and played twenty-seven games as a promising centre half before sustaining a serious back injury, he never quite lost the style of a teacher. Even when delivering the kind of news he had for me in Moscow, the impression was not of a tough enforcer who could effortlessly get down to the level and language of battle-hardened professionals, or even a lad like me, who had spent just a few years around such characters.

When he was eventually knighted in 1978, long after he was detached from the running of the England team, it was for his theories and the organisation of coaching rather than the dynamic impact of it. His manual on coaching became a standard work.

He seemed to be drawn into the wider issues of the game, especially the need for a national system of coaching, in a way that Ramsey never would be, and maybe this was understandable, considering the way football was run then, when the final word on team selection belonged to men without any practical experience of the game.

If this point needs underlining, maybe it is enough to say that, some years later, one FA councillor came into the England dressing room, nudged me and asked the name of a player who was standing a few yards away. A little stunned, I said it was Gordon Milne, a key figure in the rise of Bill Shankly's Liverpool and someone who always acquitted himself well when he was called to the national team.

So Winterbottom had to do the best he could in a position that, today, seems especially hopeless when you think that Europe's leading football nation, Italy, had won two World Cups by the end of the thirties, largely because they had put their trust in the strong and visionary coach Vittorio Pozzo, who had absolute control of both selection and tactics. When his *Azzurri* played against England, he was amazed to discover that one of the most influential football nations had never appointed a permanent team manager – a situation that existed until Winterbottom came out of the RAF and was given limited powers – and instead were happy to be 'assisted' from time to time by guest club managers, including the great Herbert Chapman of Huddersfield Town and Arsenal.

Pozzo was the father of Italian football while England, you might have said, had so many interfering uncles. They enjoyed the prestige and the international travel but, when you got right down to it, they were in so many ways no more than the privileged tourists who sat at the front of the planes and the buses, and, in some cases, wouldn't be able to recognise a new player if he didn't happen to be wearing a number on his back.

Walter, I realised over the five years I knew him as England's manager, was in no position to overturn a system that was so entrenched. For that to happen, the demand had to come from someone such as Ramsey, who had succeeded in professional club management and would only agree to lead England if he had those powers he believed were essential if he was to do the job. Without such control, Ramsey would no more have taken the job than he would have appeared willingly in public in the clothes he might wear while pottering in his Ipswich garden.

But then, of course, I listened respectfully when Walter told me where I had gone wrong against the Yugoslavs and what I had to do if I was to come back into the reckoning.

The lecture was delivered on one of the training pitches that surround the great Lenin Sports Palace in Moscow after I learned that Robson would be taking my place. My inevitable disappointment was compounded by the fact that I had been much taken and inspired by the scale of the Lenin complex. The huge stands, which catered for more than a 100,000 spectators, reached up into the sky, and the surrounding facilities included cycle tracks and swimming pools. I didn't know much about politics but I was quite moved to think that all this had been built for young sportsmen and women, and I could not avoid making comparisons with home, where such a complex was unknown.

We had the Crystal Palace in England but this in Moscow was on an entirely different level. I was suddenly eager to perform in such a setting, and put behind me the bad Belgrade experience. I thought, 'This will be a great match against a team drawn from a vast nation.' The Soviets seemed to be building towards a time when they might exploit the promise that had been displayed so excitingly on a post-war tour of England by the Moscow Dynamo team.

Walter wasn't heavy handed but he didn't ease back on his point that a lot more was expected of me. 'This is what I would like you to do, this is how I want you to improve,' he kept saying. He added that I had come into an environment where I could learn from some of the best players in the game, and if somewhere inside me a voice was saying that I was not unfamiliar with great players – how could I be after being part of the Busby Babes? – and I received excellent personal coaching from Murphy, I didn't feel it was a situation in which I could push that case. Robson was a good player and I couldn't argue that he didn't deserve a chance.

When we went to the Lenin Stadium, after touring the Kremlin, and I took my place in the stand, I found myself reflecting – as I had done a year earlier in the Bernabeu in Madrid when I watched a dazzling master-class from di Stefano in the semi-final of the European Cup – that sometimes it is necessary to sit back for a while and just concentrate on those things that could make you a better player and a more mature person. I had to tell myself that I was still learning the game and I should be patient. Sometimes it was necessary to learn your lessons and wait for your next opportunity.

Long before the end of the game, which finished in a 1–1 draw, I had once again been taken out of myself by a performance of great brilliance from Tom Finney. Here, I knew now, after the briefest time as one of his team-mates, was a player who never made claims for himself off the field but never neglected the chance to impose himself while he was on it. Nobody had been more frustrated than he was in Belgrade, and the rare disappointment of a poor performance was falling away with every advance on the Russian goal.

He told me that the great thing about football was that you always had the chance to improve if you came to it with the right head and the right heart. Although, at the age of thirty-six, he was drawing near to the end of his career, without ever winning a major prize, and having been denied the chance by his club to improve himself when an Italian club came to Preston offering terms way beyond anything he had ever known, there was a staggering consistency in his determination to use every morsel of his talent.

He had a vast supply of it and it can never have been better displayed than against the USSR. Watching his command of the ball, and the strength and creativity he brought to everything he did, I could only regret all over again my failure to maintain my form and goal-scoring touch in Belgrade, which had denied me the privilege of playing alongside him in such an impressive stadium.

If I wanted to be part of the coming World Cup in Sweden, I had to respond in the best way I could – and accept that Winterbottom, who was by nature a kindly man, was explaining to me that international football was not something you could walk into as though it was something you had been doing for half your life. There was a line you had to cross, and although many football writers had proclaimed that I had done that, and Jimmy Murphy made it clear that he felt my services were being wasted by England, I could not afford to believe everything I read or heard, even if it came from someone I respected as much as Murphy.

Whenever I could step aside from the controversy over whether I should be playing – and of course, whatever else was going on his head, a young footballer has a natural instinct to play, especially when he is training each day – I enjoyed my time in Gothenburg, where we were based for the tournament. The days could scarcely have passed more pleasantly in our hotel, the Park Avenue, near to the city centre. Each morning we strolled through the park to our training ground, which we shared with the Brazilians, who were bussed in from their hotel secluded in the countryside.

Though Walter did not impose a hard regime, it did seem to us that the Brazilians were on a rather looser rein. Often we saw them in the park in their yellow training shirts and sometimes one or two of them had a beautiful Swedish lady on their arm.

The manager made it clear that on those nights when we were not watching the unfolding World Cup we were expected to be back in the hotel before 10 p.m. This meant that we were free to enjoy all the fun of the fair, literally, at a nearby recreational park, where families went to relax in the evenings. There was music and rides and I would often go there with Don Howe, the West Bromwich full back who was nearest to my age. Don had survived the mauling in Belgrade, and would play throughout the World Cup, and from time to time he hinted that he thought that I would probably be involved by the end of the tournament.

In the meantime, away from the fairground attractions, there was nothing to do but enjoy the good food at the Park Avenue, the warm northern sunshine and watch football's premier tournament in the hope that my companions – and also my great teacher Murphy – would make a good impact.

Jimmy was there at the World Cup as manager of Wales, and he later told me, after making the same point to the press, that if the great John Charles had stayed fit, and he could have borrowed my services while they were being neglected by England, he might have believed more in his chances of some extraordinary achievement. He reckoned that with that combination, Wales might at least have got beyond the quarter-finals.

Naturally, while moving around Sweden in the role of a tourist, I took a strong interest in the progress of my mentor's team. I thought of his fierce leadership of United's all-conquering youth team, the thoroughness of his preparation and the way he seemed to get inside all of our heads so easily. I knew the Welsh had the ability to play some impressive football. As well as the formidable talent of John Charles, they had his brother Mel, a strong centre half, Ivor Allchurch, a fine inside forward with a lovely easy touch, and Tottenham's Cliff Jones, a winger who on his best days was peerless. Among Jones's admirers was my future team-mate George Cohen, who told me, 'I feared no one as much as Jones. I prided myself on being quick, but not when I played against Cliffie. He had blinding pace and terrific control.'

I was in no doubt about how hard Wales would be driven. Despite some severe injury problems, they opened well with a draw against Hungary. The Hungarians still retained some of the aura of the great team that had so shattered the belief of England at Wembley in November 1953 and in the Nep Stadium in Budapest six months later before going to Switzerland as runaway favourites for the World Cup of 1954, only to be ambushed by West Germany, whom they had pulverised in a group game.

Ferenc Puskas had fled the country in the revolution of 1956, but the Magnificent Magyars still had such players as goalkeeper Gyula Grosics, Karoly Sandor, Jozsef Bozsik and the father of all deep-lying centre forwards, Nandor Hidegkuti. But the great man was thirty-six now and it seemed he carried the captaincy of the team more as a burden than an honour.

Although Bozsik surprised Welsh goalkeeper Jack Kelsey with a speculative shot after just four minutes, Murphy's men refused to be subdued, and soon enough Big John showed why he would always be revered in Italy, particularly in Turin, the home of his club, Juventus. In the twenty-sixth minute he equalised with a soaring leap to meet a corner, and the Hungarians, made aware of the threat he posed, started the process of kicking him out of the tournament. The Mexican referee failed, shockingly, to protect him – and also denied a strong penalty appeal from Allchurch. It was at such times that I feared Jimmy Murphy would burst a blood vessel.

As long as Charles's fitness held, the possibility of Jimmy making a real impact as a coach and, particularly, a motivator remained high. When you thought of all the pressure he had been under in the months before, keeping Manchester United together so brilliantly, that would have been quite amazing in what it said about both his passion for the game and his ability to battle through the most difficult circumstances. It seemed that the man who had wept in despair in a back corridor of the hospital in Munich, before accepting Busby's plea that he must keep the club going and drive it out of the ashes, simply did not know how to stop fighting.

Wales allowed Mexico a late equaliser in the second game, after Ivor Allchurch had given them the lead from a corner by my United team-mate Colin Webster. They then drew with the hosts and eventual finalists, Sweden, and did no better partly because Charles, slowed by the treatment he had received from Hungary, was largely neutralised by the great centre half Bengt Gustavsson. The three draws meant Wales were required to meet the Hungarians again in a play-off for a place in the quarter-finals.

Goals from the consistent Allchurch and Terry Medwin, who would be a member of Tottenham's Double team a few years later, eventually carried Wales through. This was after the

Hungarians' rising star, Lajos Tichy, had scored a goal to put his team ahead, but the real damage to Murphy's cause was inflicted by some cynical defending. The job of hacking John Charles on to the sidelines was finally accomplished, and he was missing when Wales faced their biggest ever challenge in the shape of a quarter-final against Brazil.

Brazil were strong at all points of their team. Didi was immense in midfield, Garrincha, 'Little Bird', almost unplayable on the wing, and Pelé, finding his feet so excitingly in only his second World Cup game, scored after seventy-three minutes. They played some beautiful football and applied much pressure to goalkeeper Kelsey. He was defiant, however, and you could not help wondering what might have happened if the Welsh had been at full strength for what was the most important match in that country's football history.

Later, Jimmy Murphy remained strongly critical of my absence from the England team, and he returned to his point that he would not have hesitated to use me in all his matches. Putting modesty aside, I have to record that it was true that Wales, for all their competitiveness against some strong football nations, had scored a mere two goals in their three group games, one less than I had managed in my first two games for England against Scotland and Portugal.

This did not hurt my confidence in the future, especially as England failed to convert their superiority in front of goal in their final group match, a 2–2 draw with a much weaker Austrian team.

In the first game, against USSR, also a 2–2 draw, Finney was hampered by an injured ankle and although he managed to score a late equaliser from the penalty spot – after an indignant Lev Yashin had thrown his cap at the Hungarian referee Istvan Zsolt – he couldn't come near to the dominance he had shown a few weeks earlier at the Lenin Stadium. It was his last World Cup appearance and his subsequent absence was as crippling a blow to England as the disappearance of Charles had been to Wales.

Inevitably, there was much speculation that Finney's bad luck would be to my advantage. The press made the first of many calls to bring back the 'Bobby Dazzler' but Walter Winterbottom and his selectors appeared locked into the view that my chance of World Cup action had come and gone amid the bad omens of Belgrade.

Liverpool winger Alan A'Court filled the vacancy against Brazil, who were still one match away from making the introduction of the prodigies Pelé and Garrincha, but he had little chance to shine in an England performance that was, maybe inevitably, most concerned with shutting down the creative brilliance of the strolling Didi. The player was at the centre of everything his team did in the days before the arrival of Pelé, soon be christened the 'Black Pearl'.

Yet with Bill Slater and Tommy Banks doing well in support of Billy Wright, the double threat of Brazil's Jose Altafini 'Mazola' and Vava was held off, sometimes a little desperately it is true, and the goalless draw meant that the anticipated victory over Austria would have carried England clean through into a quarter-final against Sweden.

Instead, the Austrian draw necessitated a play-off with the USSR, which they won 1–0, before losing 2–0 to the Swedes. Had it been England suffering defeat at the hands of the hosts, there may have been some fierce questions raised at home by the fact that Sweden were coached by an Englishman, George Raynor, who had received little honour in his homeland. Raynor had played in the lower divisions of English football, but abroad he was almost instantly recognised as outstanding coaching material. He won head coaching jobs at AIK of Stockholm and Lazio of Rome, but it was as the manager of Sweden that his work was most admired as being consistently brilliant.

He handled waves of great Swedish players, including Nils Liedholm, Gunnar Gren, Gunnar Nordahl and Kurt Hamrin, and landed the 1948 Olympic football gold medal in London. That was a dramatic advertisement for his ability in his own country, but his best job opportunites at home make rather bizarre reading – trainer at Aldershot (from where he joined Sweden), Coventry (a high point), Doncaster Rovers and Skegness Town.

This paltry appreciation of his talents showed no improvement when, two years later in the World Cup in Brazil, where England suffered the humiliation of defeat by the amateurs of the USA in the mining town of Belo Horizonte – a result that made me cry out in disbelief when I heard it in my classroom – Sweden beat the pre-war holders, Italy, and finished in third place overall. This was at the time when the wise men of the England selection committee decided they could do without Stanley Matthews against the Americans. Sweden, for their part, had had to do without Liedholm, Gren and Nordahl, among others, throughout the tournament because they had been snapped up by Italian clubs after their Olympic win and were thus ineligible for selection because of Sweden's strange belief that only amateur players should represent their country.

Eight years later, the Swedes having abandoned their amateurs-only rule, the Italian-based superstars Raynor had already done so much to nurture, were back in the national team, and Sweden were again comfortably outstripping the English performance.

Although Walter resisted the call for my return, he did decide to shake up England before the game with the Russians. He brought back Ronnie Clayton, for Eddie Clamp, and gave first caps to Clamp's Wolves club-mate Peter Broadbent and Chelsea's twenty-year-old winger Peter Brabrook in place of Bobby Robson and Bryan Douglas. England fought hard but the new blood was repulsed by the disciplined Russians, whose key performance came from Yuri Voinov, a hard, tactically adept defender who gave Johnny Haynes little breathing space.

The rest of the tournament was dominated by the rising pride of Sweden, who made it to the final, and the emergence of Pelé. I went home full of appreciation for the new sensation of the game and, perhaps understandably, quite a few questions about what place a Swedish adventure might have occupied in my football life if I had found the net in Belgrade.

One leading English football writer produced a postscript that encouraged the belief that my exile from the team was unlikely to be permanent. He bucked up the part of me that had yearned to be something more than a fascinated, close-up observer in Sweden. The tournament had showed me so much about the difference between playing club football, even against players such as di Stefano and Gento, and the international version.

I did, I have to admit all these years later, feel a surge of pride when I read, 'There were too many simple, straightforward players earning their prosaic bread and butter in our attack and that is why we failed. Without the injured Finney, no curtain call for Charlton, and with Stanley Matthews twiddling his thumbs, unwanted, elsewhere, we lacked the vital sparks that count.'

I put down the newspaper with a small gulp because I realised it didn't matter how many shadows had come across my view of football, I did know that out on the pitch was still the most natural place for me to be. Many years later, I read how Malcolm Allison always believed that the field of play was an island, where he could leave behind all the troubles and worries of life. It was somewhere that allowed him, as it did me, to do the thing that he did best, and only that. Malcolm, a brilliant, innovative coach, had been impressed by the Russian team when, as a young national serviceman, he saw them training in the Prater Woods of Vienna, and he had a vision of what the

English game might be that he shared with the sportswriters analysing the World Cup effort.

There was no question, though, about what Brazil had brought to the land of pale northern light in their march towards their first World Cup triumph. They had broken new football ground as surely as the Hungarians had promised to do earlier in the decade. Their rhythm was beautiful and mocked the belief that it couldn't travel across the ocean with success. Most of all, more than their fierce focus on the task and their wonderful skill, they had brought the little lad who would dominate the game as no one has done before him or since.

He took hold of the ball as if it was solely his possession and his right. People were trying to kick him but they couldn't touch him, and still less frighten him. He lifted the ball over their heads and he popped it into the net as though it was the easiest thing in the world.

I would see Pelé again, soon enough, out on the field, and there would be still more dramatic revelations. It is not, after all, so common that someone proclaims his genius in the most remarkable way the first time you meet him.

3

PELE

PELE FIRST ANNOUNCED himself to me in that Swedish summer he claimed for his own, as he did to the rest of the world beyond Brazil, where he was already known to be potentially the greatest phenomenon in all their football history. But then, seeing him was not quite the same as playing against him.

The most indelible mark he left on my consciousness came after the formalities and handshakes at the Maracana Stadium in Rio nearly a year after his triumph in Stockholm. None of his subsequent achievements, and of course so many of them took us beyond the limits of what was considered possible from one individual player, would obscure the memory of his first astonishing impact on me out on the field.

His reputation was already immense, and a great roar of anticipation rolled down from the vast terraces as he received the ball on the edge of the centre circle, but I refused to be intimidated. Aware that my England defensive team-mates were alert and holding their positions behind me, I said to myself, 'Okay, come on Pelé, come on then, show us what you can do.'

He might have been reading my mind because he did that precisely, and more dramatically than I could ever have imagined or feared. He didn't do what he so often did, play a simple pass and then move into a position where his desired pattern could develop and he could seek out a place of maximum danger to the opposition. No, on this occasion he committed

48

himself to something rather more spectacular. He sold me a perfect dummy and raced on our goal, leaving me struggling in his wake. With hardly a change of stride he sent me one way, and then went another. It was as if I'd been foolish enough to try to catch a gust of wind.

The biggest embarrassment, though, was that just before he fired the ball past our goalkeeper, Eddie Hopkinson of Bolton Wanderers, he shouted, 'Goal!' or, as they say in Brazil, 'Goooo . . . aaaall!'

First he made the cry of triumph and then he made his shot. It was not the normal sequence of events. He hit the ball from about thirty yards and it just looped inside the post. Hopkinson was dumbfounded and I looked at my boots, sighed and said, 'Bloody Hell.'

It was maybe the most extraordinary thing I had ever heard or seen on a football field, and without doubt it was the most unanswerable statement. It wasn't bombast or speculation. It was an announcement of impending fact. He knew it, and before the ball reached the net, I knew it, and several other things, too.

This was an eighteen-year-old footballer who lived to play the game and who had come so quickly to the belief that there was nothing on a football field beyond his powers.

I had fought my way back into the England team, partly because of the press clamour, no doubt, but also because, after a summer's rest and the chance to disperse some of the worst demons of Munich, I was enjoying my football again – and scoring the kind of goals that had first helped to establish my reputation.

It was comfortable once more to be in the colours of United. I felt on top of what I was doing and this transferred fairly seamlessly to the renewed challenge of establishing myself with England. I wanted it more surely now, and I believed I could cope with it much more easily than in those first anxious months after Munich. But then what Pelé did, the brilliance and the swagger of it, told me that for all my ability, and the acclaim I was receiving as generously as ever before from the English press, here was somebody out on a plane of his own. Down the years, nothing would diminish for me the meaning of that extraordinary encounter with an opponent who was so clearly capable of making his own rules.

Right from the start, he knew that all eyes were upon him, he was at the centre of every show, and he loved that. He is just the same today whenever I see him, as I do frequently, around the football world. Although such a key part of his brilliance and effectiveness on the field was that he understood perfectly the principles of teamwork, there has always been a big part of him that has responded, and indeed gloried, in all the attention he has received. The man who could effortlessly make superb chances for his team-mates – as he did so memorably for Carlos Alberto in the 1970 World Cup final – without ever thinking of his own opportunities if a fellow player was in a better position to score, would always love the fact that he caused a stir whenever he walked into a room. There was a simplicity, even a humility, about the ball Pelé sent squarely into the path of Carlos Alberto for that final goal against Italy – the one they called the 'President's Goal' because the Brazilian head of state had predicted a haul of four goals.

Pelé could do the unthinkable but he was also prepared to restrict himself to the simplest move if he considered it the best option. So many gifted players lack this understanding that they can never be more than a member of a team, which is why they remained gifted rather than great. For Carlos Alberto, he made a little dummy and then waited for the run from the full back before rolling the ball into his path. Carlos Alberto didn't have to break his stride. However, beyond the touchline, Pelé has never been inclined to be self-effacing.

A great smile still transforms his face, which in repose can often be deeply reflective, even sad, at the first ripple of applause, whether it comes in the street or at some public occasion when he is sitting among kings and presidents. His lustre seems to grow with the years.

He invariably brings an entourage of five or six people, and they know their duties. Some of them precede him, making sure that everything is right and that everyone is aware that he will be arriving in a few minutes. There is another certainty. He will always be a little late, but then that is the privilege of royalty and the most popular celebrities, and don't they have a duty to bring anticipation to a fine point?

On the field, everything came out of his own mind and instincts, as though he was creating a new game as he went along. Who can forget the phenomenal goal he almost scored in the World Cup of Mexico 1970, when both he and his team-mates hit a level of imagination and execution that is unlikely ever to be surpassed?

Earlier in the tournament he showed how deeply he was exploring his game, and his confidence, when he went for goal from inside his own half against Czechoslovakia. He failed narrowly but his audacity took away everyone's breath, and set an example that David Beckham, among others, would eventually follow with success. I don't think anything Pelé did was ever taught, and the ultimate evidence of that was what he so nearly achieved against the fine Uruguay goalkeeper Ladislao Mazurkiewicz. It was surely beyond imitation.

Tostao, a fantastically subtle player, made the through pass and Pelé came on to it at an angle. Before touching the ball, he dummied Mazurkiewicz, as he had me at the Maracana eleven years earlier, and when his shot bounced an inch the wrong side of the far post, I found myself saying, 'You bugger, how do you think about coming up with a dummy like that?'

There will always be debate about who is the best player football has ever seen, but as far as I'm concerned, after watching,

and in many cases playing with and against, the greatest footballers of the last sixty years or so, I don't believe anyone but
Pelé could have conceived and executed such a move.

Ferenc Puskas and Diego Maradona will always have their
supporters, as will my United team-mate George Best. Maradona
was an astonishing dribbler, with tremendous control of the
ball, as was Georgie, and there is no doubt that in terms of
innovation, and sheer brilliant thinking and execution, it is very
hard to ignore the claims of Johan Cruyff.

If you ask me who was the most precise passer I ever saw
on the international field, I would have to say Michel Platini
of France. And, in my mind, Alfredo di Stefano will always be
a challenger for the top spot, because he played in my position,
and I saw a lot of him when I was coming into the game. Yet,
the years only seem to entrench Pelé ever more deeply as the
player who had all the assets you would ever want – and then
a little more. He saw everything – and he did everything.

Back in 1959, with his fame still in the foothills, he probably
felt there was no better place to announce his love of centre
stage than in the Maracana, the temple of Brazilian football,
and against an England team who had been alone in defying
the brilliance of its emerging force in Sweden the year before.
Much had been made of this in the build-up to our game.
Would the English, having escaped with a draw in the World
Cup group game, finally be obliged to bend the knee? The
match was painted as a little unfinished business for the new
world champions.

For us, unfortunately, it came at the start of another ordeal
stretching out on various patches of foreign soil, fresh indica-
tors that, for all the talent and experience of Finney, Haynes
and Wright, England were still as far away as ever from truly
challenging the strongest teams in the world.

My return to the team in the first match after the disappointment of the World Cup, a 3–3 draw against Northern

Ireland in Belfast in October, had gone well enough but there were few encouraging signs that we might be moving back towards our old status as one of international football's most formidable teams.

For me, though, there was definitely a surge of the old belief in what I could do, and it was confirmed when I opened the 1958–59 season with a hat-trick against Chelsea at Old Trafford. We won 5–2, and despite grim predictions that the effects of Munich – no longer countered by the first wave of emotion that carried us all the way to a Wembley Cup final against Bolton in the previous spring – would begin to bite more deeply, United were in second place in the League after five games, including a 6–1 thrashing of Blackburn Rovers at Old Trafford.

The two goals I scored against my England team-mates Bryan Douglas and Ronnie Clayton took my season's total to eight and I was able to maintain that scoring rhythm throughout the season. My final total of twenty-nine goals left me eight ahead of superb marksman Dennis Viollet. Against all expectations, United finished in second place in the table, six points behind defending champions Wolves and five in front of third-placed Arsenal. For both United and me, this was an achievement beyond any reasonable hope.

It was supposed to be a time of desperate survival, but un-accountably there was a tingle of optimism in the air, and in the seventh league game, before my own people at St James' Park, I scored again to rescue a draw that at one point had seemed beyond us. I almost scored a winner, which, against the flow of the game, would have been rather outrageous. But it would have registered a certain truth. It would have said that we were alive again, and open to good fortune as well as bad.

As I had suspected in the wake of England's disgrace in Belgrade a few months earlier, consistent scoring would always play a key part in my international career, and from that perspective it was probably inevitable that I would reclaim an England shirt. My club form, and scoring touch, was good, and when I scored a hat-trick against Poland in an Under-23 international in September, Walter Winterbottom recalled me to the full England team. For the Under-23s I played at inside left, along-side Joe Baker, who was making a great impact north of the border with Hibernian, and when the goals began to flow I had the strongest sense that I would be returning to the senior England team.

I had felt extremely comfortable on the ball against Poland, and no doubt it was reassuring to have my Old Trafford team-mates Wilf McGuinness and Albert Scanlon alongside me. However, if I wouldn't say I quite felt the old man of the team – I was still short of my twenty-first birthday – I had shared a room with Billy Wright, Tommy Finney had laid a goal on for me at Hampden Park, and, of course, I was a connoisseur of haggis. Yes, I had covered a little of the football territory now, I had been up and down, and my mood had not been so posi-tive or confident for quite some time.

The potential of the national team was underlined by the quality displayed against the youth of Poland. But it was to take the arrival of Alf Ramsey a few years later before it was fully released.

Jimmy Greaves, arguably the most natural goal-scorer the nation has ever produced, found the net, and also announcing his international credentials in his first representative game was the quick and skilful Joe Baker.

There was a warm feeling at Old Trafford a few days later when the news came that my friend and team-mate Wilf McGuinness would be joining me on my return to the England team at Windsor Park.

Wilf might have fallen with my other close friends at Munich had he not missed the trip through injury, but his escape was one key reason why the team had managed to remain competitive.

He had also provided huge support to me as I came to terms

with the tragedy and the demands it was making on all who survived it. Wilf was a ferociously committed player, as hard as nails on the field, but also a romantic, and he and his family had embraced me as warmly as Eddie Colman and his parents had done when I arrived in Manchester as a wide-eyed fifteen-year-old. Now, as a veteran of three internationals (and a World Cup spent in close proximity with the top players of England, everywhere except on the pitch), I could briefly take him by the hand – not that Wilf was ever in much need of guidance. I had never met anyone so dedicated to his career – and to his club – and the way he responded to the challenge of replacing Duncan Edwards in the United team – surely the most awesome challenge any player could have faced – told me that he had a great career ahead of him, for both his club and his country.

Heart-breaking injury would intrude into this confident belief soon enough, but even today it has not diluted his extraordinary passion for the game. Wilf offered me more than personal support. He showed me what it was to be embraced by a firm set of values along with a love for football, and never, despite the worst of luck, did he abandon the feelings that shaped his life.

The Northern Irish match of October 1958, which would be heralded as a triumphant return for me – my two goals took my total for England to five in four matches – was not so good for Walter Winterbottom after the anticlimax of the World Cup campaign. The team showed three changes from the one that had failed to score against the USSR in the play-off game in Gothenburg. McGuinness came in for Bill Slater, Tom Finney was back on the left wing in place of his understudy Alan A'Court and I replaced Derek Kevan.

Our team hotel had a wonderful view of the Mountains of Mourne, and in the relaxing and enjoyable build-up to the game, Tommy Banks continued to enhance his reputation as the team comic. The tough, blunt Lancastrian took his club job of marking Matthews, Finney and Bobby Mitchell, Newcastle's virtuoso left winger, far more seriously than he ever took himself.

However, when kick-off came at Windsor Park, on a wet night with a wild wind, it was soon clear we were not about to produce a convincing performance. I cannot remember another pitch that held to your feet so discouragingly. My two goals – Finney scored the other – provided a deceptive dressing for an unsatisfactory performance. Whenever I think back to that game, there is one overwhelming memory. It is of a ball so weighty we might have been playing with a cannonball. The team never struck an overall rhythm or cohesion. We played in small spurts and for long stretches of the game I felt no more comfortable than I had in Belgrade.

It was thus surprising, and perhaps confirmation of my early belief that in international football a goal, however it is scored, and in whatever context, tends to disguise quite a number of sins, that Winterbottom came up to me afterwards to say, 'Well done, Bobby, I thought you had a great game.'

Perhaps Walter was clutching for some relief from the pressure of his situation. This was England's seventh game without a win, a run of futility that had started in Belgrade, and the immediate future was not exactly filled with the promise of easy victories. Our next match was against the USSR, whom we had failed to beat three times the previous season.

Then we had to play Wales at Villa Park, Scotland, no doubt still feeling the pain of our victory at Hampden on my debut, and Italy, who always put a lot of pride into their performances at Wembley. None of this was guaranteed to send us confidently into the jaws of the Maracana, where Pelé awaited us, in the spring.

There was no doubt that the World Cup in Sweden had compounded the failure in Switzerland four years earlier and confirmed that England were drifting towards the margins of the international game, a situation that would have been unthinkable when Finney, now aged thirty-six, first came surging into the team twelve years earlier.

He scored in his first game, a 7–2 win over Northern Ireland in September 1946, and then a few days later struck home the only goal in a victory over the Republic of Ireland. England were impregnable at home then, and when they travelled abroad, enormous crowds showed up to see such legends as Stanley Matthews, Wilf Mannion and Raich Carter, as well as the emerging Finney.

The high point of Finney's England career was probably in Lisbon in 1950, when he scored four goals in a 5–3 defeat of Portugal. Even by his own standards, he was said to be quite extraordinary that day.

Now he was claiming his seventy-sixth cap, playing against the USSR in front of sceptical fans who had little optimism for the future. No one knew it would be Finney's last game for England. He still played beautifully, as we had seen most dramatically in Moscow just five months earlier, but the years and a persistent groin injury were beginning to bite into even this most competitive of natures. In the circumstances, it was just as well that Johnny Haynes, who had been held up to me so highly by Walter Winterbottom, put in one of his most magnificent performances.

Haynes displayed all the virtues that had been extolled by Walter, the teacher of football, in Moscow – and more. We won 5–0 and Johnny Haynes was at the heart of every move. He scored three goals with crushing authority and was especially brilliant in that area where Winterbottom had said I had to show most improvement. His reading of the game was uncanny. Lying deep, he carved opened the Russian defence quite effortlessly with long and brilliantly accurate passing, and then, at almost the moment of delivery, he was moving forward to pick up returned passes and bear down on goal.

If there had been a flicker of doubt in my mind when Winterbottom offered Haynes as the perfect model for a young midfielder, they were swept aside now, just as my reservations that nobody could be as good as the Duncan Edwards painted by Jimmy Murphy when we first met were pulverised the first time I saw my United club-mate out on the field.

After our Wembley victory, and the mastery of Haynes, I was surprised and disappointed by the cool reaction to an individual and team performance that I thought was outstanding, quite the best I had known since joining up with the national team.

I had moved over to inside right and much enjoyed the chance to operate between the guile of Bryan Douglas and the wonderfully committed presence of Nat Lofthouse, who had been christened the Lion of Vienna for his heroic, two-goal performance in the 3–2 win over a powerful Austrian team six years earlier.

Like Finney, Lofthouse was coming to the end of his playing days in that October 1958 – he would play just once more for England – but he too carried some of the best of football values, and his finest days had also come at a time when no one would have believed the national team would one day go seven games without a win.

Lofthouse was immense in the air against the terrified defence of the USSR. You could only mourn the fact that he had been absent from the game that had mattered so much more in Sweden, when England failed to produce anything like the pressure he so consistently generated at Wembley with his work in the air and his powerful runs. There was a limit to how many of those runs the ruggedly built thirty-four-year-old could make, but he brought an old pro's timing, and great courage, to his work, and I was delighted when he scored the fifth goal near the end, my own tally having moved forward from the penalty spot.

So the subdued reaction of the morning papers amazed me.

In the past there had been no reluctance to celebrate spectacular performances, as I had found to my benefit after my
scoring debut against Scotland. I could only conclude that we
were paying a price for a long period of disappointment. Perhaps
the press and the public were reserving their judgement. Maybe
they were saying, 'Yes, this was fine, but what will you do for
your next turn?'

Soon enough that would be a rather embarrassing question,
but not before continued media scrutiny and pressure forced
home the view that England were entering a critical climate.
Impatience with our failure to prove that we could operate on
the same level as the world's leading teams was beginning to
bite home. Brazil, and before them Hungary, and even little
Sweden, had shown new possibilities of what could be done.
Old assumptions about our own place in the football world,
how it was so set in tradition, were clearly under more pressure than ever before.

Suddenly, the close season tour of the Americas, starting in
Rio and finishing in Los Angeles, was not so much a challenge
as an investigation. First, though, we had to negotiate a few
more potential disasters. Johnny Haynes was injured for the
game against Wales at Villa Park in November, and we were
thankful for two goals from Peter Broadbent, which helped us
to a 2–2. Then for me there was another batch of favourable
headlines when I scored the only goal against Scotland at
Wembley in April 1959. It was a sweet and unusual goal because
I scored it with my head. Haynes, fit and in commanding form
again, started the move with a pass to Broadbent, who switched
the play to Douglas on the right wing. When I saw Douglas's
cross curling towards the six-yard line, I threw myself forward
and upwards to head past the advancing Scottish goalkeeper,
Bill Brown.

Unlike Tommy Younger, Brown did not rush to congratulate
me, but I did receive a warm embrace from Billy Wright, who

had prepared me so well for that first challenge against the Scots. He was playing his 100th game for England and I was pleased that I helped to make it a winning occasion.

I scored another goal, along with my new United team-mate Warren Bradley, in the 2–2 draw with Italy at Wembley on the eve of our flight to Rio, but again the critics were under-whelmed, despite the fact that a good Italian side had scored their goals while we were down to ten men because of injury to Ron Flowers. I was happy with my own performance and delighted with the goal, which came from a pass by Haynes, a side-step from me and a shot from just outside the penalty area.

That should have put me in the best of moods as the team bus carried us to Heathrow airport, but it was a little discon-certing to read in the press that in South America we would be torn to pieces.

4

FLIGHT OF FANCY

ANOTHER WORRY THAT I suppose was always going to grow, beyond the threat of whatever Pelé or Garrincha might do to us when we faced them in the Maracana, filled my mind on the ride to Heathrow. I tried to push it into the margins, along with those more day-to-day emotions of sadness and loss, but in the end, it was always there. Once more it was crowding me as we made our way through the check-in desk and passport control to the plane that would carry us on our twenty-four-hour journey.

No amount of banter from my team-mates, and at the start of such a trip there is always plenty of that, could provide more than the most fleeting diversion. It was so basic, this nagging apprehension that even today, after having travelled so many millions of air miles, I still feel it in my bones, at least to some extent. Before facing the football trial painted so darkly in the morning newspapers, first we had to get to South America, and with the Munich tragedy still not much more than a year old, this was my particular concern. I had looked at the itinerary with more than a little anxiety, counted up the flying time and visualised many lonely hours. For me, the idea of sleeping through some of the longest flights of the infant international air routes seemed as ambitious as making Pelé look like some routine football talent.

However my moods fluctuated, there was still the hard tug

at the pit of my stomach when it came to getting on a plane. England had already carried me through the first bouts of fear with relatively brief flights to Yugoslavia, Russia and Sweden, but what I faced now was of a much different order – my first long-haul flight.

First, we flew down the West African coast to Dakar in Senegal and then re-fuelled and headed out across the Atlantic. There were still an awful lot of flying hours ahead of me, eleven in total, in that propeller-engined aircraft we'd boarded in Dakar for the flight to Rio de Janeiro. Every so often I looked out of the window and saw the engines glowing red.

From time to time I would calculate how many hours were left, and thus how many miles, and where roughly we were in the crossing of the ocean that seemed, as my team-mates, one by one, drifted from their card games and their books into sleep, to have no end. I remember announcing to myself, 'Well, we've been going five hours now, so we're halfway between Africa and South America.' It was not as reassuring as I had hoped.

At such times, I called up all the statistics I knew that underlined how safe flying really was, even in those early days of airlines. By then, I could quote them as though they were some catechism drawn up expressly for me. Didn't everyone know it was far more dangerous to get into a car or cross a busy road? But statistics are only statistics, as Munich had so devastatingly shown. They were in abeyance, after all, when the cabin went so quiet on our third attempt at take-off and the plane kept churning on through the runway slush, until it collided with the house and burst into flames.

On that flight to South America, and on so many others afterwards, when we hit a bout of turbulence or an engine suddenly made unfamiliar noises, I told myself that I couldn't but fly. You couldn't be a top-class footballer and not get on a plane. The alternative was to hide away and give up everything that had coloured so many of my dreams.

There was so much to see in the world, so many sensations to experience, and even the occasional stutter of the droning engines did not take away entirely the tingles of excitement that came when I thought of what awaited me in such exotic places as Rio, Lima, the capital of Peru lying beyond the Andes on the Pacific coast, Mexico City and, finally, Los Angeles, the home of the stars whom my United team-mates and I watched so often, using our free passes to the city-centre cinemas.

I had to measure such experiences against the drag of apprehension at flight time. I had to tell myself that I couldn't give in to feelings that were at first quite natural but could, easily enough, threaten to become both unshakeable and irrational. More recently, I had to sympathise with Dennis Bergkamp, the Dutch player who missed important games for his club, Arsenal, because he couldn't face the prospect of short-haul flights in Europe. But then my instinct to offer advice or help was restrained by the fact that Bergkamp was a mature person – and no one knows better than I do that this is an intensely personal problem.

On the flights to Dakar and Rio I also recalled the visit of an American air force general to the hospital in Munich. 'Well, boys,' he said, 'it's going to be hard for you the next time you get in a plane, but try to remember this old guy. I've survived six crashes. Once I came down in New York. Usually it's pilot error. Mechanical problems are much less frequent with the improvement in testing. But, in the end, you have to consider the alternative to flying. In today's world it just means that you're not going anywhere.' He was a craggy character and, in his matter of fact way, he was reassuring. He couldn't take away all the dread that came to me when I walked up the steps to board an airliner, but what he could do was make it a part of life that just had to be negotiated, something that simply had to be done.

And then when you did it, and suffered it, there were astonishing rewards for a young footballer who, as a boy playing for

Northumberland Schoolboys, longed for his team to be drawn away so that he could stay in some fancy hotel in somewhere like Hull.

For a little while, any kind of ordeal we might face in the Maracana, or the anxieties I had been forced to confront in the air, were a small price to pay for experiencing the wonders of Rio. In all the travel that has been such a big part of my life since those days, nothing has quite carried the impact of landfall in Brazil. We stayed in a hotel overlooking Copacabana and the view was quite mesmerising. Huge rollers came pounding in to the beach, making rag dolls of the lithe young people who had walked across the sand to meet them as though governed by some samba beat going on in their heads.

Five years later, when Alf Ramsey led us back there to play in the Brazilian Jubilee Tournament, a dangerous reality did intrude into this picture of paradise. Johnny 'Budgie' Byrne, a highly-skilled contender for a striking role in the coming World Cup challenge back home in England, found himself in serious difficulties amid the rollers. He waved and shouted, though his cries were lost in the roar of the waves and at these perilous moments he was at risk of paying a heavy price for a lifetime of larking and practical joking. It was only later we would learn of his panic when he felt so powerless against the weight of the sea. He said he felt like a piece of paper blown about in a cyclone. At the time we thought that, once again, he was kidding. Budgie was a bit of an extrovert and this seemed to be one of his larks. 'What a card, that Budgie,' someone said, but the truth was he had been hit by a couple of huge waves and they had taken away his strength. Fortunately, he was deposited safely on the sand by a more gentle current and managed to drag himself away from danger. He was, though, a little more subdued then usual that night.

In 1959, I might have been in a trance, staring out at a cloudless blue sky framing the statue of Christ the Redeemer, and watching the planes dipping in from around Sugar Loaf Mountain.

Rio was seething with life. The streets were electric, the traffic crazy. During the next few days, we got the chance to swim in the blue ocean and climb up to the peak of Corcovado to take a closer look at the statue that dominates the landscape of the city. (On my most recent trip, nearly fifty years later, it still had the power to take my breath away.) We had one training session on an island, and from the boat we saw a stingray rise up above the waves, and I remember thinking, 'What a fantastic world football is showing me.'

If I have tried to explain the pain of Munich and its lingering effects, I also hope I have conveyed the excitement I felt in Rio. Already, I had seen and been touched by so much and now here was a wonderful part of the world to experience and, it seemed to me in my enthusiasm for all these new sights, almost inhale.

But then I was reminded quickly enough that I wasn't a tourist. Walter Winterbottom told us we had to train in the broiling heat at the Fluminense ground. Thousands of inquisitive local people came to watch us work, perhaps wondering why we hadn't decided to do it in the cool evening. However, on the eve of the game, the rain came, and as we got our first sight of the blue and grey sweep of the Maracana, and anticipated it filled by 200,000 fans – we were told at least 500,000 would have been happy to pay the price of admission – we could only be grateful for the break in the weather. Billy Wright wiped the rain from his face and said, 'Every drop is worth a guinea to us.'

When Pelé and Didi got on the ball, requiring as many as three of us to contain them, our captain's estimate of the value of the rain did not seem excessive. Indeed, it was disturbing to imagine our difficulties if the day of the match had not been cool and overcast. As it was, we were stretched to our seams by the virtuosity of players who had already built vast reputations

– and amazed by the rather stunning evidence of the depth of Brazilian talent.

Brazil fielded three players who had not been sighted in the World Cup-winning campaign in Sweden, and two of them, Julinho and Canhoteiro, immediately proved that they would have been assets for any team in the world. Julinho, who had featured prominently in the 1954 tournament, was playing in Garrincha's place and showed much of the same ability to beat a man quite effortlessly. He scored inside two minutes, unleashing all kinds of explosions on the vast terraces, and Canhoteiro further undermined us by his determination not to be shaken off the ball as he ran directly at our defence. Jimmy Armfield was playing at left back with Don Howe on the right, and Wright took position in the middle of Ronnie Clayton and Ron Flowers.

Pelé was oozing confidence in his now established role as the young messiah of Brazil, and the prospect was of a terrible humiliation, something to put alongside the convulsion in Belgrade that had cast such a shadow over our World Cup challenge and pushed me on to the sidelines.

Yet for a while, and in defiance of all those grim forecasts that accompanied us on the flight to Rio, our nerve held. Although the ball control of our opponents was quite masterful and at times threatened to sweep us aside, Wright and his co-defenders refused to panic. Another great difficulty was that when we did win the ball, we found Brazil's defence to be as formidable as their attack. The full backs, Djalma and Nilton Santos, seemed to have added still more to the authority they had displayed in Sweden, and the players in the half-back line, Zito, Bellini and Orlando, were as hard in the tackle as they were smooth and easy in distributing the ball.

At times, the invitation to collapse could not have been more pressing, but somehow we staved off the worst possibilities. Indeed, on several occasions we managed to hit back at the Brazilian masters. A shot of mine was one of two efforts that hit the woodwork and, in the end, a 2–0 loss was far from the predicted disaster. That would come in Lima, with another one following in Mexico City, but in the meantime we could tell ourselves that we had survived the Maracana without disgrace.

I had plenty of time to tell myself this on the mostly sleepless 2,500-mile flight to Peru, and it was one point of encouragement as I looked down on the snow-covered peaks of the Andes. Winterbottom had us training, this time at the national stadium, within a few hours of arriving to a welcome by a party of pupils from a local school. The children were so immaculate in their blazers they might have come from some posh prep school in England, although soon enough we would be reminded we were a long way from home and under considerable pressure to perform.

Winterbottom made one change from the Maracana team and it was an historic one. Peter Broadbent, a player I admired very much for his combination of fine craft and drive, gave way to the still teenaged scoring phenomenon Jimmy Greaves.

Greaves had scored for Chelsea as a seventeen-year-old debutant, and it was maybe a commentary on the caution of English football, and the strange selection policies and methods that were in place at the time, that this great instinctive talent had been considered far too inexperienced to be selected for the World Cup in Sweden. That was the same tournament that Pelé came to dominate, at the age of seventeen, and I sat out as a twenty-year-old who had, all modesty aside, proved that he could score goals at the highest level. The point becomes more relevant when you remember that the curse of England in Sweden was a failure to find the net, not least in the goalless draw with Brazil.

Eventually, the claims of Jimmy Greaves to play for England would be at the centre of a huge national debate when he vied with Geoff Hurst for a place in the 1966 final with West Germany, but at the dawn of his international career in Peru, there did not seem to be the merest puff of cloud covering his name in the clear blue sky.

Against Peru, he did what for him had already become almost inevitable. He scored our only goal in a 4–1 defeat that fulfilled the worst prophecies of the occupants of the press box, but when Greaves struck home with a typical piece of opportunism and the most natural skill, you didn't have to be clairvoyant to know that soon enough all kinds of scoring records would be at his mercy. He still holds the Chelsea record against all-comers, from the legendary Tommy Lawton to a striking phenomenon of today, Didier Drogba. At the age of twenty-one, Greaves scored forty-one league goals in the 1960–61 season for Chelsea and by then had amassed over a hundred for the club. At twenty-three, the same age as another legend, Dixie Dean, he had notched up two hundred overall. Even during the period that most would assume to be among the rare failures in a dazzling career, his brief and unhappy stay with AC Milan in Italy, he achieved nine goals in fourteen matches – an excellent scoring rate in any league, but quite superb in defence-dominated Italy.

Greaves's performance, though, was a rare point of optimism in Lima's beautiful stadium. Mostly, the match was a shattering experience. Maybe we were suffering some of the effects of the arduous flights at the end of a long English season – the swift transfer from a plane seat to another unfamiliar training ground had become more than usually irksome. The more Peru developed their passing game, and showed off some impressive individual skills, the more we fell away from the best of our game.

But it wasn't only their ability on the ball that hindered our performance. I was particularly irritated by some of the marking I received. Time after time, as I tried to knock the ball past the defender and go, he would just step into my path without making any attempt to get the ball, or he would pull me back. Every member of our team – except perhaps Greaves, whom I was partnering in the centre – had some reason for regret when we left the field, weary and only too aware of the inevitable tone of the reports that were already being wired back to the national newspapers. I was particularly angry. It is bad enough to be beaten, and well beaten, but when you also feel that you haven't been given the chance to play, it is even harder to take.

The manner of our defeat gnawed at me so strongly as we suffered the final ordeal of the day – the routine post-game reception, which, in those days, was always staged by the home FA – that I finally gave way to my frustration. I did something that the secretary of the FA, the former referee Sir Stanley Rous would have considered not only reprehensible but also unthinkable in an international player who was now the owner of ten caps.

I went up to the referee, who spoke perfect English while rejecting my appeals for some protection during the game, and said, 'Can we have a little chat? I want to clear a few things up, and one thing in particular. Isn't it right that when I knock the ball past a defender and he grabs me, it's obstruction – and a free kick?'

The referee just nodded and said, 'Yes.'

So, naturally, I said, 'But then why didn't you penalise a defender who was breaking the rules?'

'Oh, I'm sorry, we don't do that here,' he replied. He was quite dismissive and I realised quickly enough the conversation was as futile as some of our exchanges in the heat of the game. I walked away, shaking my head and saying to myself, 'Well, that's bloody good, isn't it?'

Worse was to follow in the high altitude of Mexico City. At 7,000 feet, we struggled, quite literally, to breathe and the situation was so difficult that our trainer, Harold Shepherdson, brought oxygen cylinders to our dressing room at the University City Stadium. It didn't help sufficiently as we slipped to our third straight defeat in the shadow of the volcanic peaks of

Iztaccihuatl and Popocatapetl. Walter Winterbottom made two changes in a fruitless attempt to win at least a small spurt of approval from our critics. I was moved out to the left wing in place of Doug Holden, who moved to the right to take over from Norman Deeley, Derek Kevan returned to the team for the first time since the World Cup in Sweden, and Wilf McGuinness won his second cap at the expense of Ron Flowers.

Kevan scored a good early goal and it was encouraging that the Mexicans, despite plenty of running power and some hard tackling, were plainly not in the class of the Peruvians. But soon enough the thin air and the rough pitch began to neutralise our efforts. The field was flinty and the Mexicans were determined not to surrender an inch of their own soil. Long before the end of the game, every breath had the effect of a dagger plunged into your chest.

The Mexicans equalised shortly before half-time and when they took the lead soon after the restart, it was clear we were beaten. Where we had dared to dream in Rio, we were now firmly caught in a nightmare that permitted no escape.

All we could do, against a very modestly talented team, was limit the damage. We lost 2–1 and returned dispiritedly to our hotel to pack our bags for the last leg of a trip that, in football terms, had carried us from one impossible situation to another. Los Angeles at least offered some diversion, a little star-gazing perhaps along Hollywood Boulevard, and a sharp drop in pressure when we played against the United States.

If anyone was thinking that our predecessors, including Tom Finney, Wilf Mannion, Roy Bentley and Stan Mortensen, probably felt the same way when they faced the part-time and amateur Americans in the 1950 World Cup in Brazil, the game England lost 1–0, they didn't say it. But then Billy Wright, a survivor of that humiliating day in the mining town of Belo Horizonte, would have been more than human if he hadn't suffered a terrible attack of *déjà vu* when another American team, much less organised and committed than the winners of 1950, he said, leaped into the lead. This was much to the delight of the excitable public address commentator, who had enlisted Bobby Robson from our squad to give him some rudimentary insight into the rules and the strategies of 'soccerball'.

It did not help that we were playing in front of a large crowd in a small stadium with a pitch of mostly uncut grass – and a baseball diamond. I was playing on the wing again, which meant that I was obliged to run over the soil of the pitcher's mound.

You could only worry at the latest head of derision surely building in the press box, and the disgrace we faced after being feted by British residents at a lavish Hollywood party. As in Rio, we were being brought down to earth with some force. Apart from the hospitality, and the flattering presence of some expatriate film stars, we had been given some fleeting but unforgettable glimpses of the glamorous side of life in Los Angeles. We walked down Sunset Boulevard, went to the magnificent Hollywood Park racetrack, saw the Dodgers play and were dazzled by Sammy Davis's one-man show.

It was something of an anticlimax to arrive in the neighbourhood stadium with its blaring public address, long grass and clear, almost mocking, evidence that its primary purpose was hosting the much more serious business of baseball. When the announcer yelled his excitement at the American goal, I felt a great shudder running through my body.

I said to myself, 'This can't be happening again. Surely. This is terrible. We are England. We deserve to play on a proper pitch.' But then I concluded that what we deserved didn't really matter. What we had to do was win. We pulled ourselves together, realising the situation we had put ourselves in was just ridiculous, and in the end, won 8–1. Maybe my horror at the possibility of being involved in such a shameful defeat was reflected in the fact that I scored three of the goals. The others came from Flowers, two, Bradley, Kevan and Haynes. They were the result of a fierce collective decision. However farcical the situation, winning was a matter of pride, and this was a feeling that took hold of every member of the team.

One of my goals was a penalty and I can do no more to stress how important I felt it was to score than recall the words of the announcer. They remain as shrill today as they were nearly fifty years ago. As I prepared to take the kick, he cried out, 'Our goalkeeper has done well, he's saved a lot of shots, but you know he cannot move until Bobby Charlton takes his kick.'

I placed the ball perfectly, smacking it along the ground, but it slowed in the tall grass and the announcer yelled, 'The goalie's saved it . . .' and then, after pausing long enough for it to trickle over the line, he added, 'almost.'

Later, when we went to the official reception, we were told something I have heard quite relentlessly down the decades. 'Soccer is going to take off here in the next ten years,' said the president of the federation.

These days, with regular US participation in the World Cup finals, such a declaration has to be taken more seriously, but still you have to wonder if the game that is such a huge part of the culture of so much of the rest of the world will ever overcome the weight of traditional American sports to become a passion. By way of contrast, in Brazil, we saw that Pelé was able to impose so much more than his talent on his fellow countrymen. He had claimed for himself a national dream in winning the World Cup.

As we checked out of the Ambassador's Hotel in Hollywood, such musings were not high in my thoughts. American 'soccer' would just have to take its chances in a wider world. It was enough, for the moment at least, that England had avoided an ambush and one last broadside from the critics. I felt very strongly that it was time to put an end to the ridicule.

5

AFICIONADO

IT WAS ALL very well my declaring that English football had to turn a new page as I packed my souvenirs and memories and looked out on the Californian sunshine, but of course the delivery of action rather than words was far from guaranteed. I could also tell myself we had too much tradition and too much talent to spend the rest of our lives in the margins of international football. However, over the next few years, we would have to produce a lot more than good intentions, however heartfelt. A major reappraisal of the way we selected and ran the national team was overdue. Most profoundly of all, we had to look at the way we played the game.

England may have escaped from the tall grass in Los Angeles with a little honour and rescued prestige, but the homecoming message awaiting us at Heathrow could hardly have been harsher. Criticism was still pouring from the sports pages. Squally days lay ahead for Walter Winterbottom, and for all the players who had failed to compete with teams occupying considerably lower rungs of the football ladder than the world champions, Brazil. No one was exempt, we were told. No one's survival was guaranteed. England's top players had been living on their reputations for too long. It was time to be held to account, and for some new thinking.

When I got over the hostility of much of the writing, and the feeling that some of the comments were a bit unfair on players who were, inevitably, tired after a long season, and had faced some difficult conditions, especially in Mexico, I could see some elements of truth in the criticism.

We did have gifted players, but did we have a proper system to develop them? Did we have the revolutionary methods of training and preparation that had put certain teams, including Brazil and Italy, and even such small nations as Hungary and Austria and largely amateur Sweden, on a different level of competitiveness? No one in authority seemed to be asking these questions with enough force or urgency, and if members of the press were increasingly impatient, perhaps they had a point, and perhaps it was being too easily dismissed or ignored by the council men of the Football Association. In England, the home of the game, we couldn't begin to point to the kind of facilities that had taken my breath away in Moscow a year earlier.

And it wasn't just in terms of custom-built bricks and mortar that we were behind. It seemed that not only had the Brazilians developed new training methods, but there were fantastic stories that they were employing psychologists. Perhaps, you were forced to speculate, this was one reason why Pelé, for instance, could be so confidently released as a crucial factor in a World Cup at such a tender age.

For England, the challenge was even more fundamental than the undoubtedly important task of preparing young players for a smooth arrival in international football. The success of the Brazilians in Sweden had shown us that the game was changing at a fast rate, and we had undoubtedly been left behind in certain key areas. In our game, players such as Ron Flowers and Eddie Clamp represented classic strength at half back. They were big and tough, and Flowers, particularly, had a good eye for goal. But they were not players of pace and subtlety. Commanding in the domestic game, they did not have the touch and vision of Zito of Brazil or Josef Masopust of Czechoslovakia. Early in the fifties, we still believed that we had a right to be the dominant force in the game we had given the world, and even when this old idea had first been questioned by the humiliating exit from the 1950 World Cup – England's first entry into the tournament – and then splintered by the sensational performance of Hungary at Wembley in 1953, we were slow to accept that our way had been first studied and then surpassed.

Aside from mutterings in the dressing room and some campaigning from the press box, there was little movement to change an absurd selection system despite evidence of malaise accumulating at a dismaying rate. We were still capable of producing some exceptional performances, but developing a consistent pattern was an entirely different matter. The concept of moulding a compatible team, rather than random attempts to pick from what was considered the best of current form – and the leaning of selectors to the cause of their own club players – was still something for future consideration rather than immediate action.

Regardless of these failings, a youngster such as myself, who had already been so impressed by the qualities of ageing players including Tom Finney and Lofthouse, had to believe that there was still much quality in English football. In the company of Johnny Haynes and the man who was considered the likeliest candidate to replace Billy Wright as captain, Blackburn Rovers' Ronnie Clayton, I dared to imagine I might be part of a more successful epoch. It was certainly true that England could still produce talent that might be confidently placed on the world stage. Jimmy Greaves was a prime example.

What wasn't in doubt, however, was that no one in the English game, from administrators through managers and coaches to the players, could any longer believe in a natural right to succeed. For me, that truth was nearer to home than I might have imagined when I left Los Angeles filled with such a firm resolve to help transform the image of the national team. In just a matter of months I had discovered, all over again, that few in the game had a more pressing need to look at themselves than I had.

During the 1959–60 season, I was returned for a while to the ghostly world of reserve football, and the sobering experience of being able to pick out individual cries of impatience and complaint from the terraces. 'You're bloody finished, Charlton,' was one of the more encouraging yells that still echo down the years. It was an unnerving experience. I had got used to playing in front of vast crowds, who generate a single roar of noise. With insults raining down, I knew this wasn't a place I wanted to hang around.

Fortunately, I was soon able to look back on that time, and ponder on the theory that sometimes it is possible to grow strong at the broken places, that an injection of adversity at the age of twenty-one is probably a lot better than the regrets that can come a few years later if you have been allowed to run away with yourself. With all the laudatory headlines that followed my emergence as an England player, there was maybe a chance that it might have happened to me. But just as there was no hint of a soft landing after the England trip, no relief was forthcoming in the new season. Complaints about the image of English football on its journey through the Americas growled on, and bit deep in the newspapers, and the call for new blood and new vision was even louder and more intense than the one that greeted failure in the Swedish World Cup. The Brazilians were on the mountain top but where were we? We were still stuck in the foothills. The evidence, we were told, was overwhelming.

No one could complain. It's true that the logistics of the tour were tough and the challenge had come at the end of another long season, marked by crowded fixtures and pitches that would have left the modern player aghast, but this was the world we inhabited and accepted and in which we had to be judged.

For me, the harshest perspective came in one of those reserve games, at home to Stoke City, to which I had been banished, along with Wilf McGuinness, goalkeeper Harry Gregg and Warren Bradley, after a poor, losing performance against Everton at the end of November. Busby decided the team needed a shake-up, a reminder that just because Wilf and Warren had joined me in the England team, and Harry Gregg had been accorded hero status at Old Trafford for some time, it didn't mean that any of us were guaranteed places. I was required to stew on this statement of fact for three matches in front of thin terraces and that new and often very critical, even derisive, audience.

In my case, this was a brief interruption in the belief that my future as a top international was assured. But for Wilf it was the tragic professional turning point in his tremendous effort to replace Duncan Edwards in both the United and England teams. He broke his leg during that period in the reserves in a way that you realised immediately would not permit any routine recovery. A Stoke player attempted to kick the ball with Wilf in close attendance, but instead connected with his opponent's leg. It was an accident, you could see that clearly enough, but that was little consolation to Wilf as his leg snapped sickeningly. The dread of every professional had become a reality for my friend who, more than anyone I knew, loved the game so deeply and had never stopped giving thanks that he could play it in the shirt of his beloved Manchester United, and then England.

He slaved, over years not months, to regain full fitness and all the confidence and ambition of the performances that had carried him into the national team. In the end, he had to admit that the task was beyond him, but before that concession he underlined to everyone at Old Trafford, and in the England set-up, the folly of taking anything for granted. You might think, so soon after Munich, no football club on earth was less in need of such a lesson, but the truth in football is that complacency can grow quickly, and fatally, on the back of even just a few weeks of high performance. One exceptional match, one burst of acclaim, can banish all your doubts, make you feel indestructible.

Wilf's fate threw a huge shadow across some of the happier conclusions that had come at the end of the long journey of early summer and balanced the disappointments that had accumulated on the field. If the road from Rio to Los Angeles had brought frustrations and trials, it had also given me experiences of, and an appetite for, a much wider world, and I would always be able to draw upon them.

I see now that in some ways it made me a different person, more aware of and interested in the teeming life that went on beyond the touchlines of a football pitch. For one thing, I became, despite a forest of raised eyebrows down the years, not least from my wife and daughters, and perhaps never more so than in these days of political correctness, a lifelong aficionado in the purest sense of the term. In Mexico, I fell in love with bullfighting. I fell in love with the colour and the swirl of the music, the drama and the courage of the matadors. It was something completely out of my experience – I could never have imagined any of it when I played football in the streets and parks of Ashington and took the bus to Newcastle with Jack. It was strange and disturbing but also fascinating in a way that would never wane. It was so different, it may as well have been happening on another planet.

Yes, I could see it was cruel on the bulls, but as Ernest Hemingway said in his *Death in the Afternoon* – a book I devoured in my new enthusiasm – everything depended on your emotional response, whether you identified with the man or the animal.

Instinctively, I put myself in the place of the matador. I saw a challenge that went beyond the parameters of a football field, where it only felt a little like death to lose a huge match. For us, the consequences of failure never included the prospect of a sudden dimming of the light and the loss of your life.

People might shake their heads but the truth is that, for me, it was instant absorption. It took me away from the depression that came so hard with defeat by a much inferior Mexican team. I was moping in the hotel when someone asked, 'Does anyone want to see a bullfight?' Why not?

I felt as though I was entering a different world when I took my place on the high terracing in the *sol* section, where you feel the blast of the sun, avoided by those who pay for the more expensive *sombra* tickets. *Sol y sombra*, sun and shade, seemed to be just one more dividing line between rich and poor in a city where beggars cooked scraps of food at the doors of a breathtaking cathedral where a high altar is made of solid gold.

The Plaza de Toros in Mexico City is the biggest in the world and the atmosphere in the late afternoon could be compared to anything I had experienced in the Bernabeu in Madrid, the Lenin Stadium in Moscow and even the Maracana. This had another dimension, of course, in the possibility of a man dying. The sand could soon be streaked with the blood not only of the bulls, but of one of those colourfully dressed little figures, standing in the face of a great beast.

Yes, I know well enough now something I was first discovering on that Mexican afternoon. The bullfight is not a sporting contest, evenly balanced between two competitors, because of course it could never be that. The bull would win every time in such even circumstances, but again this is not the issue. The bull is not a competitor but the object of a ritual, the purpose of which is not winning or losing but defining a man's courage. Ironically, human courage is always best and most cleanly displayed when the bull is the bravest of his breed. The matador receives assistance from the picadors and the banderilleros, but his performance is always rated on the courage with which he works and the boldness of his kill, which brings the moment of ultimate danger when he goes in over the horns.

The closer the matador works to the horns, the greater the appreciation of the crowd. From fight to fight on that first afternoon, my understanding of this developed, but nothing I had seen before the entry of the final bull prepared me for what was to follow.

The bull was reluctant and refused to come out into the sunlight to do what it had been bred to do. The more it was prodded and cajoled, the less willing it seemed to be. The crowd howled and waved white handkerchiefs of protest in the direction of the president's box. Then, suddenly, the sand was covered by young men and boys who had climbed over the barricades to make their protest. Mayhem ensued when steers were sent into the ring to draw out the bull, which was still resisting all efforts to lure him into the action.

It was sheer tumult. When the bull finally came out, it was greeted with jeers and whistles, and some of the boys grabbed it by the tail. The worst possible conditions were being created for the matador, who must have been experiencing terrible professional dread – facing a reluctant, tricky and unpredictable animal. Inevitably, the matador's work was unclassical to the point of being messy, but the usual protests were far less strident, not because of the nature of the bull but because of the tragedy it brought. Two boys were hit as the bull whirled about in an effort to scatter those who were baiting it, and it was plain by the way they went down and were carried from the ring that they were seriously injured, and perhaps even dead.

This, you may think, was no spectacle to glorify, and later, when I talked with my team-mates, I had to agree that I had been disturbed by much of what I had seen. Why would the boys expose themselves to such danger? Perhaps to some degree because of boredom, an urge to find some excitement, however hazardous. This is a problem that has become apparent in differently expressed ways in many cultures. It is one reason why, in recent years, I have been persuaded of the need for my club, Manchester United, to act as a bridge between young people mired in the problems of debt and drugs and professional counsellors who can provide them with some help.

In that Mexican bullring, two youths risked death in some dangerous pursuit of excitement. Today, many of their English counterparts get involved in the risks that come with binge drinking and the violence that, almost inevitably, seems to follow. Nearly fifty years ago I was in no position to make any such analysis. I just knew that two young lives had been imperilled, and maybe lost, because of some fleeting madness in the last of the sun.

Yet, for all my reservations, the excitement and emotions of the experience touched me in an enduring way. Down the years, whenever I have spent time in Spain or Mexico, I have always kept more than half an eye open for a chance to go to the bullring. One came in 1982 in Spain when I was covering the England World Cup group. I have never seen such big and brave bulls as I did in Bilbao at that time. On one occasion I went down to the place where the animals were brought after being dragged from the ring. A bull was about to be loaded on to a truck and taken to the meat market. I couldn't help but think, 'Well, this is how the great beasts and all their courage finish up. Tomorrow, they'll be on the menus of the best restaurants in town.'

Once in Seville, I ordered oxtail and was told by the waiter when he served it that the animal from which it came had been killed in the bullring the night before. It didn't taste less good for that, I have to admit, and no one needs to tell me that parts of the bullfight are cruel. They have to be if the matador is not to walk out into the ring to face certain death.

No doubt campaigns against bullfighting will continue to gather force – motions to ban it have been tabled in the European

Parliament – and will probably reach the same conclusion as the one against fox hunting did in this country. In my head, I can accept that this is may be right because the cruelty involved is something you cannot easily discount. However, emotionally, the part I cannot fail to celebrate, and be moved by, is the courage of those men who can go out there with such nerve and bravery and operate at the heart of an old culture that is so much part of them.

I wouldn't claim to be an expert but I loved Hemingway's stories of the famous *toreros* and was as saddened by the poignancy of many of their lives as I have always been by the accounts of great boxing champions facing hard times after knowing so much glory. Manolete, perhaps the greatest bull-fighter of all, died on a windy afternoon in the Linares bullring and the nation was plunged into mourning. Just as Garrincha touched the soul of Brazil – his funeral brought crowds of weeping countrymen and women into the streets – Manolete had got to the very heart of what so many Spaniards consider to be the best of themselves.

I suppose what is most compelling about a matador is how he is expected to define his character every time he goes to work. He can be flamboyant, brilliant, but if he is not in control of himself, if he betrays too many nerves at the most vital moments, he loses the crowd. He is like a hugely talented foot-baller who cannot deliver when it matters most, and we know that history can be harsh on such figures. Hemingway pointed out that the windows of a matador's soul were his feet. If they fluttered at the moment of the kill, they betrayed a lack of control and self-confidence, but if they were perfectly still, they spoke of mastery.

There had been so much to think about on the long flight home from Los Angeles. As I replayed the vivid experience of South America, I remembered how my grandfather Tanner had promised me that if I stuck to my football, if I always remembered how lucky I was to have been given natural gifts, the world would be at my feet. I could see that he was right, and I could only marvel that I had seen so much, so quickly.

What I couldn't have imagined then, of course, was that my travelling would not stop when my playing days were over. As an ambassador for Fifa, the Football Association, Manchester United and various World Cup campaigns, including one on behalf of Japan, and through work for the Laureus organisation, I have come to know almost every corner of the world. I thought about this recently when I went to Cambodia with the American skateboard star and entrepreneur Tony Hawk. We were contributing to the world-wide campaign to clear landmines, which, we were shocked to learn when we visited the notorious killing fields of the Pol Pot days, would take another hundred years to remove from that country if the current rate of progress was not dramatically accelerated.

Again, I could only be astounded that the young man who was so thrilled by that enormous stingray rising out of the ocean off Rio, and who discovered a new world and a whole new set of emotions in the Plaza de Toros in Mexico City, should be asked to cover so much territory and still, at such a mature age, be invited to see so many new things and make so many discoveries. My companion, Tony, I sensed, was maybe not given to such reflections. In America, he became a cult figure among teenagers through the artistry and daring of his performance on a skateboard, and then, after becoming a hero of the youth of the streets, he had shrewdly marketed his ability and his image and reached multi-millionaire status. Spending time with him in Cambodia reminded me of the first impact America had made on me. He seemed so undaunted by any new situation, any new set of challenges, and he put me in mind of all those assertions by American 'soccer' men that very soon they would get a handle on the world game and become a major force.

But the difference between the success of the skateboard star and the unfulfilled ambitions of the soccer men was clear enough to me. Tony Hawk swept to fame and fortune on the back of something new that could be claimed as American because it had been spawned on native streets. On my first visits to America, it was easy to see that, with football, they were toying with something beyond their culture, and until they accepted that they couldn't re-make it from its foundations, their progress would inevitably be limited.

My early impression of American 'soccer' was that it lacked seriousness. I recall seeing an American-made documentary on Brazil's brilliant game, full of exclamations, such as 'Wow', but very little insight. Yes, the narrator seemed to be saying, there is some spectacle here, and maybe it could be compared to some tribal dance. That impression was nurtured in the circus-like atmosphere of the little baseball ground in California, and confirmed when I returned on a Manchester United tour the following year, when we played matches in Fall River, Massachusetts, St Louis and New York.

We were told we were ambassadors who had to sell the game on its 'last frontier' but it wasn't easy to take our missionary roles too seriously when one of our opponents in St Louis appeared wearing a bandana, holding in place a large red feather. It didn't help when we heard him tell his team-mates, 'Hey, we've got to hassle these guys. We've got to get in their faces.' It was even worse in Fall River when one young American fouled Bill Foulkes, of all people. Initially, the man who always felt like granite on those unfortunate occasions when you could not avoid colliding with him in practice matches, was stunned.

'Right,' he said, 'if that's the way you want it.'

I remember looking at my feet and saying, 'Oh, dear me.' Foulkes spent the rest of the match chasing the kid, but if the boy wasn't the wisest opponent I had ever encountered, he was one of the fastest and, mercifully for him, he escaped unscathed.

The point I made to Americans back then was that, however

hard they tried to develop football in their own country, it would be no good unless they produced major players of their own rather than importing ageing stars. The best way would be to make sure their most talented young players experienced the game at its highest level in Europe. Young English athletes, golfers and fighters were always being advised to spend time in America, where coaching and competition were at the highest level in the world. Five decades on, it is at last happening, and the result is that the presence of America in a World Cup is no longer a novelty – their players are becoming hardened to serious challenges in Germany, Italy and England. However, it is still optimistic to believe that 'soccer' will ever be one of the major sports in a land where that status, you have to suspect, will always be reserved for that which can truly be said to have been born in the USA.

During those early travels in America, the idea of me, or any of my United team-mates, imparting ambassadorial advice on any subject was a little bizarre. After a few days in New York we were confined to our hotel. This was not because of any curfew imposed by the club. We had simply run out of money. Dazzled by America, we had spent all our allowance on flashy ties and socks, and our experience of being in the country tailed off into nothing more adventurous than watching television. This did have one benefit, however, when the news announcer said that they were joining a reporting team in the street outside our Manhattan hotel. Someone had been shot down.

I remember thinking, 'Well, America is really quite a complex place.'

But then, isn't everywhere when you're twenty-two and learning so much and in such a great hurry?

6

SHATTERED HOPES

NO ONE EVER came into the England team with more confidence, at least on the face of it, than my fellow north-easterner Brian Clough – or learned more quickly that sometimes it doesn't matter how much speed, aggressive instinct or self-belief you have if it is not accompanied by some good luck.

This was particularly true at a time when the England team was picked from game to game, result to result, and there was an ever-rising clamour to seek out new stars who would return the nation to its proper place at the front rank of international football. The belief seemed to be that England merely had to unveil their version of Pelé and all would be well. There was far less talk of developing a team, of having a manager or head coach who could go his own way, follow his instincts, and await the verdict of not one game but something that could be recognised as a pattern – or not.

As I see it now, mulling over the twelve years of almost unbroken selection I enjoyed on the way to 106 caps, it was a period of so many shattered hopes for English players who had reason to believe that they were set for years of glory on the international field. Of course, nothing will ever be guaranteed in football, and not all the talented players in the land could play for their country, but perhaps they were entitled to longer and closer examinations.

The names changed and the faces were different, but almost

Schoolboy dreams come true.

19 April 1958. Captains Billy Wright and Tommy Docherty shake hands before my first full cap.

I was registered to play. But I didn't.

VIᵀᴴ WORLD CHAMPIONSHIP - JULES RIMET CUP 1958
SWEDEN - SVERIGE

Identity card - Legitimationskort
Player - Spelare

Name: Charlton

Christian name: R.

Country: England

FÉDÉRATION INTERNATIONALE
DE FOOTBALL ASSOCIATION
General Secretary

F.I.F.A.

(P.T.O.)

With Billy Wright on the way to Belgrade in May '58. Haunted by memories and soon to be haunted by the score line.

Sweden 1958 World Cup squad (see end of book for names).

ing home after my
...day' in Sweden.

October 1958. Back in the England
set-up and welcomed at training by the
legends Billy Wright, Johnny Haynes,
Tom Finney and Nat Lofthouse.

Training in the
Brazilian heat.
Rio captivated
me in May '59.
As did Pelé
when we faced
him in the
Maracana.

Scoring, unusually for me, with my
head, against Scotland in April '59.

Brian Clough (fourth left) was a classic example of the revolving door selection policy. Here, with Walter Winterbottom (far left), two days before facing Sweden in his second and last game for England.

Wembley '61. There is no whisky bottle in the Craw's Nest commemorating this match. England 9 Scotland 3.

e 1962 World Cup squad
end of book for names).

Heading to the top of the mountain, our World Cup HQ at the Braden Copper Company.

May 1962. England 1 Hungary 2.

2 June 1962. England 3 Argentina 1.

June 1962.
gland 1 Brazil 3.
hat if…Garrincha
d not become a
otballing magician
at day.

The arrival of Alf Ramsey. With Bobby Smith, Jimmy Greaves and Maurice Norman in April '63, before his second game in charge, against Scotland.

Relaxing in the shade of Sugar Loaf Mountain during the Brazilian Jubilee Tournament of '64. Alf assured us that despite being on the receiving end of a 5–1 thumping, we should not fear Brazil in the World Cup in two years' time.

April 1965. Jack's growing reputation
Leeds United and his fierce will to
were recognised by Alf with a first
against Scotland a day after this
ll across the Wembley turf.

apping shirts after the 2–2 draw
h the irrepressible Denis Law.

June 1966. 27 England hopefuls gathered at Lilleshall in Shropshire for a one-day trainin[g] camp. Of these, 22 would make the World Cup squad (see end of book for names).

Following Lilleshall, the chosen 22 headed off for a four-game Europe[an] tour. It wasn't all hard work.

FOT.

By. 4628 HAVNE- og KANALRUNDFARTEN København 196[6]

all of them shared an expression that seemed to say their time had arrived. In so many instances that time was shockingly brief. One bad performance, an injury at precisely the wrong moment, or perhaps a timely argument on behalf of a rival in the selection room, and an England career might be over, and with it possibilities that, for one reason or another, were never allowed to grow on the vine.

So it was with Brian Clough. He went on to prove himself unique in other ways, but he was all but unknown in the white shirt of his country. In more favourable circumstances, things may have turned out very differently. Brian was, frankly, not the easiest person to get along with when he arrived in the dressing room for the game against Wales at Ninian Park in Cardiff in October 1959 – our first test since suffering the indignities of the Americas. This was the 'New England' the press had been calling for so loudly. Walter Winterbottom and the selectors had announced five new caps as their investment in a brighter future, but there was no doubt that most eyes would be on Clough when he ran out against the Welsh.

As a player, he would always be remembered as a relentless scorer of goals – 197 for Middlesbrough in 213 games, an astonishing rate, and, equally impressively, 54 in 61 for Sunderland. His manner, even back then, could be sharp and abrasive. Undoubtedly, this was a player with a special hunger and determination to succeed after becoming a professional only after his national service. He was quick, and there was no doubt he deserved his chance. In Cardiff, Jimmy Greaves played on his right side and I played on his left, and although both of us had considerably more experience than this twenty-four-year-old who had not performed in the First Division, he was not exactly deferential to his younger team-mates. I was less than overwhelmed by one of his post-match comments to the press. He announced, 'It was bloody awful having to play between Jimmy Greaves and Bobby Charlton.' I had to look twice at the comment and ask myself, 'What does he mean by that?' Then I thought that maybe he was judging everything by the standards of the Second Division.

If Cloughie could easily get under your skin, there was no questioning that he had both a remarkable talent and personality. He seemed to be saying that he would take the game and life on his own terms. It was an exceptional position to take in those days when footballers were still governed by restrictions on pay and freedom of contract that would simply not have been tolerated in other walks of life.

So his chance came and went, Clough quickly falling by the wayside, a victim of his failure to make a scoring impact on his two appearances for England, and also a run of injuries that grew in seriousness. In that long build-up to the 1962 World Cup in Chile, Winterbottom experimented with a wide range of strikers of differing styles. Joe Baker was the first to step into Clough's briefly occupied place, and he was followed by Tottenham's powerful Bobby Smith, Gerry Hitchens of Villa and then Internazionale, Burnley's Ray Pointer and, another classic old-style England centre forward, Ray Crawford of Ipswich.

If it is true what they say about a frustrated playing career supplying the strongest motivation for outstanding coaches and managers, Clough is probably one of the most powerful examples. We can never know how he would have performed as manager of England, which he said before his death was his one unfulfilled ambition in football. There has to be a strong suspicion that, like Sir Alf Ramsey, he would have been able to transfer his brilliant success at club level, which included two European Cups with Nottingham Forest, to the international stage. Clough's supreme talent in life, after his instinct to score goals, was to get the best out of a player who might not, in other eyes, have been a natural claimant for a place at the top of football. So many of his former players have said that, when they look back, they sometimes wonder how it was they played so hard for a man who could at times treat them harshly, and always made his own rules, and mostly they agree he had both a force and a mystery about him that they could never quite predict.

If some people believe Clough carried a chip on his shoulder over his misfortunes as a player – his career came to an end, effectively, on Boxing Day 1964, when he was aged twenty-nine and playing for Sunderland in the modest surrounds of Gigg Lane, Bury – there is no doubt he was able to turn it into one made of football gold. Who knows, Clough's chip might have proved as effective in the service of England as the one some said Ramsey had over the class system he encountered at a Football Association controlled by rich businessmen and lawyers and, in one case, a very lordly Oxford professor.

Such possibilities, of course, lay some way off in the future. For now, England's structure was not such that it was able to profit from professionals of the quality and ruthlessness of a Ramsey or a Clough. In the meantime, one could only reflect after our paths crossed so briefly, that Clough was a player of striking ability and character and that he was, maybe, another example of a talented player who never had the chance to settle into a team that had been moulded over the months and the years rather than a policy of random selection.

Clough disappeared – as I did – after our next match resulted in a jolting defeat by Sweden at Wembley when we seemed to have established easy control, but while I would reappear, albeit in a radically different role, Clough was gone from England's colours forever. I often wonder whether his life, and the drinking that finally dimmed his brilliance, might have been affected, become more balanced, if he had found more satisfaction as a player. Would he have attacked his later life quite so ferociously? We can be sure that he came to Ninian Park with the highest of hopes. A few weeks earlier he had scored all five of the Football League's goals against the Irish League.

All five newcomers at Ninian Park were soon to understand

that their international status could be withdrawn as quickly as it had been bestowed. In fact if someone had wanted to build up a case against England's selection policy, if they were looking for examples of how it worked against the building of a sense of team and confidence, they could do a lot worse than make a study of the game against Wales.

Like Clough, the young, tough Trevor Smith, centre half of Birmingham City, would play just one more game before being sent back to the wilderness, never to return. For Smith, a classic stopper, the demotion was also painful. Much less extrovert than Clough, he was nevertheless a strong character, who for several years had been seen as the natural successor to Billy Wright. When the England captain bade his farewell in Los Angeles, after winning his 105th cap, it seemed Smith was taking his place by right.

He had served an impressive apprenticeship with the England Under-23 team, winning an exceptional fifteen caps at that level, and had played for England B against West Germany at the age of eighteen. But then his full international career was over almost before it began – and not without some misfortune. He pulled a calf muscle early in the Welsh game and had to fight hard to get through the match. In the defeat by Sweden, which led inevitably to another unfurling of headlines about the latest crisis of the England team, he suffered a second bout of bad luck. Agne Simonsson, whose brilliant play in the 1958 World Cup led to his signing by Real Madrid, was at the peak of his game, tugging Smith and his co-defenders about the field almost at will. Smith, like the rest of the England team, had a poor game, but when you thought of how much consistent effort he had put into winning his first caps, his fate did seem very harsh.

Unfortunately, the same could also be said for two more of Clough's fellow debutants, Stoke City left back Tony Allen and Middlesbrough winger Edwin Holliday. Allen, who was not yet twenty, had been playing so well for his Second Division team that he won the vote over a future England captain, Jimmy Armfield. A local hero, Allen, who had attended the same Potteries school as Stanley Matthews, appeared to have survived the misadventure against Sweden when he was picked for the next game, against Northern Ireland at Wembley. But this would be the end of a run that had promised so much. He was missing from the team facing Scotland at Hampden Park and it is hard to imagine an absence that could have cost him more. His place was taken by Ray Wilson and, predictably enough for anyone who had seen the tremendous development of the man from Derbyshire with his local club Huddersfield Town, it was obvious, even to the selection committee, that the vacancy had been filled.

Holliday, a cousin of Colin Grainger, the Sheffield United and Sunderland winger who had brought a lot of promise, and scored three goals, in seven appearances for England in the mid-fifties, made his exit with Allen after Belfast. 'New England' had been stillborn and had reverted to the same old shifting England in less than a handful of matches. Only John Connelly, my future team-mate at Old Trafford, returned from oblivion, having been left out after four games. In all, Connelly won twenty England caps, the reward for speed, considerable skill and enough toughness to take him into scoring positions, however formidable the opposition.

My own position at the time of the Welsh game that marked the beginning of so many brief international careers, was odd. At the age of twenty-two, I could fairly class myself as one of the veterans of a team in which, with Johnny Haynes out injured, twenty-six-year-old Ron Flowers was the oldest player and the average age was the same as my own. Only stand-in captain Ronnie Clayton had more caps, with thirty-one against my thir-teen. That should probably have given me some sense of secu-rity, along with an early goal from Greaves. In the absence of Haynes, though, I had new responsibilities. I was the designated 'schemer' and although the role was unfamiliar – and the task of reproducing the Haynes game sat heavy on my shoulders – we were able to develop some decent rhythm. We had plenty of width and with Greaves, Clough and Connelly looking for scoring opportunities, the Welsh defence was never able to relax. However, they proved durable enough to prevent any further scoring, and near the end teenaged striker Graham Moore, who would eventually arrive at United via Chelsea, struck home the Welsh equaliser.

After all the ballyhoo about young blood and new English ambition, a 1–1 draw was not the result to lift the pressure on Winterbottom and the selection committee, but neither was it sufficiently dire to justify the bout of wholesale changes and the resulting ridicule. So, with Haynes still injured, the new men were invited to take a drink at the last chance saloon when Sweden visited Wembley eleven days later. What I didn't realise was that, when I also retained my place, I was on the guest list for both the game and the saloon.

We started well against Sweden, as we had against Wales, and when Connelly put us into the lead after eight minutes, the shadow of Haynes lifted a little. Unfortunately, it returned just as soon as the Swedes applied some serious pressure and Simonsson began to explain to the Wembley crowd why it was Madrid considered him fit to keep company with Alfredo di Stefano and Francisco Gento. I scored late in the game, but it was one of those that have to be listed in the category of forlorn gestures. The Swedes had already scored three unanswered goals, and when Haynes returned to the team for the next game against Northern Ireland, my place was taken by Ray Parry of Bolton Wanderers.

Here was another case study of long years of waiting and the brevity of a player's opportunity to prove himself for England. Parry, who was two years older than I was, had collected a cup-winner's medal at Wembley the previous year when United's run from the ruins of Munich finally touched reality. More remarkably, seven years earlier, Parry had made football history when he became the youngest player ever to appear in a First Division game. He was just fifteen years and 267 days when he lined up against, of all teams, Stan Cullis's fierce Wolves. It was an astonishing statement of trust in a young player, and down the years Parry had proved himself an inside forward of craft. But then, like so many others, he had to demonstrate all that experience and ability in a small fraction of time. For him it was two games, a narrow win against Northern Ireland and then a draw at Hampden Park in April 1960.

For me, the five-month span of Ray Parry's international experience was also career-changing, and in a way I couldn't have imagined. I returned to the England team for that Hampden game in the spring a changed player and, perhaps after the trauma of Wilf McGuinness's shattering injury, a somewhat different man. Certainly, I was a reluctant left winger, the position I'd been moved to by my club and now my country. But if I was less than enthusiastic, I was successful, and so, after the surprise of being left out of United's first team for the first time since I had emerged from Munich amid a blaze of headlines, my instinct was to subdue my protests. Yes, I saw myself as a natural creative midfielder, perhaps in time indeed the heir to Johnny Haynes, but I had to admit that I had some of the natural attributes of a winger. I was quick, I could go by a defender and, most vitally for United, and my own chances of an England return, I discovered that going wide didn't mean that I couldn't score goals.

I scored two in my first shift as United's new left winger in March 1960. I also crossed for Alex Dawson to score the other goal in a 3–1 defeat of Nottingham Forest – an important win after a crushing defeat at home to Wolves and an early exit from the FA Cup at the hands of Sheffield Wednesday. I scored three more in my next three games, and although I was goalless in

the 5–0 defeat of Fulham at Craven Cottage, I had the satisfaction of making chances despite the attention of an up-and-
coming full back who was both formidably quick and so
physically hard you could shut your eyes and imagine you had
just collided with Bill Foulkes. His name was George Cohen,
and I remembered him well from his superb performance as a
teenager when we drew 2–2 in an FA Cup semi-final at Villa
Park eighteen months earlier. Cohen was still four years away
from his England debut, a delay that was probably caused by
his touch on the ball not comparing with that of Blackpool's
stylish Jimmy Armfield. However, in the matter of quick,
rigorous defence his progress was becoming relentless. My
bruises were soothed, however, by the most welcome of headlines: 'Charlton set for England return'.

Rather amazingly, when you consider the selection policy at
the time and the ever-extending chorus line of England hopefuls, I went on to have an unbroken run of twenty-five caps on
the left wing. I took it as another example of how a kind fate
had picked me out for special favours. What, I wonder now,
might have happened to my England career if George Best had
arrived at Old Trafford a few years earlier, or Albert Scanlon,
the reigning left winger, hadn't lost so much in the Munich crash
that was ultimately beyond recovery? I am not so falsely modest
as to say that I didn't have enough of that natural talent my
grandfather Tanner celebrated so enthusiastically to force myself
back into the reckoning somehow and in any circumstances, but
the solution to one of the problems facing Matt Busby and Jimmy
Murphy as they rebuilt United after Munich might just have
been custom-built for my immediate needs. They and England
needed a left winger at that time, and I was given the job.

Still, and for all its short-term advantages, my love for the
number eleven shirt was never warm – and certainly never
enduring. Indeed, when Best's star rose over Old Trafford, and
Busby, the 'Old Man', told me I could return to the grazing of

the midfield pasture I had always regarded as my natural home, I was filled with the same relief as when my mother Cissie, who was concerned that for one reason or another football might fail my hopes, told me that I could abandon my grammar school education and devote myself entirely to my career at Manchester United.

When I did eventually return to the midfield for both United and England, it was with the sense that I had emerged as a finished article. I had played in all the key attacking roles with varying degrees of success and finally knew my place as a footballer. It was probably not entirely coincidental in the case of England that the career of the great Haynes, damaged by a car crash, had largely passed. Haynes had been invoked as the model I must follow when Walter Winterbottom told me that I was dropped from the England team after the defeat in Belgrade – after scoring three goals in my first three matches – and at the time I felt no resentment. I could only admire his ability to read a game, his immaculate passing, both long and short, and the wonderful masking of his intentions, which often sent at least half a defence running in the wrong direction. But if Haynes was a superb example of how to play midfield, he was for me also something of a shadow.

The problem, no doubt, was mine. Haynes had staked out his ground and won the admiration of all his contemporaries. My own ground, by comparison, could scarcely have been more uncertain. On the many occasions I played with the great man, I never felt I managed to dovetail with him to either his or my satisfaction. So I moved from role to role, now a classic inside forward, now a striker, now a deep-lying playmaker trying to aim passes into the path of the new scoring specialist, Jimmy Greaves. But despite passing success, a healthy number of goals and more than a few favourable headlines, I still could not look up and say, 'At last I've found my place, I know my role.' When I was dropped by England, then sent into the United reserves to hear the cry from the terraces that, at the age of twenty-two, I had maybe run my course, I might have been excused for asking, not *if* I could play, but *where* I should do it. For that period, it seemed the left wing was the answer.

Murphy, the old pro, naturally said he saw mutual advantage in the move. The new challenge would bring into play some of my best assets – and the club could do with some kind of new injection along at least one of the flanks. All his old advice swirled back into life – use your speed, put the defender on his back foot, exploit all your advantages. It worked as sweetly as either of us could have hoped, and impressed the England selectors, yet still many times I heard Jimmy's piercing voice yelling at me as though I was his only concern. This was invariably when I grew frustrated at the lack of action and the infrequency of the passes I was receiving and went looking for the ball inside. Someone said that the left wing could be the coldest place on the field, partly because most players were naturally right-footed and often saw a pass to the right winger as the easier, safer option. I was more inclined to believe that than another theory that the reason for the longevity of Matthews, Finney and Liverpool's long-serving winger Billy Liddell was that they were able to take a little breather and recharge their batteries much more often than players in any other position. I was particularly unimpressed with this argument one afternoon at Nottingham Forest, when I convinced myself that the old clock was moving so slowly it was about to stop.

There was another concern. Although my work level dropped hugely when I moved to the left wing, I would often feel wearier than if I had been covering much more ground in the midfield.

A lot of these reservations, however, were put in abeyance when I heard the news that I would be returning with England to Hampden Park, the place where my international career had opened so warmly two years earlier. If yet another insight is needed into the rate of change in the England team, the almost constant state of flux, it is maybe enough to note that I was one of only three England players to survive from our 4–0 victory in 1958. Ronnie Clayton was the only one to retain his position, at right half, Bill Slater being moved to the middle to replace the retired Billy Wright. I filled the position that had been occupied, so helpfully for my arrival in the England scoring records, by the illustrious Tom Finney.

This time we were nothing like so productive – I scored one penalty but missed two others (one a retake) in the 1–1 draw – but if I was able to do enough on the wing to keep my place, it seemed that England's old prestige in the world had slid into what was beginning to look like an unshakeable mediocrity. The statistics spoke of this as volubly as any critic. In the two years since the great bowl of Hampden had been reduced to a nervy silence by the brilliance of Finney and Haynes, and I had volleyed home my first goal, England had played nineteen games and won just five – friendly victories over Portugal, the Soviet Union and the United States, and two wins out of six against the allegedly weaker nations of the Home International Championship.

This surely underlined a malaise that many believed would not be overcome until the national team was put on a new footing – when the FA councillors could finally be convinced that their power was running grievously beyond their knowledge and experience of the realities of professional football.

With the trial of another World Cup just two years away, Walter Winterbottom could hardly be optimistic, and this was before we went from Hampden to Wembley to be held by Yugoslavia, and then to Madrid and Budapest, where we lost 3–0 and 2–0.

A lifeline had been run out to me on the left wing but it was hard to see where England, who scarcely a decade ago had earned a standing ovation in Turin for a majestic 4–0 victory over Italy, the reigning champions from pre-war, would find salvation.

The team that Walter Winterbottom was able to unleash on the Italians that day reads like a roll call of lost greatness. Take, for instance, the legendary giant Frank Swift in goal, who became a football writer and died in the plane crash I survived. Then there was Neil Franklin providing a beautifully balanced fulcrum in defence. A master player, Franklin left English football two years later, at the peak of his powers, after being lured to Bogota in Colombia by the breathtaking offer of £5,000 a year and a £35 win bonus, which was nearly twice the maximum wage that could be paid by his club, Stoke City. Matthews and Finney were on the wings, Wilf Mannion was the playmaker and the striking was left to Tommy Lawton and Stan Mortensen.

You could flick through the records of that time and see why such a convulsion was caused by England's shocking exit from the 1950 World Cup – Lisbon, 25 May 1947, Portugal 0 England 10 (Lawton 4, Mortensen 4, Finney, Matthews); Paris, 22 May 1949, France 1 England 3 (Johnny Morris 2, Billy Wright); Brussels, 18 May 1950, Belgium 1 England 4 (Jimmy Mullen, Mortensen, Mannion, Bentley).

The Brussels game was England's last before leaving for Brazil and the World Cup. It was the culmination of six games, all won, that had been played quite ferociously after the shock of losing the nation's first home game to 'foreign' opposition, the Republic of Ireland at Goodison Park. England scored twenty-five goals against seven.

Mannion was a leading creator. Some years later, I'm proud to say I played in an unofficial testimonial match for him. It was a wet night but, although he could no longer cover the ground so well, his control was miraculous. I thought of the time more than a decade earlier when I saw him mesmerise Old Trafford with a sublime performance. Both United and Mannion's Middlesbrough had made a floundering start to that 1953–54 season but I had gone along with some pals from the youth team, saying, 'Well, we must see United's first win of the season.' It seemed like a reasonable forecast when United took a 2–0 lead but then something quite amazing happened. Mannion simply took hold of the game. He nursed his team to a 2–2 draw with one of the best individual performances I have ever seen. Every pass seemed to go straight to the heart of United's defence.

Before then, at the end of the previous season, he had scored twice in one of United's heaviest defeats of the Busby era, a 5–0 thrashing at Ayresome Park. A report noted that he was so unplayable it seemed odd that he had not been included in England's summer tour party the year before, even at the age of thirty-four. But odd to whom? Not, presumably, the men in the committee room, who were at the height of their power as selectors at a time before public and press began to demand more freedom of action for the professional in charge of the team. It must have seemed then that you could stick a pin in a list of the leading players, or accept the fervent recommendation of a selector on behalf of one of his club's boys, and still come up with a team more than capable of competing with the best in the world.

There may have been a compelling argument for Mannion's inclusion even at his age, but the fact was that the inside forwards who were sent ahead of him, Ivor Broadis, Eddie Baily and Jackie Sewell, were all good enough to contribute to England's draw with Italy in Florence and their victories over Austria in Vienna and Switzerland in Zurich.

But that was 1952. By 1960 a very different picture was being painted. With results so discouraging in the first shadows of another World Cup, Walter Winterbottom must have wondered if such players would ever come again. And there was another question. If they did, would anyone upstairs notice?

7

REVITALISING ENGLAND

In 1960, ENGLAND did not need a messiah. Johnny Haynes had, after all, been that for some time, and in neither of the last two World Cups could it be said that the team lacked potentially inspirational figures. In Switzerland in 1954 they started with Stanley Matthews and Tom Finney on the flanks and my United team-mates Roger Byrne and Tommy Taylor, who would shortly be joined by the potentially phenomenal Duncan Edwards. In Sweden in 1958, Tom Finney was still around, and in luminous form despite reaching his mid-thirties, and Haynes was seen as one of the world's most gifted creative players. No, the most pressing requirement was a sense of growing cohesion – and an understanding that many teams were displaying new levels of tactical innovation.

We needed to believe that we, too, could be part of the football revolution, and the 3–0 defeat by Spain in May did not encourage such thoughts. A week later we arrived in the Nep Stadium in Budapest, not a place to stimulate much English optimism, not after the events that unfolded there in the spring of 1954. What happened then was the ruthless dissection of a myth that sprang up, at least in some quarters, after the sensational performance of Ferenc Puskas's Hungary at Wembley on a dank day six months earlier, on 25 November 1953 to be precise.

There, Hungary, instantly christened the Magnificent Magyars, beat England 6–3 and although some, including a certain Alf Ramsey, England's right back, claimed that the score was a distortion, others argued that it was the shining of an extremely harsh light on the decline of our footballing prowess. The more hopeful theory was that with less eccentric selection – George Robb of Tottenham, for example, had been preferred to Tom Finney – and a more tightly organised defence, aware of the new Hungarian system using a deep-lying centre forward, a role brilliantly executed by Nandor Hidegkuti, the humiliation would not have happened and would, anyway, be avenged in Budapest.

That was the great myth and the Hungarians reacted to it with contempt in the following May. Finney was restored to the England side and Ivor Broadis scored a goal. Unfortunately, the Hungarians scored seven. It was not so much a defeat as a formal undressing.

By the time we arrived in Budapest in the spring of 1960, much of the bloom had gone from the Hungarian team who had promised to hold a master-class at the 1954 World Cup in Switzerland but instead were unaccountably beaten in the final by West Germany, a result that was all the harder to comprehend because they had earlier thrashed the new champions 8–3 in a group game. But then Puskas had been injured before the final and probably shouldn't have played. When I lined up against them, with my Manchester United team-mate Dennis Viollet on my inside, winning his first cap, and Joe Baker making his fifth attempt to convince the selectors that the centre forward spot should be his alone, the Hungarians had only a haunting memory of the great man after his break for freedom during the 1956 revolution. Puskas was out of the country, playing for his club Honved, when the fighting erupted and the Russian tanks rolled in. Eventually, he managed to arrange for his family to join him in pursuit of a new life and finally, after some nomadic months and much negotiation with suitors from all over Europe, he settled in Madrid where, of course, he played so brilliantly for Real. But if the Hungarians were not what they were, they were still too good for us and their 2–0 win suggested that in two years' time they would be a force in Chile.

The kings may have gone, but there were some impressive pretenders, including forwards Florian Albert and Lajos Tichy, and much hope was being attached to the tremendous progress of a prodigy of a centre half, Kalman Meszoly. Walter Winterbottom must have envied his Hungarian opposite number Lajos Baroti's potential to construct another great team from the ruins of the old as we flew home from another discouraging foreign mission – two games, two losses, no goals scored, five conceded.

It was not the strongest foundation on which to build for the challenge facing us in the World Cup in South America, and indeed it provoked some doubt about whether we would even make the finals. Although our three-team qualification group included Luxembourg, whom we were expected to beat, there was no certainty that we would overcome our other opponents, Portugal. The importation of brilliant individuals, such as Mario Coluna and the fast-rising young Eusebio, from Portuguese African colonies, meant the country was far from the feeble force pulverised by Lawton and Mortensen, Matthews and Finney. Where, now, could Winterbottom turn after so many new permutations had been reduced to dust?

Perhaps he decided that in this new world of football, of changing formations and the clearest evidence that in terms of ball skills and tactical subtleties many rival nations had passed us by, we needed, as another embattled public figure, Prime Minister John Major, would later say, 'to get back to basics'.

If we were to exploit some traditional, and possibly still viable, strength, we needed someone up front who could bring a little fear to a foreign defence in an old-fashioned way. Winterbottom and the selectors decided this need might be answered by Bobby Smith.

A more cynical view is also possible. As well as his known and impressive assets, Smith, a big, strong, huge-hearted lad from North Yorkshire, was the man of the moment as he led Bill Nicholson's Spurs into what would prove a successful challenge for the Double of League and FA Cup. So he had the force of headlines pushing his selection, a sense that he might put some beef – and some not inconsiderable quality – into the faltering England cause.

Whatever the driving force behind the decision, Smith's selection was quickly proved to have considerable merit. Six months after our pallid efforts in Madrid and Budapest, our failure to suggest that we could make any kind of impact on the coming World Cup, and a year after sneaking a 2–1 win over Northern Ireland at Wembley, we were winning 5–2 in Belfast. Smith took the place of the quick and skilful Baker, who was paying for his lack of impact in front of goal, and Jimmy Greaves was brought back into the team at the expense of Viollet. Greaves scored twice and Smith made a huge splash, scoring once and generally terrifying the Irish defence.

A strong case could be made for reserved judgement – there had been too many disappointments over the last few years to read too much into one victory, however refreshing – but soon the evidence was building impressively. England had found new life, and some of their old strength.

Smith, the idol of White Hart Lane for his perpetual willingness to do battle, was the catalyst as we surged into a run of consistent success – and power.

Here are the results that so quickly transformed the assessment of England's chances of making any kind of flourish in Chile – England 9 Luxembourg 0, England 4 Spain 2, England 5 Wales 1, England 9 Scotland 3, England 8 Mexico 0, England 1 Portugal 1, England 3 Italy 2.

The friendly victory over Italy had the extra psychological value of being played in Rome, and in Lisbon, the draw with a strong and talented Portugal represented a big qualifying step towards Chile.

England were alive again and it was a conclusion not seriously disturbed by a weary performance in the last game of the summer tour, which brought defeat by Austria in Vienna. Smith didn't maintain his scoring form and lost his place on the final stretch of the road to the World Cup, but looking back now, the memory of his impact, which did so much to make the whole nation feel better about its football, is still vivid.

Smith followed his goal in Belfast with two against both Luxembourg and Spain, and he scored again in the demolition of Wales at Wembley. Two more came against Scotland. He scored eight in five games, and if it is sad to recall that he was absent when the World Cup squad assembled a year later, no one could doubt that he had performed a major service for the team. He had reminded everyone that if you were strong enough in your approach, if you believed in your ability, a lot more could be achieved than you might ever imagine.

Bobby Smith came from the best traditions of English football and I can give him no higher praise than to say, when I played with him, he always reminded me of Nat Lofthouse.

This is a statement of approval, and affection, prompted by something dearest to the heart of a midfielder. It is that when you send the ball forward to a big man who is wrestling with the defence, you always hope to get it back so that you can develop the rhythm of the attack. How many times have you seen a midfielder throw up his arms in frustration after making an unrewarded run for the return? If you ever saw Johnny Haynes, you would have seen the gesture often enough, and if you happened to be on the field, you would be left in no doubt about his views on the pass that never came. My own body language was explicit enough, but probably less so in the presence of Lofthouse and Smith and, later, Roger Hunt and Geoff Hurst.

When you sent the ball forward to Lofthouse, you knew that

he was good enough to control it – and strong enough to resist any defensive challenge and get it back to you in a good position. It was the same with Smith. Clearly, he was a winner. He came into the England team, as so many did in those days, on a wave of club success, but once he arrived you felt an immediate benefit. You could begin to say with confidence, 'We have a force, we can apply genuine pressure,' and that's a vital factor for any team who are struggling to find their way.

Lofthouse played for Bolton Wanderers at Newcastle in the first top-flight match I ever went to see, and the impression he made on me that day was confirmed every time I saw him. Down the years, that led to a comparison with John Charles. In certain respects, such as heading the ball, it wasn't reaching too far to say that Lofthouse had more than a touch of the great Welshman, although not in the scale of his talent. That couldn't be so, because Charles was both uniquely strong and skilled, with a silky touch that, in such a big man, was quite staggering. Lofthouse wasn't as tall as Charles, but the way he used his head, with adroitness and precision, was what you would expect of a highly talented player.

Smith had a little of that, plus the biggest of competitive hearts. It was easy to see why he was so popular among the fans at White Hart Lane – and so highly valued by his fellow Yorkshireman, manager Bill Nicholson. Spurs were a team of great subtlety, including such players as Danny Blanchflower and John White, but Smith gave them another dimension, a hard determination to get the job done whatever the circumstances. For a little while, he seemed to be the answer to many of Walter Winterbottom's prayers.

For Smith, though, there was one problem he couldn't ultimately master, despite that burst of eight goals in five matches. One big lesson of the Swedish World Cup had been absorbed deeply enough by Winterbottom. Whatever reservations existed about his ability to deal with hardened pros, Walter was a football man who looked into the trends of the world game with much knowledge and insight. The Brazilians had won with 4–2–4, a system that relied heavily on the superb movement and versatility of their squad, but it was clear to the England manager that defences generally had become both harder and more sophisticated, and that against them something new had to be deployed.

With this in mind, Winterbottom had been drawn, as Italian football would be in his wake, to a most serious rival to Smith, the supremely English striker: Gerry Hitchens, a former Shropshire miner and centre forward of Aston Villa.

I had played army football with Hitchens before we both graduated to the First Division with our clubs, and I knew him to be a quick attacker with good skill and plenty of determination. These qualities, soon to be showcased in the England team, persuaded Internazionale Milan that he should join the emigration to Italian football that included my future United team-mate Denis Law and Jimmy Greaves. Other strikers were tried in the build-up to Chile, including Ray Pointer of Burnley and Ray Charnley of Blackpool, but the arrival of Hitchens was most costly to Smith.

His impact, on and off the field, was one that couldn't be ignored. He scored after just ninety seconds of his debut against Mexico at Wembley in May 1961, a flying start to the 8–0 win in which I was able to avenge the humiliation of defeat in Mexico City two years earlier with a hat-trick. Then, after giving way to a scoreless Smith in the 1–1 World Cup qualifier with Portugal in Lisbon, he resurfaced in Rome to score two in the 3–2 defeat of Italy. There, in the sunshine of the Eternal City, Hitchens, who died tragically early while playing in a charity football game in North Wales at the age of forty-eight, looked, in his sharply cut suit and brightly coloured tie, the star of the Italian football scene he would be part of later that summer.

He appeared very much at home in Italy and it was an impression that was justified down the years. While Greaves and Law retreated quickly to English football, confessing that they felt like fish out of water, Hitchens dug himself into the Italian scene and prospered for the best part of a decade, moving on from Internazionale to Torino, Atalanta and then, before his shockingly brief retirement from a game in which he had proved a successful pioneer in the pursuit of better terms for English players, Cagliari.

The confidence and verve of Hitchens' performance in England's win against Italy, would surely get him on the plane to Chile.

For Bobby Smith, there was no longer any such certainty, a bleak fact underlined for him by Winterbottom's decision to give three caps to Ray Pointer and two to Ray Crawford before the party for Chile was announced. Yet, on the eve of the announcement, Smith was handed one last chance to scramble his way on to the plane. He would play against Scotland at Hampden Park, and he no doubt concluded as he dressed for what might have proved to be the most important game of his career, that he could hardly have been given a more dramatic setting to restate his case.

He and Stan Anderson were in that most precarious of situations in that time when selection could be as fleeting as a gust of wind. An impressive goal, a few passages of eye-catching play to capture the interest of the press or the attention of a selector, and who knew, an unpromising fate might suddenly be changed. Anderson had won his first cap in the previous game, a 3–1 friendly against Austria at Wembley, and had shown some neat control and a nice touch on the ball. But did he have the weight and presence for a World Cup? That question was bound to be asked as we ran out before a crowd of 132,000.

Apparently, he did. He was named the following day alongside three other half 'wing-halves', two of great experience, Bobby Robson and Ron Flowers, and one who was relatively unknown to the wider football audience but who within the game was beginning to feature on the grapevine very impressively indeed.

Smith was missing and you couldn't help but feel for the big-hearted and extremely able man who had done so much to give England a surge of spirit when it was most needed. He paid for the day when the Scots rose up and won 2–0, when the 'little birds' on the terracing sang an entirely different song from the one to which they gave voice on the day Tom Finney sped down the left wing to serve the pass that enabled me to open my scoring for England.

Anderson made the plane, but he never played for England again. Smith did reappear, winning eight more caps and scoring five more goals after he was restored to the team by the new manager, Alf Ramsey, the year after the World Cup. He scored two in Ramsey's anti-climactic first game, a 5–2 European Nations Cup qualifier defeat by France in Paris, one in a 4–2 friendly win against Czechoslovakia in Bratislava, two more against Wales at Ninian Park, and, finally, one in an 8–3 slaughter of Northern Ireland at Wembley. Smith played as he had always done, with fight and power, but then Ramsey, in that way of his that did not permit much hope of reappraisal once his mind had been made up, decided he had to widen his search for the centre forward to help him win football's greatest prize.

A stream of fresh contenders would pass by Ramsey's analytical gaze – Johnny 'Budgie' Byrne of West Ham, surviving his scare in the waves of Copacabana, fluently skilful; Barry Bridges, a sleek product of a young Chelsea team that was promising to touch the stars; Fred Pickering, a converted full back from Blackburn Rovers, displaying a powerful scoring touch at Everton; Mick Jones, the strong and wonderfully hearted leader of the Sheffield United and, later, Leeds United line; and Frank Wignall, a key figure in a fine, emerging Nottingham Forest team.

All of them had their moments, those surges of blood that indicated here might be the answer to any team's most fundamental demand – a striker to round off all the work and the planning and the hopes. Each had a target as clear as the one presented to Bobby Smith when he was picked out as the man to revive England, and performed well enough to take him heartbreakingly close to the prize of a place in a World Cup. All of them failed because, like Smith, they couldn't announce clearly enough that they had a vital and unanswerable edge over all their rivals.

Such a thing, of course, demands certain qualities. One of them is a confidence that sometimes cannot be distinguished from arrogance. It is a way of holding yourself on the field, knowing with instinct and certainty what is happening around you – and what is most likely to happen next.

Sometimes just one appearance in the shirt of your country is enough to prove that you have all of that. One outing can show that you were born to operate at the peak of the game. The least famous of those 'wing-halves', and indeed of all the players included in the party for Chile, was able to do this when we stopped on the way to the World Cup to play a friendly match against Peru in Lima, that place where three years earlier a 4–1 defeat had bitten so deeply into my bones.

This time we won, easing back, 4–0. Jimmy Greaves delivered a warning shot of serious intent with a hat-trick. Maurice Norman, of Spurs, claimed his first cap with an authority that ensured his place was not threatened throughout the World Cup. I won my thirty-fifth cap and was sufficiently happy with proceedings that I felt no need to seek out the referee and make a bitter protest. But for many, including me, the most lingering memory was the performance of the blond boy from East London, who was also winning his first cap. He oozed class and if he wasn't notably quick, he seemed to have all the time in the world. He had just passed his twenty-first birthday and his maturity was staggering in someone so young. He was, of course, Bobby Moore.

8

AULD FRIENDS

IN ONE OF my favourite Scottish watering holes, the Craw's Nest at Anstruther, the proprietor Sandy Bowman proudly displays a single malt whisky labelled Wembley, 1967. You may not be surprised to learn that there is no companion bottle marked, Wembley, 1961.

This of course may be pure oversight, absolutely nothing to do with the fact that in 1967, in the spring following our World Cup success of the previous summer, we lost 3–2 to Scotland. Large parts of the pitch were dug up, and the goalposts dismantled, amid scenes of great celebration. In Scottish eyes, the match, officially a combined Home International Championship and a European Championship qualifier, was transformed, at the moment of victory, into a play-off for the world title.

On my visits to the Craw's Nest, I always point out that a similar commemoration of the 1961 match, when things went less well for Scotland, might provide a little historical balance. So far my suggestion has not been taken up but each year I check, mostly in a spirit of supreme optimism.

I'm linking these two events now, slightly out of chronological progression, because in all the strivings for world conquest that became a theme of my international career under both Walter Winterbottom and Alf Ramsey, there was always a vibrant sub-plot, one that has, in my opinion regrettably, long gone from the lives of leading English and Scottish professionals.

Playing Scotland was always separate from everything else I did as an international player. It always had a point and a focus of its own, hence my retaliatory questioning about the missing bottle of single malt in the Craw's Nest. In that other spring, the one of 1961, when our main aim was a place in those World Cup finals in Chile, we beat Scotland 9–3. This is not to gloat, merely to say that it was one of the most extraordinary games I ever played against Scotland, which is also to say it was one of the most extraordinary games I ever played.

It was remarkable for many things, and not least the fluency of our attack, because this wasn't a Scottish team that had been assembled casually on some Glasgow street corner. Certainly the Scots had four debutants, but they also had two candidates for any World XI you might care to choose in Dave Mackay, one of the most formidable players I would meet at club or international level, and my future United team-mate Denis Law, who was emerging as a major player with Manchester City and would shortly be signed by Torino. Since we were not yet club-mates, Denis did not feel obliged to kick me at the first oppor-tunity as a ritual statement that, before any other football allegiance, he would always be Scottish, but he was no less committed for that. They also had the Celtic centre half Billy McNeill, who would lead his club to Britain's first European Cup in 1967, and the excellent Rangers pair, Eric Caldow and Davie Wilson at left back and outside left.

Yet in a line-up that did not appear to offer any easy pick-ings – Scotland had given us a severe examination in a 1–1 draw at Hampden the previous spring – there were two victims of the harshest fate, as towards the end of the game Jimmy Greaves (3), Bobby Smith (2), Johnny Haynes (2), Bryan Douglas and Bobby Robson scored almost at will.

Even when I think of it all these many years later, I cannot suppress a wave of sympathy for the Celtic goalkeeper, Frank Haffey. Apparently, even as the crowd streamed out of the stadium, he was already the victim of sharp, cruel Glaswegian wit. One joke, it is said, had a tartan-bedecked fan saying to his friend, 'What time is it, Jimmy?' only to receive the reply, 'Nearly ten past Haffey.'

Inevitably, perhaps, the goalkeeper, who was winning his second cap, never played for Scotland again. As one of the agents of his downfall – I didn't score but Rangers' right back Bobby Shearer was, as I expected after playing against him in a Football League versus Scottish League game earlier that season, very vulnerable to my pace – I feel, even at this distance, obliged to point out that Haffey was considerably more than a hapless incompetent parachuted into a nightmarish experience in one of the world's great stadiums, a place where a Scottish footballer would least like to fail. He played 201 times for Celtic and kept 61 clean sheets, a formidable statistic even though his club operated from a position of considerable strength in the Scottish game.

Following the shock of the defeat, Haffey did not become a shell of a man, which, in the context of some of the fiercest, tribal aspects of Scottish life, might easily have been the case. However, in 1964, after breaking his ankle in a game against Partick Thistle in the previous November, he did leave the country, playing briefly for Swindon before leaving for Australia. How he fared at the hands of a large Scottish expatriate community down under, I do not know, but the circumstantial evidence suggests that his essential self-belief was not seriously damaged. He did, after all, become a cabaret singer in his adopted country when he finally put away the gloves.

Likewise, Bobby Shearer, a big red-headed lad who had a fine career with Rangers, was not unduly bowed by the mauling I was able to deliver as Haynes, Robson and Douglas created acres of space in the Scottish defence.

Having won the inter-league match in Glasgow, the Scots decided to go with the same team at Wembley and it was a serious mistake. Certainly, I had seen the possibilities of playing against Shearer. He was slow on the turn, and that meant at Wembley I was able to play in optimum circumstances for a winger who had speed and could disguise the way he intended to go. The experience, from a strictly English perspective, was perfect. The scoreline may have been a little harsh on the Scots – at one point it was merely 3–2 in our favour – because it was quite close until we ran away with it at the end, when everything we did seemed to turn to gold. Every pass was threaded to within an inch of its target and, because it was clear I had the beating of Shearer, I had never before seen so much of the ball.

Yet in the end – and this can be the ultimate cruelty of football – only the shortcomings of Frank Haffey are remembered. One moment of his agony stood out above all others. He dropped the ball – it was as though this experienced goalkeeper was encountering the unimaginable horror of losing control of his hands – and then desperately tried to retrieve it as it rolled slowly over the line. The cameras were close in and had never been so unforgiving.

Many years later, Shearer, who died in 2006, came up to me when we were both playing in a Variety Club golf tournament in Scotland, and asked, 'Do you remember me?'

I could not help myself from replying, 'How could I forget you? Bobby,' I added, 'you were the first full back, and the last actually, I ever saw kick the ball into the stand for no reason.'

There was a reason, though, and it was deeply embedded in the British football of the day. Back then, a player such as Bobby, tough and strong but not particularly skilful, was told that if a simple pass wasn't on, he had just one obligation and that was to hoof the ball out of harm's way. In fact, there was an echo of this a decade later. Don Revie, a hugely skilled player in his own time who had assembled a squad of outstanding versatility at Leeds United, reputedly delivered the sternest of rebukes to his brilliantly gifted left back Terry Cooper for deciding, in an especially critical moment near the end of the game, to play his way out of trouble rather than aiming for a spot high on the terracing.

Shearer, and at that moment at Elland Road, Revie, belonged to a tradition that differed from the new style Cooper had decided to follow, and it was one with which we were equally familiar in English club football. It was probably most rigorously exemplified at Bolton Wanderers by my former England team-mate Tommy Banks, and Roy Hartle. Off the field, Banks was the wry humorist and Hartle a perfect gentleman who would eventually become a local councillor. Whenever I saw him he was the essence of politeness, invariably saying, 'Bobby, how is your good lady?' However, Banks and Hartle left such niceties in the dressing room.

Once I recall Hartle shaking every bone in the body of my United team-mate Mark 'Pancho' Pearson with a tackle guaranteed to make a strong man weep. Pearson was carried very gingerly to the touchline and after some repairs came limping back on the field. Banks's greeting was not encouraging. He shouted, 'Roy, lad, when you've finished with him, chip him over to me.'

Playing against Law, Billy Bremner of Leeds and Bobby Lennox of Celtic when they had the blue shirts on their backs could be a similarly challenging experience. This was never more so that on the Wembley afternoon when, still undefeated after our World Cup triumph, we faced Scotland, six years after the match when Frank Haffey's football world fell apart. Right from the start it was a wild game with heavy tackling on both sides that earned little or no rebuke from the German referee, Gerd Schulenburg. Our first misfortune came when Jack was injured in an accidental collision with Bobby Lennox. This left Jack hobbling at centre forward for the rest of the match, although remarkably it did not prevent him from scoring one of our goals. The tempo of the game was extraordinary, not least due to the fact that Alf Ramsey enjoyed losing to the Scots about as much as he might enjoy root canal work at the dentist's. His determination to beat the team from over the border was all the more powerful because he knew the taste of defeat – as manager of England, he lost his first two matches against the Scots.

The wounds ran very deep and perhaps partly explained his notorious reaction to a cheery greeting from a Scottish reporter when he arrived in Glasgow for one of those early battles. 'Welcome to Scotland,' said Jim Rodger of the *Scottish Daily Express*. Ramsey levelled an icy stare at the journalist and declared, 'You must be bloody joking,' or, it must be added for the sake of absolute accuracy, something largely to that effect.

But however hard we had been exhorted, the Scots brought their own special motivation. They also had the brilliant enigma, Jimmy Baxter. Although his career was already beginning to run off course, taking with it one of the most sublime talents ever produced in these islands, he found within himself a rare force and the best of his touch this day. Denis Law bundled in the first Scottish goal after a shot from Willie Wallace bounced off Gordon Banks, and the others came from Lennox and Jim McCalliog, Sheffield Wednesday's clever player. Geoff Hurst added to Jack's goal, but we just couldn't find a way to stem the Scottish tide.

The English dressing room, presided over by a tight-lipped Ramsey, was a sombre place after the game. We had done all we could, and despite the Scottish cries of jubilation, we still believed we were champions of the world, but nobody needed to tell us that some desperate months lay ahead.

I remember thinking as I walked off the field, and the goalposts were disappearing beneath a Scottish swarm, 'Oh, my God, we are the world champions but now we face a year of hell.'

Deep down, you couldn't begrudge the Scots their moment because here was a football nation who had never enjoyed the results that the quality of their native talent had so long promised.

We had a fierce rivalry but, speaking for myself, I can say it didn't descend into raw animosity, nothing, certainly, that could ever be placed in the category of England versus Argentina, or United versus Estudiantes. Indeed, after playing twelve matches against the Scots, winning five, losing four and drawing three, I have to say that nothing in my competitive life gave me so much sustained pleasure. Sometimes the results were hard to take, sometimes Scottish passion, and let's be honest, triumphalism, provoked some bitter English reaction, but not to the point where you lost the value of games always played as though they were the most important challenges in the world.

However, it is probably true to say that the balance of competition and respect was never more precarious than on that afternoon when we walked off Wembley in the face of a Scottish invasion.

We had approached the match with some apprehension. We knew that as champions of the world we had never before provoked such Scottish determination. It wasn't a match as much as part of a fervent tribal war. You had a picture of the clans gathering uproariously in the railway stations, and some of them not making it beyond the border as they were thrown off the trains at Carlisle. From the moment of kick-off, we knew how committed the Scottish nation was to this single football match.

When the final whistle went, I sighed and took a deep breath, my thoughts turning to the reaction of Denis Law and Paddy Crerand when I arrived back at Old Trafford, and how a reigning world champion would be told, in the briskest terms, that he had lost his bragging rights.

Denis, after all, had confessed to going out to play golf the afternoon England faced West Germany in the World Cup final out of the fear that he would be required to watch the 'Sassenach bastards' claim world football's most sought-after prize. I did comfort myself a little by recalling that when Nobby Stiles, John Connelly and I returned to United for pre-season training after the World Cup final, Denis had the grace to come up to each of us individually and offer his congratulations.

Still, that was a gesture made after some long weeks of reflection. In the heat of Wembley battle, no one had been more determined to press home the Scottish advantage. Every run he made, every leap in the penalty box, emphasised his search for one more goal, one more strike at the heart of England. Jim Baxter, Scotland's other star on one of the nation's most famous days, showed an entirely different approach. He preferred to make a statement about Scottish skill, holding the ball and at one point producing an outrageous display of 'keepy-uppy'. The Scottish fans were ecstatic. Others wondered if the Scottish maverick was somehow crossing a line, taunting for the vindictive sake of it, but that was an argument that would have won little or no support north of the border.

If you wanted to find a symbol of both the glory and the frailty of Scottish football, its sublime ability to create the most gifted footballers and its capacity to betray itself at the most vital moments, there was an overwhelming case not to pass over Jimmy Baxter.

In some ways, he was similar to the highly gifted but often erratic Celtic winger Jimmy Johnstone, another player Scots hold so closely to their hearts. But if Johnstone benefited from the guidance and discipline of his club manager Jock Stein, the genius, and self-destructiveness, of Baxter often seemed beyond such restraint. His progress from Raith Rovers to Rangers and then, with the ebbing of the prime of his talent and the last pretences of personal discipline, to Sunderland and Nottingham

Forest, was the story of tragic waste. It is one that carries an obvious comparison to that of my United team-mate George Best, but again there is a difference. George's career, and life, like Jimmy's, was tragically foreshortened by a lack of discipline, but George did have some years of the highest achievement, including the run to the 1968 European Cup, before trailing away into the margins of the game.

Jimmy and I did our national service at the same time and so I got an early glimpse of his skills in a few army games. His talent was breathtaking, as easily displayed as it was rich and deep. Like Denis Law, he had something that leaped out at you. You might call it competitive arrogance. It seemed to proclaim, 'Do not come near to me, do not touch me, because it will do you no good.' It certainly didn't that day at Wembley when England tried to overcome the disruption that followed Jack's injury.

For Baxter, I imagine now, it was more than anything a gesture of defiance against those who said that his career should have amounted to a lot more. 'Look what I can still do,' he seemed to be saying with every stroke of the ball. When he flicked it in the air and invited Nobby Stiles, the tamer of Eusebio and another dozen great players, to do his best, or his worst, he presented the picture of an ultimate football rebel, a man going his own way but determined that he should be remembered at least for one extraordinary day.

There were, of course, many great days, and that only increased the anguish when his career dribbled away, and then, later, in another echo of George Best, when he died after the controversy that followed the decision to give him a liver transplant in spite of his drinking habits.

Spectacular though his performance was in 1967, he always insisted that he had played better four years earlier when Scotland won 2–1 at Wembley and he scored both the goals. As one of his beaten opponents, I would have to agree. The

Scots were severely handicapped by the early disaster of Eric Caldow's broken leg, but Baxter was undeterred. He scored one beautiful goal and converted a penalty – the first of his career – and was never far away from the heart of a match he had plainly decided he had the ability to dominate. For Scotland, you could only feel sad that he had not reached that conclusion more often, and that such ambition was too frequently lost in the march of his often wayward days.

On Scotland's most cherished day at Wembley, at a time of vindication, the seeds of fresh frustration were sown. The win gave them a brilliant start to their European Championship qualifying campaign, which for the first time was merged with the Home International Championship. What better way could there be for them to underline their belief that they had assumed the mantle of world champions than by excluding England from international football's second most important tournament? Yet that extremely practical goal was lost along the way, and most disastrously in Belfast, where Scotland were defeated by Northern Ireland. They were now obliged to beat us at Hampden, but after parading their skills so extravagantly at Wembley, the task was beyond them.

Scotland could do no better than draw, which meant that we were through to meet Spain in the European Championship. We defeated them home and away, only to come unstuck against Yugoslavia in the semi-final. This can only have been of passing solace to the frustrated Scots, as no doubt was their brilliant victory over the powerful Dutch team eleven years later in the World Cup of Argentina, when Archie Gemmill, a classic little Scottish midfielder, scored a brilliant individual goal – another cry of defiance but competitively meaningless after a draw with Iran and a loss to Peru.

For many years, a deeper worry existed for the Scots, but fortunately it is one that has been softened by more recent results. For so long it seemed that if England had lost many competitive values, if they were finding it increasingly hard to make any kind of impact on the major tournaments, a trend culminating in the failure to qualify for this year's European Championship finals, Scotland might have actually lost its football soul. While England still manage to produce, spasmodically admittedly, players of potentially world-class talent, such as Michael Owen, Paul Scholes, David Beckham, Steven Gerrard and Wayne Rooney, where were the new Laws and Baxters, St Johns and Gemmills?

The old supply line from the boys clubs seemed to have been cut, a disaster magnified, for followers of the national team, by the ability of clubs to invest a sudden gush of television money on European players, many of them of questionable quality. The result was shattering for those who remembered the glory of Jock Stein's Celtic drawn exclusively from Glasgow and its environs.

Now, after the thrilling run that took Scotland so close to qualification for the 2008 European Championship finals, something seems to be stirring. Perhaps the ghosts of Baxter and Johnstone are on the march – and perhaps, who knows, there could be another day when a bottle of single malt is put down behind the bar of the Craw's Nest. For me, as always, it would be no great hardship to take a wee dram.

9

A PLACE ON THE
MOUNTAIN TOP

As WE FLEW down over the Andes into Santiago, the capital of
Chile, in May 1962, I was immensely heartened by our showing
in Lima – much more so than I, or anyone else connected with
the team, could have imagined two weeks earlier at Wembley.

With the squad selected, and all the individual hopes and
fears resolved, the game against Switzerland was supposed to
be an occasion for a statement of intent, even celebration.
Gone now, surely, were the inhibitions brought by tension and
self-doubt. We had made it to the greatest show on the football planet. We had survived the risks of injury and capricious
form, got past the selection committee room and the politics
and now we had to proclaim the fact that we really could
compete with reigning champions Brazil and their stars, Pelé
and Garrincha.

That hope did not seem misguided when we started strongly,
and imaginatively, against the Swiss, fellow World Cup qualifiers, and John Connelly, Gerry Hitchens and Ron Flowers
scored a goal each. Hitchens had won the race with Ray Pointer
for the number-one striker's place, despite Pointer scoring one
of the two goals against Portugal the previous October, a result
that ensured our qualification. But in the second half all that
buoyancy dribbled away quite shockingly. The Swiss took control

almost completely. They scored and suddenly the field seemed to be filled with red shirts.

It was the most hollow of 3–1 victories and the food for thought it offered might have proved indigestible without the uplift of Lima and the evidence that match provided that maybe England were finally acquiring players with the temperament – and the steel – to make an impact beyond the borders of their own football. Maybe the performance against Switzerland was a throwback, an aberration, and instead we were heading for better days.

The players who sprang to mind in that regard were Bobby Moore and Ray Wilson, who at twenty-seven was six years older than the future captain of England but who played with a passion and a sharpness that announced him as every inch one of the new wave of modern defenders. If Moore was so cool he might have been carrying the wisdom of the football ages, Wilson was hard and direct and superbly fit, a quality noted by the Huddersfield Town manager Bill Shankly when he decided to convert him from an apprentice railwayman to a full-time full back of tremendous defensive instincts and an easy ability to go on the overlap.

I soon became close with my fellow northerner. He had a dry and sometimes dark humour, befitting a man who would eventually become an undertaker. But it was the young prodigy 'Mooro' who did most to convey a wider sense of new possibilities, new depth, as we were transported via a single-gauge railway track up a mountain to our World Cup headquarters at the American Braden Copper Company.

It was on the flight to Lima that I heard Winterbottom was thinking of giving Moore his first cap with a view to making him a cornerstone of the team. My reaction could not have been less complicated – 'This is good, this is the way we should be going.' I had seen a little of him in the colours of West Ham and although I hadn't studied his game closely, I was impressed.

Beyond any of the specifics of his play, the tackling, the passing, the heading, there was the composure. It made you think, almost subliminally, 'Hey, this kid knows what he's doing, he is at home.'

Many others must have reached the same conclusion because his name had quickly infiltrated the corners of the game. His great advocate and mentor was Malcolm Allison, who would later for a while so colour my life as the coach of Manchester City, and the sad irony for 'Big Mal' was that his protégé quickly took his place in the West Ham team.

When I saw how easily Moore fitted in with England, and noted the assurance that seemed to spread around him, I thought, 'This is definitely one for 1966. This is a lad who's going to be around for a long time.'

Perhaps out of natural optimism, and a conviction that there was enough quality in English football eventually to bear fruit at the highest level, I had refused to believe, even in the wake of the most discouraging performances – and there was no question about the one against Switzerland falling into that category – that we were condemned to unbroken futility. I also thought that if the dismal pattern was to be broken, surely our best chance would come in England in four years' time. We would have every advantage then. Chile offered the opportunity to show that we had both the quality and the character to respond to the challenge.

What I didn't quite realise, as our little train clanked up the mountainside, was how many fresh lessons had to be learned about keeping twenty-odd players, nearly half of whom had very little chance of getting into the action, primed to produce the best of themselves if they were required – and at the same time contributing to the spirit of the squad.

One of the problems that became increasingly evident in Chile was a lack of that unity that is so essential if the days are to pass easily and a competitive focus is to be maintained. Much later I read a report that said when Bryan Douglas, a key player of great experience and skill, arrived at the Braden Copper Company, he sat down on his bag and confessed, 'I feel homesick already.' He was perhaps missing his Blackburn team-mate Ronnie Clayton, whose companionship he had enjoyed for so long on England travels, but even though his comment was news to me, I was aware that for some in the squad, the South American days dragged terribly. I do recall one player, who didn't play in the tournament, saying, 'Don't score today, lads, let's go home at the first opportunity.'

No doubt he was not entirely serious but it was not a mood to encourage the kind of commitment that goes into winning a World Cup. Perhaps it was another sign that, in the future, there would be an unanswerable case for stronger leadership, unencumbered by a committee and provided by a professional who better understood the psychology of the average player, detached from the support of his family and friends and, as so often is the case even with the most gifted and experienced individuals, uncertain about himself and his chances of making the right impact.

As I have tried to make clear, I had the highest respect for Walter Winterbottom's knowledge of the game, and his gentlemanly manner. But if I am honest, I also have to say it struck me very clearly that he could be remote from the anxieties and preoccupations of the players, and if this was so, there was a very good reason for it. He had never been in charge of a professional team, day in and day out. He had never been obliged to understand, and sometimes sort out, the problems, real or imagined, that prevented players giving of their best. This may sound a little harsh, an offloading of responsibility perhaps, but one thing was evident enough to me during the course of the tournament. It was that the squad lacked any real sense of unity and purpose, a problem increased by the effects of homesickness, particularly in some of the fringe players.

I became increasingly influenced, and impressed, by Winterbottom's assistant coach, Jimmy Adamson. He was still idealistic about the game but also hard-headed about what should be demanded from players who had been picked by their country. Here was a professional player who had immersed himself in football and done tremendous work, on and off the field, at Burnley, the little Lancashire town club set in the moors, which, amazingly, was competing with the strongest clubs in the land. He believed that, as a World Cup came every four years, every professional of ambition, who wanted to look back on his career with pride, must embrace the challenge of it, not to some degree but with a hundred per cent involvement.

With this attitude firmly lodged in my mind, Ray Wilson, who although several years older had won twenty-four fewer caps, was a natural companion for me. Football had given him travel and experiences way beyond the expectations of the average railwayman, and his attitude was that while he played the game he would give it everything he had. This didn't involve him in any great statements about what he intended to do, he didn't have a lot to say for himself, but when he spoke, his words were all the more valuable for that. He was mostly quiet and when we whiled away some of the hours on the Chilean mountain top, if he talked much it was usually about his love of the countryside and how he had already fulfilled one ambition by walking the length of the Pennines. He had started off in the south, around Uttoxeter, and finished at the northern limit, exhilarated by the days on the moors, breathing air free from grit or soot. For him, the Braden Copper Company was almost home from home.

For me, the days of preparation passed by easily enough. I was struck by the reach of the American dollar into these Chilean mountains, how it made a little colony, complete with a golf course, a training pitch, a swimming pool and gardens, for the men who tapped the mineral wealth of another country. In those days, Chile was so poor that when their World Cup organising committee made its case to world football's ruling body, Fifa, one plea was, apparently, 'We have nothing else, so why not give us the World Cup? Give us one thing at least that we can be proud of.' This plea became all the more poignant after the country suffered a serious earthquake in 1960, followed by one of less severity in 1961.

However poor the country and its people, it had great beauty, and efforts to charm the outside world with dancing displays before every game were always touching. So, too, was the little band that welcomed us to the mining camp, and the way our train had been festooned with union flags. Such feeling was especially warm when you considered the gulf between rich and poor. It was something you couldn't avoid as you passed some of the shacks that existed in Rancagua, on one occasion on the way to a sumptuous reception at the palatial home of the mayor of the town, where nothing was spared in the display of drinks and food. It was hard to imagine what would have been made of such opulence by the children we had just seen running, and laughing, in the unpaved streets.

Facilities at the camp were not luxurious but they were more than adequate. The rooms were clean and with our train taking us down the mountain for the group games in the mining company town in the valley, we could not complain of any inconvenience beyond the inevitable tug of boredom and, it had maybe to be whispered, the missing of loved ones. My wife Norma was pregnant with our first daughter, Suzanne, and, of course, she was very much in my thoughts. My family situation was one reason to discourage an apparent backdoor approach to sign me by the famous Buenos Aires club Boca Juniors. I said that, apart from my loyalty to Manchester United, there was no question of my moving my wife at such a time. After a pause, the intermediary snapped back that there was absolutely no problem. The club could easily arrange for Norma to have the baby at the British embassy, which of course meant that, if it was a boy, he would be qualified to play for England.

More seriously, I found myself thinking back on all that I had seen in the four years since my spectator's role in the World Cup in Sweden, and also what chance I would have given myself, in the ruins of Munich, of being the twenty-four-year-old owner of thirty-five England caps, a haul second only to that of Johnny Haynes, who had fifty-one to back up his status as the most celebrated player in English football.

My collection of caps at such a young age was a great honour – and gave me an intense awareness of the need to meet the latest challenge that had been placed before me. I thought of all the players who had strived to be at this place on the mountain, good players, but who failed, and those who had, like me, made it but now fretted about whether they would be equal to the tasks they had been given. I thought of the wave of Wolves players, of whom Ronnie Flowers was now the sole survivor, and how his team-mates Eddie Clamp, Bill Slater, Peter Broadbent and Norman Deeley might have fared if the fortunes of their club, so long a mighty fortress in the Black Country, had not begun to ebb.

Broadbent had shown tremendous promise a few years earlier. I admired him for his skill and for his neatness and composure in front of goal, but in the end he probably suffered for the lack of a little more pace. Later, I was pleased to hear that he had some compensation in his success in business.

Blackburn Rovers were another club who had begun to slip away from their old heights, and you had to wonder if that had maybe hurt the prospects of Ronnie Clayton, who for so long had seemed a likely leader of the team. He wasn't in the class of Johnny Haynes as a creative player, but he did see the whole picture of a game, and he wasn't afraid to put his foot in if things turned rough. He was always ready to fight for his team, and he was another about whom it was natural to think, 'Well, it could have turned out so differently for him.'

In the end, you could only be grateful for your own good

luck – and hope that in the next few weeks the doubts would fall away with the approach of the first of our three group games against Hungary, Argentina and Bulgaria. More than anything, I hoped that all of us could raise ourselves up to the level that was necessary if we were going to force ourselves into contention and live with the best, the teams who believed that they had a chance of challenging the standard set so brilliantly in Sweden by Brazil.

Certainly, if we were very honest, it had to be accepted that it wouldn't be enough to do what we had been doing for so long, that is playing our own game in the belief that one day it would prove good enough to beat the world. That was one piece of baggage we had to leave on the mountain top as we boarded the train to meet Hungary, the team who had already done so much to expose our flaws and to show the rulers of our game that time had marched on much quicker than they may have thought.

10

THE LITTLE BIRD

ALL THE MUSING on the mountain would eventually come down to one of the most familiar, and haunting, questions in football. It starts, 'What if?' In the case of Chile 1962, what if Brazil, in the absence of one genius, the injured Pelé, had not unfurled another at the peak of his powers?

Garrincha, the Little Bird, was of course no stranger to us. Four years earlier in Sweden we had seen the enormous power he generated from once crippled legs. We had seen him torture defences before but in Chile it was as though he realised that, with Pelé laid low, for a little while at least he was suddenly without a rival under the football sun.

I will always believe that, but for the astonishing and ungovernable eruption of his brilliance, we might have flown home to England with more than the equivalent fate suffered by our successors forty years later in Japan – defeat in the quarter-finals by the eventual champions Brazil.

Before that point of head-shaking conjecture, however, we had to absorb the disappointment that awaited us at the end of our first train ride into action against Hungary.

We made the journey down into the valley under a sullen sky and steady drizzle. The gloom deepened after just sixteen minutes when Lajos Tichy reminded us of the skill and imagination with which the Hungarians had invaded the game in the early fifties. He seemed to be presenting no threat as he meandered outside the box, well covered by Bobby Moore and with the other England defenders closing down space in front of goalkeeper Ron Springett's goal. Unfortunately, and shockingly, Tichy suddenly produced the kind of inspiration that had so devastatingly thrust Hungary on to the English consciousness nine years earlier at Wembley. While scarcely changing his stride, he unleashed a superb shot, sending the ball flying past Springett.

The Hungarians clearly scented blood and Karoly Sandor, a quick and tricky winger, required a brilliant save from Springett. Almost immediately, Florian Albert, the great hope of a new generation of Hungarian football, squandered a chance to kill us off – from no more than six yards.

Johnny Haynes, frustrated by our failure to settle into anything like a smooth passing game and so quickly facing another disappointment at the helm of a World Cup challenge, yelled for greater effort. If we had been stunned by Tichy's initiative, we were determined to fight our way off the ropes. Jimmy Armfield relieved some of the pressure with fine running on the overlap along the right and when I ran free on the left and crossed into the heart of the Hungarian box, goalkeeper Gyula Grosics, a veteran of the Puskas team, was knocked out in a collision with Gerry Hitchens.

We applied such pressure for most of the game but, unfortunately, on this day, the classic English tactic of the high ball encountered a near flawless response in Hungary's young master defender, Kalman Meszoly. He went on to become a foundation of the Hungarian defence – and this was the day he announced his pedigree.

He produced a near-perfect performance, dominating magnificently in the air, and it was a rare moment of dangerous exposure for a now recovered Grosics when, in the fifty-eighth minute, the goalkeeper allowed a cross by Bryan Douglas to slide from his grasp after another collision with Hitchens. Greaves was on the ball as quickly as you would have expected and his shot was goal-bound when defender Laszlo Sarosi reached out a hand and stopped it on the line. Ron Flowers converted the penalty and signalled a burst of attacking from us that, while not always perfectly orchestrated, lasted until the end of the game.

Unfortunately, it was punctuated by a moment of disaster for the penalty hero, Flowers slipping on the rain-slicked surface while covering what seemed like a most innocuous pass. Albert seized on the loose ball, rounded Springett and shot coolly past Ray Wilson, who was desperately attempting to protect an otherwise empty goal.

Our 2–1 defeat made for a solemn journey back up the mountain. This time there was no band to greet us and the union flags were limp and bedraggled in the rain. Argentina, who had beaten Bulgaria in the same stadium the day before, were our next opponents. We were told they had a new phenomenon, a player of great panache, much revered in the barrios of Buenos Aires – Jose Sanfilippo.

The Hungarians had benefited from a piece of good fortune, but Albert had converted it with a fine killer touch, and if we were honest we had to admit that they had looked more of a team. Their football was rhythmic and economical, and if in young Meszoly they had the outstanding player, they produced more evidence of depth on their way to winning the group when another young player, inside forward Janos Gorocs, appeared in the team and produced a masterful performance in the 6–1 demolition of Bulgaria. Gorocs never won the world reputation I expected after a performance I have never forgotten for its perfection, but he was a reminder to us that it wasn't only the big-name stars who represented a threat. The international game was throwing up young players who were brilliantly equipped to meet new demands on both fitness and tactical understanding. Against Bulgaria, Gorocs looked like a dazzling example of a new and fast-rising generation of players. Try as I might as I sat in the stand of the little stadium of the Braden

Copper Company, I could not find a weakness, or even a hint of one, in the performance of a young player who, fortunately, was missing when we played them in the opening game and about whom I had not even heard a whisper.

We heard a lot more than that, however, about Senor Jose Sanfilippo. Apparently, he was the toast of Buenos Aires, a player who provoked surges of applause whenever he touched the ball. For all its other eccentricities and self-destroying cynical tendencies, Argentina had always put a high value on celebrating the team rather than just one individual, but Jose Sanfilippo was a new phenomenon in his elevation above his team-mates.

There were other worries, however, before a game we had to win if we were to stay in the tournament. Under a new hard-line coach, Juan Carlos Lorenzo, the Argentines had put a lot of iron into their game – at least, that is one way of putting it – and we had seen plenty of evidence of this in their opening victory over Bulgaria. Having been swept out of the 1958 World Cup in a humiliating 6–1 defeat by Czechoslovakia, the Argentines had decided that their new football had to be a lot quicker – and a lot tougher.

Walter Winterbottom had decided to replace the battling, and, after the Hungarian game, somewhat battered, Gerry Hitchens with the tall Alan Peacock, and in his team talk he said we had to show plenty of bite against a team who would try to employ some of the intimidation that had worked against the Bulgarians. Ron Flowers and Maurice Norman ensured we did that, but even more profitably we outplayed the Argentines.

I had one of my best games for England at outside left, going by my marker, Vladislao Cap, without too much difficulty on the way to making the first and scoring the second in a 3–1 win. For the opener, Peacock, on his debut, met my cross to beat goalkeeper Antonio Roma, but captain Ruben Navarro handled and Flowers drove home the penalty. Before half-time

I scored the second with a low shot to the far post after inviting the defence to believe that I was again planning to go round the full back. Jimmy Greaves scored the third in the 68th minute, emphasising that the Hungarian defeat was not the death sentence some had feared – and Johnny Haynes had been right to tell the English press, with great feeling, that they had been too quick to write off our chances.

Sanfilippo? He scored a late, meaningless goal, which did nothing to stop him falling from the pinnacle of the new celebrity culture that would be, with the ultimate profit of victory in 1978, dismantled for the next twenty years – until its inevitable reinstatement with the astonishing rise of Diego Maradona in Mexico in 1986. The new and controversial coach Lorenzo had much work to do but he decided quickly that he would do it without a Sanfilippo, who, I had to conclude, had been lauded quite ridiculously. No doubt he had some basic skill, and he was certainly not averse to displaying it, but here it seemed we had a classic case of show before substance. How many times down the years have players been celebrated not for what they do but what they promise to do? Between the two, there is all the difference in the world.

Lorenzo's consolation was that, even on a very bad day for his team, there was some evidence that he had a foundation on which to build, supplied not least by a tall, forceful young midfielder named Antonio Rattin.

Our encouragement was that we were back in the World Cup. The frown that had been more or less permanently installed on the brow of the captain Haynes had eased considerably and, speaking for myself, there was the sense that maybe we could indeed compete with some of the best teams in the world.

That mood, however, scarcely survived our next match against Bulgaria – until this day I have always believed it was the worst game in which I was ever obliged to play.

The match was so bad, so depressing, so opposed to all that

I believed in and had been taught at Manchester United, that when the final whistle confirmed our place in the quarter-finals after a goalless draw with one of the least talented, least ambitious teams to have played in the World Cup, I found myself involved in a loud and angry dispute with my captain.

Before and throughout the game, Johnny Haynes had stressed that a draw was enough to take us, for the first time, into a World Cup quarter-final, and when this was confirmed, he seemed, outrageously in my opinion, to be suggesting that this was a result we were entitled to celebrate. I would have none of it and made my point heatedly. It didn't degenerate into fisticuffs but it was one of the few occasions in my career when I gave my feelings full rein.

'How can you say that was a good performance?' I demanded to know. I had spent an hour and a half running around in a game in which apparently no one wanted to score. It was dreadful and, I contended, quite dangerous.

'Bloody hell,' Haynes said, 'it's the first time we've reached the quarter-finals.'

'Yes, but we're talking about bloody Bulgaria,' I responded, 'and what kind of a disaster would it have been if they sneaked a goal? What would the press have made of that?'

The fact was that this had at one hideous moment been more than an outside possibility. It came near the end when the Bulgarian winger Ivan Kolev worked himself free and crossed perfectly to Aleksandar Kostov, who somehow managed to miss an open goal. Earlier, Georgi Sokolov missed another opportunity to score. Had either he or Kostov done so, I cannot imagine any serious football nation would ever have had to retreat from a World Cup in such disgraceful circumstances. Down the years I'm afraid my anger at events that day in Rancagua has only festered and some years ago I was somewhat relieved to read that, according to Bobby Moore, who was playing only his fourth international, I had not been guilty of any over-reaction. Bobby said, 'We would have a dozen passes at our end and then try to hit the ball up to our one forward. He was bound to lose it. So then they had a dozen passes down their end. It was one of the worst internationals of all time.'

More troubling, I believed, was that the game was a miserable betrayal of all that I thought English football should stand for. It was one thing to lose to Brazil or Hungary when, even on the worst of days, there was a little honour in it if we tried to do our best as honestly as we could. But this was altogether different. If some were in a mood of self-congratulation on the train ride home that night, I was not one of them. I did not play football to try to sneak a result against inferior opposition. That was not in any of the lessons taught by the fierce Jimmy Murphy, or any small part of the picture painted for me by my grandfather Tanner in those last hours we had together in his sick room.

My anger made for fretful sleep on my company cot on the mountain top but when the sun rose in the morning it was accompanied by an encouraging fact. However we fared against our quarter-final opponents, there would be no question of making a mockery of the football once practised by Tom Finney, Stanley Matthews and Wilf Mannion. You couldn't begin to contemplate such a game plan against the beautiful game of Brazil.

This was true, we would learn dramatically enough, even in the absence of Pelé. Brazil's progress to the quarter-finals had not been imperious, not at least after the great man had been forced to surrender to the effects of a groin injury that he had attempted to conceal from the management. This happened in the second group game, a goalless draw with Brazil's final opponents Czechoslovakia. Garrincha burst down his flank, crossed and Pelé reached to connect. As he did so, he felt the pull that he knew had ended his tournament. He had, however, already made his mark. In the opening game, a 2–0 victory over Mexico, he showed tremendous tenacity and, given his condition, great courage in fighting his way down the wing before crossing for Mario Zagallo to head home. The second goal was entirely the product of his genius. He beat four defenders, one of them nutmegged, in a run down the right and then, while surviving heavy traffic in the penalty box, he shifted the ball to his left foot before driving it home.

Such superhuman effort could not be maintained against a Czechoslovakian team brilliantly marshalled by the great Josef Masopust. Pelé hobbled out of the tournament, years later paying a moving tribute to the grace of his opponents, noting the refusal of defenders Jan Lala and Jan Popluhar to make their hardest tackles when they saw that he had been reduced to no more than nuisance value. Pelé said, 'It was one of those things I would always remember with emotion – and one of the finest things to happen in my football career.'

The departure of Pelé might have been to our advantage if Garrincha's football had not taken on a new and, we had to conclude sadly, unplayable dimension.

We had gone down to the coastal resort of Vina del Mar in good enough heart. The post-Bulgaria recriminations had spent themselves without lasting problems and with Pelé gone we felt there was some reason for optimism. We had done well against Argentina, and reminded ourselves that we were not without talent, or competitive character. Even after Garrincha produced his first extraordinary assault on our senses – and our confidence – we remained defiant. First, he swept through half the defence, demanding a desperate tackle from Haynes. Then, most remarkably of all, he outjumped Maurice Norman, who towered above him as they awaited a corner kick, and sent a header past the flabbergasted Springett.

That was an invitation to capsize but instead we hit back. Gerry Hitchens, who had come back into the side because of Peacock's injury against Bulgaria, shot past Gylmar after Jimmy

Greaves's header came back off the crossbar. At the half-time whistle, I thought, 'Garrincha is a problem but we are not out of this.' After the blind alley of the Bulgarian game, we were playing real football, operating like a real team.

Unfortunately, Garrincha was about to enter his own world, one in which we simply had no place, no more, I suspect, than would any other team in world football.

Indeed, I will always believe that if Garrincha had not been playing, we might well have beaten the world champions – the what if . . . with which I started this chapter. As it was, we could fairly claim that we had been engulfed by a single talent. His free kick eight minutes after half-time ripped through our defensive wall and the best Springett could do was push the ball into the path of Vava. It was a stunning strike, and before we could recover our composure, Garrincha had struck again. This time it was a mesmerising, curling shot from the edge of the box.

There didn't seem anything beyond the powers of Garrincha now, except, that was, his ability to catch a woolly black dog that raced on to the pitch, perhaps to celebrate another piece of virtuosity from the Brazilian. The dog swerved past Garrincha, but not Greaves, who got down on his hands and knees to trap the invader. The crowd cheered but it did not do much for our mood.

English heads hit their chests, and none more heavily than Johnny Haynes's. A marvellously gifted player, a master of passing and vision, a man who created his own extraordinary geometry on a football field, he had been denied his great ambition to lead his country to previously unknown glory.

It was a dream that fell well within the boundaries of his ability and, who knows, if Munich hadn't happened, if some of the cornerstones of a young, and potentially poised England had not been torn away, if he had been able to orchestrate a settled team rather than a constantly changing chorus line, he might have proved to be the man of destiny his exceptional talent had once promised.

Instead, he could only reflect that in his time at Fulham, the friendly little club beside the Thames, which seemed to have no greater ambition than to inhabit, happily, the margins of the English First Divison, to go its own way, playing its own idea of what football should be, he had created a legend of excellence and beauty.

My future England team-mate George Cohen, and Haynes's most loyal club-mate, still speaks reverently of the master player, and expresses his sadness that he never enjoyed the rewards that might have come if Fulham had agreed to overtures from Tottenham Hotspur and the Italian game.

For myself, I could only mourn the passing of one of the truly great English players when I recently attended his funeral in Edinburgh, a place where he had settled happily for his last years. I thought of all the times he had split a defence with a pass that seemed to come straight from the football heavens. I thought of his desperation, even his rage, to succeed in Chile, and finally, of the expression that crossed his face when it was clear that Garrincha had put an end to all his hopes.

He never again played for England, although from time to time the new manager, Alf Ramsey, toyed with the idea of his recall. That possibility was hindered by a car crash. The injuries Haynes sustained required a long and painful recovery period.

What was never in doubt, however, was that few had ever heard the call to England duty more clearly than Johnny Haynes. In the end, it was his misfortune that it had come at the wrong time, a fact confirmed on the day the Little Bird of Brazil played the game of his life.

11

JIMMY ADAMSON TALKS

BEFORE WE FLEW home, we found some time for a measure of liquid consolation that would not begin to find its way on to the agenda of a modern England World Cup team. We were invited by the press corps to have some farewell drinks, and when we gathered in a bar in Vina del Mar, they made it clear that in their reviews of our campaign the sharpest of knives had stayed in their sheaths.

This was a welcome shift after the abrasive reaction of Johnny Haynes to the criticism that followed our first defeat against Hungary. Then the picture being painted was of another no-hope World Cup campaign, something not much better than the running up of a white flag. Now, at least, the English public had been told we were flying home with a little honour – and hope for the future.

Yes, of course there were important issues to be resolved. The Football Association had to acknowledge that, in so many ways, they had been living in the past. After sixteen years, it was almost certainly time to consider the position of Walter Winterbottom and the need for a new kind of leadership. But our exclusion had not been shameful. We had beaten one of the South American powers, Argentina, and we had not buckled under the brilliance of Garrincha.

My friend Geoffrey Green, football correspondent of *The Times*, who later invited me to be godfather to his baby daughter

Ti and often helped me while away the endless hours of inter-continental flight, felt it not inappropriate to sip a Scotch in between strumming his banjo and humming some suitably upbeat songs.

Frank McGhee of the *Daily Mirror*, a man never reluctant to pass on a trenchant view, agreed with me that we had played well against Brazil after finding our nerve and some rhythm against Argentina and surviving the Bulgarian nightmare. Garrincha, Frank also agreed, would have put to the sword any team, however talented and organised, on the form he displayed against us. Sometimes it was necessary to shrug your shoulders at unkind fate and move on to the next challenge.

Such a philosophical reaction did, however, come under a little strain, when we returned home and saw that Brazil were much less irresistible in their semi-final and final matches against Chile and Czechoslovakia. Most ironically of all, Garrincha's place in the final was in some doubt after he was sent off in the Chile match. The Brazilians, apparently, waged a fierce campaign behind the scenes to have him reinstated. Not too surprisingly, given Brazil's huge significance in South American football, and the popularity of the player, they won this battle, but then they must have been terribly disappointed by Garrincha's near anonymous performance. As the Brazilians faltered against the clever, intricate game of European Player of the Year Masopust and his men – winning 3–1 only after a late surge of individual brilliance and goals from Zito and Vava in the sixty-ninth and seventy-eighth minutes – I could only argue all over again that we had not been so far away from proving ourselves a genuine force. What if, what if . . .

It was a point of view I expressed from time to time to my travelling companion on the long flight home from Santiago, via Lima and Miami. But mostly I listened because Jimmy Adamson, England's assistant coach, had impressed me as a fine, intelligent professional, and although he was very much involved in the future of his club, Burnley, there was a body of opinion that was making him one of the favourites to succeed Walter Winterbottom. As it turned out, Adamson refused the invitation after Walter resigned to become the head of the Council for Physical Recreation, having unexpectedly lost in the voting to pick a successor to Sir Stanley Rous as the secretary of the Football Association.

The history of the national team was being shaped in those post-Chile days, and it would take a huge stride in the direction of professionalism when Alf Ramsey was officially unveiled as the new manager on 1 May 1963, but during that long conversation with Adamson on the plane home, and subsequent ones when I drove over the moors to see him, I realised that here was a man capable of achieving major improvements in the way England were selected, trained and psychologically prepared.

Again, I have to stress that I do not mean this to sound like some dismissive epitaph for the Winterbottom years. For it to be so, I could hardly proclaim that England had come closer to glory in South America than many believed possible. In his last days in the job, Winterbottom, a symbol of an old, amateur world in many eyes, had almost turned himself into a national hero. On top of that, despite all the vagaries of the system, he had managed to form the nucleus of a side that I fervently believed would be extremely serious runners in the 1966 World Cup. At twenty-four, I had become the veteran of a team already feeling the impact of such talented, modern players as Bobby Moore, Ray Wilson and Jimmy Greaves.

But the more I talked to Adamson, the more I could see that a new and stronger form of leadership was required. Part of Walter would always be locked in the theoretical – it was part of him and his passion for the game. He was 'donnish' in the best sense, kind and never given to heavy-handed treatment of players or shows of bombast or ego, but it was clear that the days of the teacher would have to give way to those of the pro.

Had Adamson accepted the invitation to become the first professional to take over from Winterbottom, I have to say it was a potentially brilliant choice. On that trip back to England, time and again he referred to what he believed was the basic challenge of any player picked by his country.

'It's no good, Bobby,' he said, 'if you just roll along, hoping to play well, do what you do for your club, and think it's enough. It's not. You have to exert yourself in a way you haven't done before because this is a new test not just of your ability but of your playing character.

'You also have to remember that your responsibility increases with the degree of your ability. If you're Johnny Haynes or Bobby Charlton, you're expected to play at a certain level because you have been here many times before. So if you don't meet expectations, if somehow you don't deliver the best of yourself, the effect is much more damaging than if some new boy doesn't settle in immediately.'

I got the impression that Jimmy was a little disappointed with the overall effort in Chile. While I tended to bubble on a little about potential, Adamson kept bringing me back to the reality of performance. Potential is something that may or may not happen. Performance is the true guide to what a team can do. He was certainly appalled at the level of homesickness experienced by the squad, particularly by those players who knew they didn't have much of a chance of getting into the action. One thing for the future, he said, was much more consideration of the overall mood of the squad.

'Everyone has to feel that they have a part to play. If so-and-so plays well, it may be that he's relaxed in the company around him – and that he understands that this is a tough but relatively brief period in a player's career, and one that could easily define the rest of it. Some degree of homesickness is inevitable, but if it goes out of control, it's a symptom of other problems.'

Against the throb of the prop engines, the familiar tones of Adamson's north-east accent beat out a similarly consistent message. I could have taken notes and produced a basic manual for a working pro at any level of the game. It was impossible, as Adamson talked, not to make some comparisons between his style and background and those of the man he would shortly be asked to succeed.

Although Winterbottom had playing experience at my club, Manchester United, he had trained to be a teacher and came to the England job via a post with the RAF Association. Adamson's basic training came down a mine and playing for my home-town club, Ashington. Anyone with that kind of background is not likely to set significant store in theory, but to concentrate more on the practical business of earning a living, day in day out.

Adamson's drive to get out of the mines was as strong, and as compulsive, as Jack's, and soon it was rewarded with a regular place in the Burnley midfield and a share in the club's astonishing league title success of 1960, snatched from under the noses of such powerhouses as United and Wolves and the brilliantly rising Tottenham. Earlier in the year of the World Cup, he had been voted England's Footballer of the Year after leading Burnley to a losing cup final against the holders of the Double, Spurs.

He had never played for the full England side, but in Chile he had been entrusted with the vital role of reminding the players of their basic strengths and the need to carry them on to the field. He could do this with great authority after developing a tremendous partnership with one of the best inside forwards ever produced in the British Isles, the elegant Ulsterman Jimmy McIlroy.

On the plane he said to me, 'What you can never forget,

Bobby, and if you do, you let down both yourself and your team, is that generally speaking if you are an influential player and you play badly, if you don't give it all you have, everybody else will follow suit and play badly.

'You have to remember that you're not just in charge of yourself. If you're a good pro, you're always responsible also for your team-mates, who in some cases might not be so gifted.'

Down the years I have often wondered what Jimmy Adamson might have made of the England job if he hadn't been so immersed in the challenge of keeping Burnley, the little cotton town with a population of fewer than 100,000, in the company of the most powerful football cities in the land. When he finally took over from Harry Potts in 1970, Burnley were heralded as the Team of the Seventies. Of course, it didn't happen and the visionary Adamson soon found himself fighting a losing battle against relegation, and after battling back to the top flight, he went on to Sunderland and Sparta Amsterdam before succeeding Jock Stein at Leeds United.

The promise remained unfulfilled and I often regret that somewhere along the way our relationship tapered off. Frequently, I think it would be good to take a day off and go over to see him, and maybe I will do so one day soon. It would be fascinating to hear his thoughts on the course of an English regime that might have been his, and all the changes that have come to football since the days when he could have inherited such a big part of England's future.

Of one thing, though, I am certain. He would surely have brought valuable insights and strength to the challenge presented by the departure of Walter Winterbottom. Unlike Walter, and this for the record is something that does not have to be couched in diplomatic terms, he would have been quite specific about his requirements of individual players, and his requests would have been made in the specific language of professionals. One example of the contrast comes in the fact that throughout my years playing for Walter, he always told me I had to run. 'Keep running, Bobby,' he insisted. This flew in the face of my belief that while mobility was a basic demand, and had to be met by any player, it was not an end in itself. There were many other aspects to playing midfield with a purpose and exerting a real influence. Long before we touched down at Heathrow, Jimmy Adamson had given me the reassurance that in this, at least, I had been right.

What the conversation did most, I realise now, was help prepare me for a new and decisive phase of my career – a time when I joined Bobby Moore and Ray Wilson, my brother Jack, George Cohen and Nobby Stiles, Jimmy Greaves and Martin Peters, Gordon Banks, Geoff Hurst and Roger Hunt and a whippersnapper named Alan Ball, in giving a new and hard definition to the concepts of teamwork and ambition. It would be a few more months before that future was expressed precisely in the clipped, deliberate words of the new manager of England, but already I had a strong sense of what I had to do.

That was the bonus I took from the flight. For once, I had rather more to think about than the constancy of the engines that glowed in the long night.

12

ALF

I KNEW THAT Alf Ramsey would make many changes to the running of England when he took over from Walter Winterbottom. I knew this even though I didn't know him personally – I had never spent a second in his company before I answered, along with the rest of his first squad, his summons to the Hendon Hall Hotel in the spring of 1963, but I was very sure about what he represented.

Anyone who had played against his Ipswich Town, one of the unlikeliest First Division champions in the history of the Football League, had to know that. Behind the immaculate suits, the beautifully laundered shirts, the smart ties, clipped tones and tightly buttoned manner, there was a man who wore nothing so religiously as his beliefs about what a professional footballer should be and how he should behave.

You heard stories that his manner could be a little eccentric, or at the very least not typical of the free-and-easy style of most pros, but there could be no doubt that he had the most vital knack possessed by any manager – he carried his players with him. He was a loner, a man who threw up a wall around his private life. He was known to have lectured his fellow pros at Southampton and Spurs, and to cause resentment along with admiration when he was blunt to the point of being rude, but again and again you heard the same verdict – he knew the game, he knew players and, most of all, he understood what they needed and how they should be led.

It was enough to feel the force of his team to have these assessments confirmed. At United we were warned about what to expect before we travelled to Portman Road in their first year in the First Division – the season they shocked the big clubs by landing the title at their first attempt, leading home mighty Spurs, the Double-winning team of the previous season, and Burnley in the spring of 1962. 'Go through the list of their players and you don't see much to alarm you,' said Jimmy Murphy, 'but then go out on the field and play against them and it's a different story.'

Murphy was right about the less than overwhelming aura of the key Ipswich men. Jimmy Leadbetter was a Scottish inside forward who didn't even look like a player when Ramsey came upon him, but soon he was a converted left winger of great effect, supplying a stream of passes and crosses to the striking pair that became the twin hammers of Ipswich, Ray Crawford and Ted Phillips.

Leadbetter operated from a withdrawn position, and he did it so well, with such unbroken efficiency, that not only did his club win the title, but Crawford, a modest buy from Portsmouth, shared the Golden Boot with Derek Kevan after scoring thirty-three goals. Many years later, another outstanding and utterly original manager had similar success with a withdrawn left winger. Brian Clough won two European Cups with Nottingham Forest for many reasons – no doubt the key one was his superb ability to motivate players – but there was never much question about his tactical master-stroke. It was the use of another Scottish winger, John Robertson, who had not exactly announced his status as a major player until he came under Clough's influence. Robertson, a portly figure, executed brilliant work along the left to produce an endless supply line for the Forest strikers, and I often wondered if Clough had drawn some inspiration from Ramsey's reclamation of Jimmy Leadbetter.

Shortly before he died, many years after we had enjoyed different kinds of glory under the management of Ramsey, I met Jimmy in the street in Edinburgh. He still didn't really look like a footballer but I told him how vividly I remembered the impact of his performance when we first met. Manchester United went on to the field convinced that we had enough individual quality, and enough of a way of playing, to stop their march, but our illusions were quickly shattered. Leadbetter sought space wherever he could find it and used it with an unerring touch. We lost 4–1.

I travelled to meet Ramsey for the first time in the company of Liverpool's Roger Hunt. We had played each other that day but we soon dispensed with the details of our club collision at Anfield during the taxi ride to Lime Street railway station. We agreed that while we already knew that Ramsey was going to bring a new, and almost certainly much tougher, approach – one of his basic and successful demands before taking the job was that the selection committee, the great and shocking anachronism, had to be immediately disbanded – we didn't know how his style would touch us. We were left in doubt only very briefly, and this was particularly true for me.

Ramsey was waiting for us in the hotel lobby and when he saw me he said, 'Bobby Charlton, I want you in that room there.' Briefly, he introduced himself to Roger and me, saying that he didn't want to be referred to as Mr Ramsey but Alf. This, I would learn soon enough in the company of other senior players including Jimmy Armfield, Ron Flowers and Ray Wilson, who were also directed to the separate room, did not announce any onset of democracy.

Ramsey said, 'Gentlemen, as this is our first meeting, and you are the team's most experienced players, I want you to tell me anything that, compared to what has gone on before, would improve things. Don't hold back. I want you to tell me anything, however small you might think it is . . .'

There was, perhaps understandably, a deathly silence. Who wanted to lunge in with any opinion at this early point – and perhaps make a fool of himself in the presence of a man famous for his low toleration of views that conflicted with his own?

However, the silence wore on my nerves more quickly than it did on those of any of the others. I thought, 'I don't want him to think I'm an idiot without opinions or, if I had them, was too nervous to give them a little air.'

'Well,' I blurted, 'there is something I've often wondered about, Alf.'

'What's that, Bobby?' he snapped.

Undaunted, I continued, 'We stay here in Hendon Hall in north London and each day we travel for at least an hour to the Bank of England's training ground in Roehampton, in south-west London – and then it's another hour or so to get back. Would it not be logical to have a hotel nearer Roehampton or, alternatively, a training ground nearer to the hotel?'

A terrible pause ensued. My new manager, the man who would shape every stride of the rest of my England career, finally broke the silence. 'Bobby, I've most certainly listened to what you have to say, but I think we will leave it as it is.'

At the first opportunity I turned to Wilson, the laconic north-erner, and said, 'Ray, for heaven's sake, don't let me open my mouth ever again.'

When I thought about it, though, I suspected the exchange had served Ramsey's purpose well enough. He had felt obliged to open up the floor, it was the form of things, after all, but the point of the episode was that, however good an idea might swirl up from the discussions of the troops in the dressing room, when all was said and done and argued, it was he who would always make the decisions.

Many of those in high places at the Football Association resented the way the new manager curbed their powers, the quite brutal way he had told them that their input on selection was no longer needed and that in future they should not assume they could mingle with the players as they had done in the past, but at the team level, there was in some ways relief at this instant show of power. It made matters much less complicated. Here was a boss with ideas and imperatives of his own, and as long as he was in charge, they would not be challenged.

Inevitably, from time to time someone would be fool enough to be talked into making a new overture, some other appeal to logic, which would make the day-to-day lives of the players more congenial. And quite often that fool would be me.

The pipe-smoking Armfield – who eventually fell from favour because, some believed, he made a critical defensive error against, of all people, Scotland, which allowed Jimmy Baxter to score a decisive goal – and his successor Bobby Moore were smart enough to lay low when there were some stirrings of rebellion, however mild. Not me. I was talked into it in my role as the most capped player, the man who was maybe least at risk of losing his place if the wrong thing was said at the wrong moment. Every time it happened I swore, as I had done on that first occasion, that it would never happen again, but each time the Wilsons and other old pros eventually got their way. They manipulated me into one-on-one set-pieces I could never win.

The one that became the most notorious, the most telling and, when I look back, the most amusing, occurred soon into Ramsey's regime, just before we embarked on our first summer tour with him in 1963. The tour was an early test of Ramsey's nerve and confidence because first results had not been encouraging, although no one could begin to pass any judgement at that point. The 5–2 defeat in Paris was inflicted just days after he had been given the team, and that Scottish victory inspired by Jimmy Baxter at Wembley came soon afterwards. A degree of respectability had been achieved, and respect won from the players, by the 1–1 Wembley draw with world champions Brazil. Bryan Douglas scored our goal.

Now, though, manager and players would be thrown together for several weeks on a tour that would take us to Bratislava to play the excellent Czechoslovakia, impressive runners-up in the World Cup, Leipzig to play East Germany and Basle to play the Swiss, who had given us such an uncomfortable time at Wembley before we flew off to Chile. The trip would give us some general insights into the future and, specifically, into quite how Ramsey intended to impose his authority.

My intervention was deemed necessary by my team-mates after we were taken to Simpson's, the tailor in Piccadilly, and fitted with some rather heavy worsted suits. In the team hotel on the eve of the trip, some of the players came to me and said, 'Bobby, you must go to Alf and plead that we wear some light clothes for travelling. Have you seen the temperatures in Central Europe? They were soaring over eighty today in Czechoslovakia.'

I made my usual protest. 'Why me? Why not the captain or someone else?' I asked, only to get the usual response, 'Bobby, you're an old hand. He'll take it from you.'

So there I was again, the reluctant rebel, arguing for sweet reason, but with a familiar foreboding that I would not be doing anybody any good, and perhaps least of all myself.

'Alf, the players want to know if it would be OK if they wore their casual clothes while travelling on the tour, it's apparently going to be very hot, and keep the suits fresh for official functions.'

There was the usual pregnant silence before the manager said, 'All right, Bobby, I'll think about it.' But then, inevitably, I should have known, he spoke again before I reached the door. 'Bobby, I've thought about it, and I've decided we'll wear the suits.'

'Bloody hell,' I thought, 'I've done it again.' When I reported to my team-mates, some of whom, I noted, had hints of smiles playing on their faces, I insisted, 'That's the last time.'

If Ramsey frustrated us in our desire for simple comforts, we could see quickly enough the point of having him as our manager. He gave us an overwhelming sense that he was in charge, and that he would point the way to our success on the field. When we reached Bratislava, he was quite superb in our training preparation, doing something that I will never forget for its brilliant simplicity, for the picture it gave of one football man's understanding of the difficulty that can come when a manager is trying to transmit his ideas so that they remain strongly in focus in the heat of a big match.

Before the training session began, Alf said, 'I want you all to go to the positions you would naturally take up once the match starts.' When we did this, he looked around for a moment or two and then said, 'Right, now I'll tell you where I want you to be.' Then, position by position, he explained, very briskly, what he expected from each player. These were not, he made it clear, pieces of wisdom written in stone and carried down from the mountain top. They were the distillation of all his years in the game, an attention to detail that when he was a player was often considered quite fanatical in the dressing rooms of Southampton, Tottenham Hotspur and England but, however many feelings they ruffled, could never be rejected as outlandish or illogical.

They were underpinned by the fact that out of relatively modest talent, he made himself a brilliant full back and the winner of thirty-two England caps, a run that came to an end in the firestorm of the Wembley rout by Hungary – an afternoon that would forever condition his thinking about the need properly to prepare players in his charge.

The immediate result in Bratislava was quite spectacular. We beat the team who had pushed Garrincha and his Brazilians so hard in Santiago and were led by one of the great players in European history, Josef Masopust. We beat them 4–2 with goals from Jimmy Greaves (two), Bobby Smith and me. We beat them with hard running and craft – George Eastham taking up the scheming role left vacant by Johnny Haynes – and, as a direct result of the manager's work at the training session, a much greater certainty about where we were on the field and what we were supposed to be doing.

Most satisfying of all was that Czechoslovakia were plainly intent on protecting their reputation. They tackled hard and maintained pressure on our defence. Ray Wilson was winning his nineteenth cap and Bobby Moore his twelfth. You could feel the growth of assurance in our ranks, the sense that suddenly we were finding in ourselves a way of playing that was beginning to strip away some of the old uncertainties.

The mood of the team was so good that the details of our wardrobe did not seem so important as we travelled on to Leipzig, where we won 2–1, and Basle, where the Swiss team were simply cut to pieces. We won 8–1 and I scored a hat-trick. I also felt a tremendous sense of confidence that I had rarely known before while wearing the England shirt.

However, I would learn before long – and with most certainty on our tour the following summer – that under Alf Ramsey there would always be the need to avoid any hint of what he might consider complacency. The confirmation came, rather stunningly I felt, at the end of what was a quite epic football journey.

Even at this distance, and bearing in mind that many of the players had gone through more than fifty games in the regular season, the schedule is guaranteed to bring on more than a touch of weariness. We started the odyssey in Lisbon, after beating Uruguay 2–1 at Wembley with two goals from Johnny Byrne, then, following a 4–3 win, flew to Dublin, where we beat the Republic of Ireland 3–1, before beating the United States 10–0 in New York.

We then flew to South America to compete in Brazil's Jubilee Tournament in Rio and São Paulo. There, the first result was distinctly less encouraging, a 5–1 defeat at the Maracana at the hands of the hosts, for whom Pelé was in particularly exuberant form, but Ramsey's nerve held to the point that he declared, 'Don't worry about this result, it has come out of the worst possible circumstances for us. And I'll tell you something else. Brazil have no chance of retaining the World Cup when they come to England in two years' time.'

Although the result looked bad, the reality was indeed much less bleak than it appeared. Within thirty-six hours of boarding the plane in New York, we had been running out on to the field in Rio. We were lively for a while, and Liverpool's winger Peter Thompson, who was winning his fourth cap, was particularly impressive when he got on the ball and, in the way he had made his trademark at Anfield, ran at the Brazilian defence. But soon enough the energy was draining from us and by half-time George Cohen, perhaps the fittest man in the team, was struggling so badly that the team doctor, Alan Bass, argued that he was ill and should not continue. Without substitutes, and with the team plainly facing an ordeal of endurance in the second half, George, typically, elected to play on.

Ramsey's contention that Brazil would struggle in England was based on the belief that while stalwarts such as Djalma, Nilton Santos, Didi and Zito had grown old, the new generation lacked some of that substance, and with Garrincha struggling with injuries, Pelé, who was now being targeted ferociously in every match he played, would lack vital support. Brazil's particular softness, Ramsey was convinced, was in defence where old certainties had gone. Even Pelé needed a foundation on which to play and you did not win a World Cup without a solid defence.

The prophecy was given immediate weight in our minds when Ramsey led us into the Maracana to see Argentina, minus

Sanfilippo and looking far more formidable than the team we had outplayed in Chile, beat Brazil in a match that turned into a near riot. Pelé was involved in some fierce exchanges, which revealed that the master footballer was not without his street instincts. At one point he exchanged head butts with one of his markers, and as the huge crowd heaved and screamed, Ramsey stood up and announced, 'Gentlemen, I'm ready to go,' and marched us out of all the potential mayhem.

When we recovered our legs after the draining travel, we did better, drawing with Portugal and losing by the only goal to Argentina.

The Brazilian scoreline was an ugly but, I believed, discountable blemish on what otherwise was a highly successful tour. The squad had grown together and the authority of the manager been established in so many ways, some big and some small. Nothing could have prepared me, however, for the extraordinary conversation I had with Ramsey in a Copacabana restaurant on the eve of our return to England.

The occasion was another amiable social collision between the England players and the English press. Eventually, Ramsey would come to see the interests of the press as directly opposed to his own, but in the meantime he understood their needs and had respect for certain of the writers, notably Ken Jones, who had played professionally before joining the *Daily Mirror*, and his colleague Frank McGhee. So he was receptive when word came that the press would like to take him and the players out for an end-of-tour dinner and a few drinks. The reporters said that it had been a fantastic tour and they would like to signal the end of a hard and successful season with a little hospitality.

When we gathered in the restaurant I found myself, quite by chance, sitting next to the manager. The conversation was casual and easy, involving reporters and players, but then Ramsey turned to me and said, 'Well, Bobby, what did you think about the tour?'

Looking back, I can't believe it would have been possible for me to have been more enthusiastic, right from my opening statement that, after six years with England – and fifty-five caps – it was the best tour I had ever known. I was quite specific in my verdict on the value of more than a month – and so many thousands of miles – spent living and working closely with the men with whom I hoped to share the challenge of the World Cup.

I said I thought preparations for 1966 were coming along quite brilliantly. There was a terrific mood in the team, with some fine new players. Bobby Moore, just six games into the job, was proving a great and natural captain, George Cohen and Ray Wilson were forming a tremendous partnership at full back. The system we were developing, and the training work, had filled the players with a new confidence. All in all, I thought we were in excellent shape – and bang on schedule for a significant performance in two years' time.

And then I said, 'But of course, Alf, it's been a very long tour and I really have missed my wife and my daughter and I will be glad to see them.'

Ramsey lent forward, his face suddenly a mask, and told me, 'If I thought that was your attitude, I wouldn't have brought you on this trip.'

13

GENTLEMEN, WE WILL WIN THE WORLD CUP

HOW DO YOU get inside the mind and the heart of a man capable, on a warm and convivial Brazilian night, of making such a cold statement?

You don't. You take the best of him and you resolve to live with the rest. In the case of Alf Ramsey, you accepted that here was a man driven by exceptional forces, some of which, I had to suspect at the restaurant table in Rio, might sometimes be as unfathomable to himself as they were to the rest of us.

There was, I thought immediately, a contradiction in his suggestion that to think of your loved ones after so long on the road was somehow to betray your professional duties. Alf was an extremely private man, who was often said to be fighting demons from a humble past in Dagenham, but one fact about his life was well known. He was devoted to his wife Vicky and their daughter, and was determined to make a separate life with them away from the pressures of football.

Now he was saying that it was necessary while representing England to shut out all other thoughts and yearnings. I knew he was single-minded. His attention to detail was already a near legend in the game, and he detested defeat and any kind of failure, but this seemed to be carrying things a little too far.

This was true, at least, until I got to know him a little better and began to understand more clearly his purpose – and his obsessive commitment. He seemed to be saying the manager, the players, the coaching and medical staff, had to shut themselves off from all other influences. We would all falter if even one of us, and for the briefest time, allowed his attention to be drawn away from the next training session or team talk or, ultimately, the next match.

It was this fervent desire to make his team and his players a family, insulated against everything else in the world – except perhaps one of his favourite westerns or James Bond films, to which he led us with great enthusiasm whenever they were available – that was perhaps a leading reason why few people in the history of English sport have been analysed as relentlessly as the man who delivered the nation's only World Cup. He was the one who, at the moment of triumph, turned his back on the glory, insisting that it belonged solely to the players. It was almost as if he was saying, finally, that if at times he had given us hell, had made decisions we didn't like or perhaps agree with, it was really all for us. We had to take everything he gave to us and then, he had always believed, we would become strong.

In recent years, I have sometimes wondered about the changes that have come to football, and life, and how they are mirrored in the differences between the England of Ramsey and the one made by Sven-Goran Eriksson nearly three decades later.

It was hard not to chuckle, somewhat ruefully, of course, when trying to imagine how Ramsey would have dealt with some of the expectations of David Beckham and his generation of England players. He would not have been enthusiastic about the idea of having wives and family installed close to the team hotel for the European Championship in Portugal in 2004, for example. When the England camp disbanded, he would no doubt have blanched at the sight of the bouncy castles being removed. In Germany in 2006, he would have been appalled to know that wives and girlfriends had their own FA official deputed to deal with their needs, which included the demands of the paparazzi. By way of historic comparison, I recall Nobby Stiles confessing that he didn't have the nerve to put to Ramsey his wife Kay's request that he break training for a few days to be with her for the birth of their son Peter. He contented himself with the fleeting visit home allowed all the squad before the last days of World Cup preparation.

This is not to make any judgement, just to point out that, apart from anything else, Ramsey was a man of his age who understood that he could push his demands to limits that would not begin to be seen as acceptable today.

Even now, nearly a decade after his death, some opinion is still divided over both the man and his football. Some insist he was a tactical revolutionary who showed a genius for getting the best out of the English footballer, a school to which I will always belong, while others claim he set the game back in England with his banishing of wingers and his emphasis on rock-hard defence. Between such extremes there will always be shades of opinion and, if we want to be ultimately precise, the truth probably lies somewhere in the middle.

Similarly, there is conflict over his character. Selfless and idealistic is one theory, supported perhaps by the fact that he ended his days modestly in the house in Ipswich from where he built his managerial career. Another is that he was quirky, a bigot and an inverted snob – yet this assessment does not begin to take account of so many acts of personal kindness and concern, which, despite them not being so obvious to me that night in Rio, I benefited from as much as anybody down the years.

What could never be questioned was his patriotism and his determination, whatever the pressure, to always do what he considered right. What he was most keen to do, as I had already grasped before his Rio statement, was to sweep away the possibility of any one player feeling that somehow he was above or separate from the team. If there were any doubts about this, they were dispelled on an agonising, and mostly sleepless, night on the eve of the tour that had ended for me with Ramsey's astounding rebuke.

After the team dinner, we were told we could go out to relax over a few beers. There would, however, be a curfew. It was set at 10.30 p.m. I found myself in a bar off the Bayswater Road with a few team-mates, including Bobby Moore and Jimmy Greaves, who were in the first stages of a Londoners' alliance that, naturally enough, developed down the years.

The drinking was not ferocious but we were relaxed, which is how we had been told we ought to be, and the time was passing pleasantly. Unfortunately, the mood carried us past the curfew hour. We were not disastrously late, it was still the right side of midnight, and we didn't feel too much concern as we walked back to the hotel. We did walk briskly, though. Alf had been quite explicit about the time and already we knew well enough how much he disliked even the smallest breach of discipline. We were relieved, then, when there was no sign of a sentinel at the hotel door as we hurried to our rooms.

Unfortunately, the damage had already been done. Shortly after 10.30 Alf had sent his assistants Harold Shepherdson and Les Cocker to check all the rooms. When they reported that five beds were still unoccupied, Ramsey was apparently incensed. He told Shepherdson to get the passports of the missing players – we always handed them to Harold when we reported for a tour or the flight to a game – and place them on the pillows of the empty beds.

It was a shocking sight, the passport resting there on the white pillow – and shouting its reproach. My mind raced away towards all kinds of consequences. What would our families and friends think when the headlines bannered our shame? How would Matt Busby and Jimmy Murphy react back at Old Trafford? No doubt Jimmy would yell his criticism and Busby, far more woundingly, would deliver a phrase that he always reserved for such occasions. He would say, 'Bobby, son, this behaviour is just not Manchester United.'

When the team was assembled in the morning, with Moore and Greaves as bleary-eyed and anxious from sleeplessness as I was, Ramsey stretched the tension and the worry to its limits. He said that we had let down the whole side and that if he could have brought in five replacements without causing great inconvenience – some contenders had already left for their holidays – he would have done it without hesitation. As it was, our passports would be put to use but we had to understand that this would be the last time we would escape with a warning.

It didn't matter that Greaves was a brilliant goal-scorer, our new captain, Moore, was now an integral part of the team, and I was the most experienced England player – a team couldn't prosper if its key players felt they could make their own rules.

On the build-up to the World Cup two years later, while the team were working at the Lilleshall training centre, Nobby Stiles, Alan Ball and John Connelly made a mistake similar to the one that put us under such a cloud. They went to a local pub for a quick drink without Ramsey's specific permission. They were welcomed back to the team quarters by Wilf McGuinness, who had been appointed to the training staff in recognition of his work at Old Trafford after bravely fighting to get back into the game after breaking his leg so badly. McGuinness wore a heavy frown and said, 'You're in big trouble, lads. The boss knows you've been to the pub and he's blazing.'

Stiles and Ball were abject, but wise, in their apologies, saying that they didn't realise they had gone out of bounds and that they had been in the pub for just a few minutes. Most certainly, it wouldn't happen again. Connelly was the feisty one. He listened to the ensuing Ramsey lecture with growing exasperation before saying, 'Alf, for heaven's sake, we're just talking about a pint here. We didn't realise we were doing anything wrong.'

At this point, Wilf told me later with a twinkle in his eyes, Ramsey could not trust himself to say anything more than, 'All of you, get out of my sight.'

Looking back to those circumstances, and knowing his reservations about the value of playing his orthodox wide men before his 'wild cards' Ball and Martin Peters, I have to say it is remarkable that Connelly was the first of three wingers (Terry Paine and Ian Callaghan were the others) to play in the tournament. Maybe Ramsey was just a little impressed by Connelly's show of defiance. It was more likely, though, that Connelly was selected for his aggression and spirit, and tendency to score goals.

What wasn't in question was the idea that the team was sacred to Ramsey, and as the days ticked down to the opening of the World Cup, he made it increasingly clear that he wasn't interested in celebrating individual talent, however outstanding. He had one question and he asked it quite relentlessly – what did so-and-so mean to his team-mates? Could he be counted upon when the going was tough and the big issue of success or failure was still to be settled?

More than anything, Ramsey wanted everyone to understand that he was in charge. The details of his leadership could be irksome, requiring us to languish in heavy suits as the sweat formed on our brows in some airport terminal, or being oblivious to the players becoming bored and restless on those seemingly endless journeys around the North Circular, but the central point was quite unmissable. There would be far harder decisions down the road – one of them would involve the national hero Jimmy Greaves – but as George Cohen's presence in the team already confirmed, tough calls, such as the axing of a talented full back and captain in Jimmy Armfield, would not be shirked.

By the time the whole nation seemed to be riveted on one decision he had to make on the eve of a World Cup final – Hurst or Greaves – I had long been converted to the belief that when it really mattered, the odds invariably were on Ramsey getting it right. It wasn't a question of being a loyal supporter, one of 'his boys' – this didn't enter into it because Ramsey did not have his boys, only players he kept under constant examination. I was only too aware that although, while still in my mid-twenties, I was building towards a record number of caps, every new one I received came utterly without guarantees.

I never heard him say it but it is part of Ramsey folklore that when one senior player – the most popular choice is Geoff Hurst soon after one of his outstanding performances – called cheerily, 'See you next match, Alf,' as the team dispersed at Heathrow airport, the manager frowned severely and said, 'If selected, Geoffrey, if selected.'

Maybe the story is invented, maybe not, but there is no doubt it carries the same essential truth that was implicit in Ramsey's comment to me in Rio. No one was indispensable, no one lacked a covering player who could come in and play just as hard and, maybe, even more effectively. Even though you might say the stories of Moore, Greaves and me in London and Connelly's survival of the Lilleshall scrape contradict this view, I would not agree. Neither of the episodes was outrageous. Mistakes had been made, certainly, but did they warrant the breaking up of the team before a vital tour – or robbing England of a potentially vital player in a World Cup? I didn't think so, and my instinct was confirmed when Ramsey did face the hardest of his decisions.

Effectiveness was the key claim of any contender because it was the search for this quality that was always at the heart of his selections. I soon reached the point when I never began to second-guess a Ramsey decision about players or special tactics for a certain game because his success rate was astonishing. I might have said to myself, 'Well, that's rather an odd formation,' but then we went out and made it work. It got to the stage when, in the shadow of the World Cup, it was thought we had forgotten how to lose.

This is a sweeping statement, a rosy memory you might say, but as Ramsey tinkered and adapted, the tide of results he achieved increased the confidence in the dressing room – and that was of major significance to our chances. Some of the football was perhaps less than spectacular, owing more to hard work than inspiration, but all the time Ramsey was saying that one day it would all fall into place, one day we would be truly ready.

At times, the turnover of players was as extensive as in the Winterbottom years, and while I will always swear that Ramsey had a clear idea of his best formation, and that he unveiled it with dramatic force on a cold night in Madrid eight months before the start of the World Cup, he never quite closed the door on the idea that Terry Paine, John Connelly, Ian Callaghan or Peter Thompson could hit a vein of form that might just restore his belief in the traditional value of wing play.

If anyone should understand this, he maintained, it was surely a full back who learned his trade in the days of Matthews and Finney. Yet if this career defender knew very clearly what he wanted from the men at the back, and in the engine room of midfield, and had basically satisfied himself that he would get it when the challenge came, the final shape of his forward line was clearly a different matter.

While Jack and Nobby confirmed their places in the side, the cast list farther upfield was wide indeed. Before two members of the great West Ham triumvirate, Geoff Hurst and Martin Peters, pulled on the England shirt, the number of forwards who auditioned during the year building towards the final straight, reflected a desire to explore every viable option. The list comprised seven strikers – Jimmy Greaves, Roger Hunt, Frank Wignall, Johnny Byrne, Barry Bridges, Fred Pickering and Mick Jones. In the wing department, which was being so deeply questioned by Ramsey, the candidates were Paine, Thompson, Alan Hinton and Derek Temple, with Hinton and

Temple giving way soon enough to the challenges of John Connelly and Ian Callaghan. In midfield, the terrain to which I had returned, two contenders were George Eastham and Terry Venables, and then there was the red-haired teenager who some said belonged in a category all of his own, that of a force of nature, the inexhaustible Alan Ball. And the old master, Johnny Haynes, now recovered from his car crash, was reviving memories of the best of his game with some brilliant performances from Fulham. Later, though, I heard that this issue had already been resolved and it explained to me why Haynes had not been invited to make his claims from within Ramsey's 'New England'.

Apparently, one day after training at Roehampton, Ramsey called George Cohen to one side and asked him about the form of his club-mate.

'It's brilliant, Alf,' said George. 'He's completely recovered from his injuries.'

But Ramsey shook his head and said, 'No, George, I don't think that's quite right.'

George repeated the conversation to Haynes when he went back to Fulham and after a short pause, Johnny said, 'I'm sorry to say it, but Alf's right.'

Yet if Ramsey was sometimes accused of casting his net wide to the point of indecision, in one fundamental way he was acting from great strength. In the two years separating our party in the restaurant on Copacabana and the start of the World Cup, we played twenty-one games, winning fourteen, drawing six and losing one (3–2 to Austria at Wembley). Most significantly of all, with the manager fine-tuning to the point where he was no more than one or two positions away from his finished team, despite the large number of official contenders, we launched into a final run of seven straight wins, scoring nineteen goals and conceding four, three of them in a riotous 4–3 win at Hampden Park that gave the manager his first precious victory over Scotland.

Among our victims were West Germany, our old nemesis Yugoslavia, Finland, Norway and Denmark on a sweep through Scandinavia, and then a final victory over Poland in the citadel of Chorzow, the ground where the Poles always know they will receive their most vociferous support.

Ramsey had given us both a system and belief, and in the process he had, crucially, identified a new type of England player – one whose primary task was not necessarily to look good but to get a vital job done. It gave me immense pride that heading this list were my brother Jack and my best friend in football, Nobby Stiles.

Ramsey had not picked them out for their style, or because they had the look of natural-born England players. No, you wouldn't say that when you saw them doing their jobs for Manchester United and Leeds, but what the manager saw, I had believed for some time as I played beside Nobby and regularly crossed the Pennines to see my brother building his reputation with Don Revie's emerging team. One minute it seemed to me that Jack was a happy-go-lucky character who enjoyed football for various reasons, not least the fact that it had presented an infinitely better career choice than life down the mines, and the next he was a key player in a very hard, talented and professional team.

I remember one night going over to Elland Road and being especially struck by what a good game he was having. He had everything in the air, covered the ground tremendously well and was a threat at every set-piece won by Leeds. This was some time before he was picked for England, but I found myself thinking, 'Really, I'm not sure there is a better centre half in the game than Our Kid.' Not only did he do his work well, he was never slow to chivvy his team-mates into greater efforts.

I came to think of him as I did Nobby. Here was a real professional, nothing airy fairy, nothing for show, just a player doing his job at the highest level. They were players you could trust when the action was at its height, and it seemed to me appropriate that Ramsey should bring them into the England team at precisely the same time, at Wembley against Scotland in April 1965. Once in, it seemed to me that little short of an elephant gun was going to take them out.

Both of them are credited with career-defining comments, Jack when he expressed his wonder to Ramsey that he should be included in a team of England 'stars', and Nobby when asked to take out the great Eusebio, the reigning European Player of the Year of Benfica and Portugal. 'For the match, Alf,' Nobby was said to have replied, 'or for life?' He strongly denies saying that, but he accepts its contribution to his legend of combativeness, even though it makes a parody of a brilliant defensive performance. Jack's question to Ramsey, 'Why did you pick me among these great players?' carries us more surely into the heart of the manager's team-building methods.

'You must remember, Jack,' said Ramsey, 'I don't necessarily pick the best players but I always try to pick the best team.'

The iron that Jack and Nobby brought encouraged more stirrings of the optimism I had expressed to Jimmy Adamson on the flight home from Chile, which I felt were beginning to be justified.

With Bobby Moore so assured beside Jack, George Cohen and Ray Wilson dovetailing so brilliantly, and Gordon Banks fast laying claim to the status of the world's best goalkeeper, Ramsey had put down the basic foundation of any team – a defence of daunting strength and a fine eye for reading all points of danger.

However, there were still some strange incongruities in the job of the England manager that I would always find a little bewildering. While Ramsey wrestled with the last vital decisions going into his first World Cup line-up, this man who had shown the nerve to drive into history the old selection committee was obliged to collect expenses forms from the FA offices on the way back from training in Roehampton and then painstakingly fill them out with individual players. It took Ramsey some time to send that relic from the past the way of the selection committee, but in the meantime there was no doubt that England had never approached a major tournament so professionally, so geared for the possibility of success. Indeed, at the centre of everything Ramsey did was the declaration he made when he launched his campaign and confirmed it in the wake of that 5–1 defeat by Brazil in Rio.

'Gentlemen,' he said, 'we will win the World Cup. I believe it and you must believe it, and the nation must be made to believe it. You have the ability and the character to do it, and I'm telling you it will happen.'

Alf Ramsey never wavered from that belief, and the stronger he became in that conviction, the more we were convinced.

In many ways, it was the boldest statement ever made in the history of English football and it invited a lot of pressure. But then sometimes a footballer needs that kind of pressure, he needs to be asked to produce all of his talent and all of his character.

Alf Ramsey asked in the strongest way, and long before the World Cup of 1966 was unveiled, I was convinced he would receive – as would the nation that had craved success for so long.

14

COUNTRY LIFE

OVER THOSE DAYS and weeks of early summer 1966 it became clear to me that I wasn't alone in my confidence. It was easy to see that the same optimism had touched so many of my team-mates and, I also believed, the nation in a way that went far deeper than the propaganda that is still such a staple of the build-up to any big match or tournament.

You could feel it on the training field and in the street and, as I remembered at the start of this story, even on the quiet little beach in Majorca where Norma and I went for a couple of weeks holiday before Alf Ramsey's England gathered together for the final run-up to the World Cup. We went in the misguided belief that we could put football on hold and behave like any other young couple seeking a break from the pressures of their lives.

I have already recalled the impact of Trevor Atkinson, the journeyman pro who made such a deep impression on me in that brief interlude beside the Mediterranean, but there were many others like him who, while maybe lacking his knowledge of the game, were still both excited and confidently expectant. There was a Hertfordshire farmer, who still played some amateur football, saying, 'Bobby, you and your team-mates are playing for all of us. You will win the games and collect the trophy, but all over the country, in towns and villages, amateur players like me will be able to puff out their chests and say, "We are the champions of the world." '

This was quite something to be told. It was more than just football. For a little while at least, it was the life of the country, and this was easier to believe when you heard that the Prime Minister, Harold Wilson, had said that England's success in the World Cup had the potential to influence a general election.

At times on that holiday, the responsibility weighed a little more heavily than at others, but there was always the uplift of a cheery call from some fellow British holidaymaker, 'Good luck, Bobby, we know you can do it.'

Once, when perhaps the burden may have shown on my face, even a Spanish barman offered some encouragement, saying, 'I watched on television when you beat Spain in Madrid, and my friends and I agreed that England was *muy fuerte* – very strong.' He made a fist when he said it and that put a lift into my stride.

It was clear to me now that when Alf Ramsey, on the very day of his appointment, made his famous declaration of intent, he was offering more than a passing sound bite. He was creating a field of confidence, laying down an article of faith that was made much easier to believe by his refusal, even in the most discouraging circumstances, ever to offer even a hint of retraction.

Over the ensuing three years, this conviction about the course he had set had grown stronger and was possibly most dramatically demonstrated when Alf, having got himself involved in a discussion with some football writers, was criticised for creating tactical confusion both in the dressing room and the nation. The author of this charge, Eric Cooper, who was billed as the 'Voice of the North' by the *Daily Express*, had written one article which had particularly offended the manager when he made some tactical changes shortly before the acclaim that came with the breakthrough triumph in Madrid. It carried the headline, "It's Hoke Cokey, Alf." Outraged at the way the discussion was going, Alf promptly offered to settle the disagreement outside, although, as ever fastidious about his appearance, not before beginning to remove his perfectly tailored jacket.

In the long build-up he would always display trenchant defiance on behalf of his players, which meant, of course, that he carried them with him ever more strongly as the time of decision approached.

On returning from our family holiday, I travelled to Lilleshall in Shropshire on 6 June to join Alf's squad of twenty-eight (which ended up being twenty-seven when Everton's Brian Labone had to withdraw because of injury) for an eighteen-day training camp. The mood of unity in the squad must have been quite evident to outsiders and it was certainly noted by some of the reporters who were allowed into the centre. The World Cup was beginning to dominate both the sports and news agendas of newspapers, radio and TV.

Trainer Harold Shepherdson, a survivor of Walter Winterbottom's regimes in the 1958 and 1962 World Cups, no doubt risked accusations that he was pushing a party line when he leaped at the chance to explain this aura of intensity and commitment, but he did not contain himself in describing what might have passed well enough as a definition of a football trainer's utopia.

Shepherdson, whose other job was with Middlesbrough, had grown very close to Ramsey, and he plainly admired the way the manager had organised and motivated the players. He also told the press that he was equally impressed with the response of the troops.

'I have never known a happier, more willing bunch,' he said. 'No moaning, no slackers, everybody does anything asked of him – and more. The spirit and determination are quite amazing.'

Today the language used by Shepherdson might strike many as dated but he was speaking of players who inhabited another age, another culture, from that occupied by the England squad who were recently told by their new manager, Fabio Capello, they needed to ban their agents from the team hotel, switch off their mobile phones, dress more correctly and be a little more punctual at meal times.

Judging by some reactions, you would have thought Capello was asking his players to return to the Stone Age. In fact, he was exerting a classic old football premise that was espoused for so long by the great managers – the team who stick together, who respond to common standards and discipline, are much more likely to win together. Ramsey, I'm sure, would have nodded agreement with his Italian successor, and said that details and habits, however insignificant to some, soon enough begin to shape a state of mind.

Perhaps I should also draw a line between the belief and confidence that Ramsey was building and something quite different, which I found alarming early in 2008, when the players Capello inherited from Steve McClaren and, substantially, Sven-Goran Eriksson, failed to qualify for the European Championship. I do not blame the players entirely for the complacency that was surely a major reason for their inability to fight their way out of a group that, when it was announced, was welcomed with much relief.

What was most worrying for me was that, in the television build-up to the vital game with Croatia at Wembley, there was hardly a glancing reference to the threat presented by England's opponents. After watching the pre-game analysis, you would be forgiven for failing to remember that, in Zagreb, Croatia had inflicted a humiliating defeat, with infinitely better individual performances and much superior tactics.

Then, after another defeat – in a game we needed only to draw in order to take our place among the best teams in Europe – Michael Owen, a player I have always respected, allowed his name to go over an article that said not one individual Croat player could have expected to win a place in the England line-up. Perhaps in his belief that his team had seriously under-performed, it was not unreasonable for Owen to think such a thing.

Michael may well pass my scoring record of forty-nine goals for the national team, and if he does, I will be the first to celebrate his achievement. Yet somehow, the fact that he has set the highest standards of professional behaviour on and off the field, and been a superb scorer in club and international football, and still made such a statement – to an already disenchanted media – only seemed to underline England's plight.

Back in 1966 there was, no doubt, a greater sense that if you wanted something you had to work for it day by day. Nothing was guaranteed, not success or financial reward, and you would not have gained any plaudits for announcing that you had lost a vital match, the result of two years of planning and effort, to an apparently inferior team.

There is a limit to such comparisons made across the decades, of course, but maybe while discussing our approach to the World Cup all those years ago, just one more is permissible. It's the difference between our pre-tournament arrangements and schedules and those made for the 2002 squad, who flew to the Far East after stopping off in a resort hotel in Dubai for a relaxing week with families and girlfriends.

There was no such budget in 1966 – and no clamour to negotiate a win bonus that would stretch into the millions. In our case, there was a quick agreement in the dressing room to the suggestion by Bobby Moore that we should reject the proposal by the FA that a bonus of up to £1,500 should be paid to each player on a sliding scale, depending on the number of his appearances. Instead, we decided that each member of the twenty-two-man squad should receive £1,000 in the event of our winning. Although some players later complained, with some anger, that the Football Association had cheerfully handed over a quarter of a million pounds' worth of Corporation Tax based on their net profits, a sum that would have been reduced if they had paid the players a decent bonus, I have to say that the majority passed over the issue without too many recriminations. It was a more innocent age, when you still couldn't put a hard and fast value on glory. There was, too, a common view – one that would be seen, and probably with good reason, as naïve today. It was that winning brought its own reward, and was no less enduring for its lack of a price tag.

So, in stark contrast to Dubai, we worked through the long days in the Shropshire countryside with a sense of duty and mission, and if we missed our families, we didn't mention it to Alf or Harold or our fiercely driven trainer, Les Cocker of Leeds United.

On one occasion, Ramsey deemed that, perhaps out of our developing comradeship, we were not working hard enough, or ruthlessly enough, in our practice matches. This, we confirmed, was out of fear that we might do damage to a team-mate so near to the tournament. The manager was distinctly unimpressed. Lilleshall, unless we hadn't guessed, was not a holiday camp. It was, like it or not, a battleground of the most basic football ambition. What happened in these training matches might well influence his final choice of the party he took on the tour of Scandinavia and to the game in Poland, which without serious mishap or dismal performance, would probably constitute the final squad of twenty-two. A casual approach, a few tepid performances under his acute eye, might just be the reason why five of us would not be asked to place our passports in the safekeeping of Harold Shepherdson.

Whether or not this relative tentativeness ultimately contributed to the omission of Keith Newton, Peter Thompson, Bobby Tambling, Gordon Milne and Budgie Byrne I rather doubt because in my opinion they were all excellent players who I'm sure would have responded well to any challenge that came their way. What was certain was that we all had to sharpen up. The authority of Ramsey could not be challenged in any respect. His instructions were typically curt and explicit.

'Gentlemen,' he said, 'I would like to see more effort in these training matches. If they do not approximate the conditions of a real match, they will benefit no one, and certainly not you or me. So, I have to tell you, "go to it".'

Such an instruction didn't have to be given twice to Jack, Nobby or Ray Wilson. Suddenly, real vigour came into the games, and the shouts and groans must have reached some distant meadows. Fortunately, there were no casualties and no regrets, partly due to one swift change of policy initiated by the players. No longer did we report to the training games minus our shin pads and with our socks rolled down. Not for the first – or last – time, we had been summoned to football war by Alf Ramsey.

The more we immersed ourselves in the work, the more quickly the time passed, even though the manager was quite sparing in his indulgences beyond the regular showing of westerns and thrillers in the recreation room. On one occasion he bought us pints of beer and the experience was so heady it left me reeling.

Some of the Catholic lads gloated that at least they got to glimpse a little of the outside world when they went to mass on Sunday mornings in a neighbouring village, which perhaps inevitably provoked an upsurge of Church of England devotion in some of their team-mates. Naturally, there was a request that, in the interests of fairness and religious equality, non-Catholics should be allowed a weekly visit to the parish church. The move was countered effortlessly by the manager. Alf said that he understood the warden of Lilleshall was a lay preacher and he would be delighted to hold a service.

And so we prepared for the task in hand, grateful for the odd diversion, but essentially committed to our grand purpose. Each day, which for me usually started around 8.30 a.m. after some of the best sleep I had ever had, we were drawn into a rhythm of exercise and practice matches. It was tough exercise designed to warm us up and remove the risk of pulled muscles in the coming weeks, and the more I did it the more comfortable I became.

These were the penultimate steps along a very demanding road but each one of them seemed to deepen the satisfaction, and heighten the anticipation, of battle.

As is probably true on the eve of any battle that has ever been fought, or will be in the future, no one could be quite sure how well they would face the challenge, but when I saw the faces of veteran footballers such as Our Kid and Nobby, George Cohen and Ray Wilson, and youngsters such as Alan Ball and Martin Peters, I had the strongest sense that, for the next weeks, I could not have handpicked for myself better and more reliable company.

I was reminded of Alf Ramsey telling Jack to remember he didn't just pick the best players but those he could be sure would give everything they had for the team and the men who had come to share their destiny. As we broke camp in Shropshire to return to the wider world for forty-eight hours before embarking on possibly the toughest work of our football lives, it was not hard to believe that he had been as good as his word.

The question I kept asking myself was whether our performances in the imminent Scandinavian tour would prove we could deliver our end of the bargain. I had one other footballing issue to dwell on as we prepared to board the plane heading to Helsinki. Would the forthcoming games give any indication of the way we were going to play? After all, we'd shaken many in the football world with our tactics in a match in Madrid six months earlier.

15

4−3−3

THERE IS A vital difference between hoping to do something and then knowing with deep certainty that it is within your reach. Everything changes when, suddenly, you believe you have been given the means and shown the way. This happened on the icy-cold night of 8 December 1965, in the Bernabeu in Madrid, the place where eight years earlier, travelling with United, I had sat wide-eyed, beholding the brilliance of Alfredo di Stefano.

After our 2–0 victory over Spain, Alf Ramsey left the dressing room quickly and, looking back, I have to say it was probably just as well. Had he stayed he might have been forced to reveal again his difficulties when facing moments of emotion, or what he might consider misplaced or premature celebration. He might have had to unravel himself from the embrace of my extrovert brother Jack, or the tactile young Alan Ball, who had been playing in only his fourth international – an astonishing fact when you consider his impact on the game. He might have been forced to say something like, 'That's quite enough of that, thank you very much.'

Inside the unbending exterior of the man, though, you have to suspect it would have been a different story. This was, after all, the night Ramsey showed that he had the players – and the system – to beat the world. In the dressing room the sense of this was enormous. It was as though not just one door but a whole series of them had been opened. We had passed from the world of chance and speculation to one of the most encouraging reality.

Two-nil may not sound like a slaughter but it was, and if you doubt this, it is only because you didn't see the Spanish full backs, Reija and Sanchis, gesturing frantically to each other as the scale of their bewilderment grew. They were defenders marking empty space and phantom opponents. They were the first victims of Ramsey's Wingless Wonders.

When I saw the dismay of the Spanish defenders as we poured through their lines in what seemed like droves, I said to myself, 'We have a system now.'

The Spanish coach, Jose Villalonga, attempted to make adjustments but mostly he stood on the touchline shaking his head and, like his full backs, from time to time throwing up his arms in disbelief. Was it possible for a team who had arrived in the Spanish capital with a reputation for strength and competitiveness and some considerable organisation, but no more than that, to so dominate a game against a leading football nation?

At every level, the praise poured in and the compliments were couched in extraordinary terms, even by the standards of Fleet Street's most flamboyant sportswriter, Desmond Hackett of the *Daily Express*. Under the headline 'Ramsey's Wreckers', The Man in the Brown Bowler wrote: 'England can win the World Cup next year. They have only to match the splendour of this unforgettable night and there is not a team on earth who can master them.

'This was England's first win in Spain but it was more than a victory. It was a thrashing of painful humiliation for the Spanish. Gone were the shackles of rigid regimentation. The team moved freely and confidently and with such rare imagination that the numbers on their backs became mere identification marks on players who rose to noble heights. England's football was as smooth as the brush of a master – precise, balanced and as lovely to watch as the ballet.'

Footballers could go a lifetime without such a review. Desmond Hackett did not get to be so celebrated by his newspaper's then more than four million readers by stinting his criticism of England's footballers and boxers – he once had to wash the windows of heavyweight Jack Bodell's house because he had promised in his column he would do so in what he considered the extremely unlikely event of the man from Derbyshire winning a title fight, which he did. What was even more remarkable about Hackett's sentiments now was that they were entirely supported by Ramsey's rival, Villalonga.

He echoed the press-box belief that England had turned themselves into authentic contenders to win their first World Cup. The Spanish coach said, 'England were just phenomenal tonight. They were far superior to us in their experiment – and their performance. No team in the world could have lived with their force.'

Our exhilaration was fuelled by the fact that Ramsey had by now made it clear to us that he didn't put any particular value on winning 'friendly' matches, such as this one, but performance was everything. He needed to see that we were developing a real understanding out on the field – and have confirming evidence that out of the changes, all the examinations of different players, a genuine pattern could be picked out. In these terms, what happened in Madrid came like a gift from the cold, starry sky.

For me, the truth was that I had become increasingly comfortable playing for England. I was glad when Manchester United shifted me back to the midfield, which I had always considered my natural home, and England soon followed, but my attitude to the national team had not changed fundamentally from the time I first arrived in Troon and was taken into the care of Billy Wright, even accepting the internal struggles I was facing back then in the so recent shadow of Munich.

I always thought that playing for your club was your real business and England was the jam on the bread, a product of whatever success you had playing for the team who paid your wages. I never really felt under pressure in the England shirt. Why should I have done? I just felt lucky that I was considered good enough to play at both levels so frequently, and so by the time Alf Ramsey told us that his overwhelming priority was to win the World Cup – and that it would be the only proper measure of his success in the job – I wasn't filled with any panicky questions about whether I would be able to meet this challenge. No, there was none of that. The more Ramsey worked on his assignment, and the more I could see that he was bringing in players of substance who were plainly equal to the job he had in mind, the more I said to myself, 'Well, bring it on, then. Come on, let's have it.'

Everywhere we went after the Madrid breakthrough, Ramsey made it clear that results were secondary. It was all fine-tuning on the way to the World Cup, and the fact that the wins kept coming, and the reviews remained enthusiastic, in Hampden Park, Helsinki, Oslo, Copenhagen and Chorzow plainly did not affect Ramsey in the slightest.

Down the years, some have alleged that Ramsey never truly settled on his final formation before the start of the World Cup, and that it emerged from the circumstances of the first games in the tournament and the failures of Connelly, Paine and Callaghan to convince him that they were good enough to prevent him jettisoning the idea of traditional wide men. I don't agree. Madrid was never in my mind a happy accident. It was the basic blueprint he would return to well before the climax of the World Cup final.

In Madrid, Ramsey played nine of the players who would appear in the World Cup final. Martin Peters and, in eventually the most controversial and, for Ramsey, defining circumstances, Geoff Hurst would make it by the end of the road – and Joe Baker and George Eastham would give way.

In all the reworked debates that have come down the years,

I have never identified with a point of view more strongly than I did with the comments of George Cohen in his autobiography. George said: 'The Madrid game was a watershed for both the manager and the players. It told him that he had options – good solid options – and it told us that we had a boss who knew what he was doing, who had the nerve to absorb the odd setback without being blown off the course he had settled on right from the start.

'Certainly it was no reflection on their efforts, or their skills, that [Baker and Eastham] didn't complete the journey. They didn't make it all the way because – this seems a little amazing today when you consider the endless juggling of modern coaches, and not least Sven-Goran Eriksson [in his time with England] – Alf Ramsey had nine players already deeply installed in his plans long before the start of the big tournament. He had a few more things to try and a little more tinkering to do.'

George's analysis is strengthened by the fact that the tinkering involved Peters and Hurst, players whose absence from the team was so quickly rendered unthinkable.

When all the theorising is done, however, I always return to the most basic point of all. Never mind that we had good players, and that they had emerged from a generation who had, in many ways, developed a much more professional outlook than many of their predecessors, we could not possibly have won the World Cup without Ramsey.

He made the winning of it seem increasingly feasible because he proved quickly that he was tough enough to handle a situation that was so different from the running of a club, a fact that Don Revie later learned to his dismay when he swapped the leadership of Leeds United for that of England. Revie was a phenomenal club manager. He had his finger on every detail at Elland Road, and all the moods of players as different as Jack, Billy Bremner and Norman Hunter. But with England, he couldn't exert the same control. He had to make his points effectively in a smattering of days rather than year in and year out.

Ramsey was more economical with his time – and his words. He brought together all the different personalities, and all the vanities and the foibles of players talented enough to represent their country, and he realised straightaway there was only one way to do it. It wasn't by cajoling – as he proved on those occasions when I was elected the hapless spokesman of the players – or by negotiation. It was by catering for no one's priorities but his own. It could only be Ramsey's way.

He concluded, from his own experience, that every player needed to be told his place in the scheme of things, and be reassured that he could operate in the chosen system. Certainly, though, he didn't have to be nursed or privileged or made to feel, even for a second, his needs were any greater than those of the man sitting beside him in the dressing room or on the bus.

This was the great gift – the most important one on the road to the start of our World Cup adventure – presented to us by our manager at the Bernabeu.

Spain were one of the top football countries in the world – their opening line-up in their first group game against Argentina at Villa Park (they also drew West Germany) included such luminous names as Francisco Gento and Luis Saurez – but they couldn't begin to play us. I remember thinking, 'This is fantastic. We don't have wingers but their full backs are standing out there like lampposts. They are doing what they've always done but everything has changed.'

The Spanish coach Villalonga later developed his praise. He said, 'I don't feel so badly, you know, about the team's performance. They faced a system that they had no reason to be familiar with – and it was backed up by one of the best team performances I have ever seen. Brazil, Argentina, Germany, I believe they would all have gone the way of us tonight.'

England 1966 World Cup squad (see end of book for names).

There were few laughs in the Wembley dressing room on 11 July as we prepared to begin our campaign against Uruguay.

...and even less 24 hours later after our 0–0 draw. But the trip to Pinewood Studios to meet James Bond lifted our mood…

…as did Ray Wilson's dry wit.

16 July. England 2 Mexico 0.
Opening our account at last.

20 July. England 2 Fran
Through to the quarter

23 July. England 1 Argentina 0. Captain
Rattin refuses to leave the pitch and
Martin Peters and I refuse to get involved.

Leaping for joy. Hurst's
headed goal puts us in front
and into the semi-finals.

With the game won, for a
few moments the on-field
events were put to one side.

26 July. England 2 Portugal 1.

1–0

2–0

World Cup final beckoned.

Tears may have been in the great Eusebio's eyes, but he left the pitch with dignity and great sportsmanship.

29 July. A day away from Alf fulfilling the prophecy he made on his first day as England manager.

Ray Wilson's wife and Norma make their way to Wembley…

With hours to go before our date w[ith] destiny, it's time for Ray to pick up some new shoes. Obviously.

…while the players play for high stakes. None more so than Jimmy Greaves.

July. l-r, Moore, Cohen, Ball, Banks,
...t, Wilson, Stiles, me, Hurst, Peters, Jack.

Each one of us knew what we had to do.

Even when we went a goal
down…England 0 Germany 1.

Beckenbauer and I
were rarely apart.

England 1 Germany 1.

...land 2 Germany 1.

With seconds to go. England 2
Germany 2. 'Bobby, that's football.'

'You've won it once. Now you have to go out and win it again.'

Hurst shoots…

…and I know it is over the line. England 3 Germany 2.

England 4 Germany 2. We had to go and win it again. And we did.

The final whistle. 'What about that kidd

champions of the world.

is is for you players – you won it.'

Jimmy's reaction was wonderful.

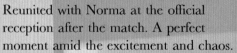

Reunited with Norma at the official reception after the match. A perfect moment amid the excitement and chaos.

On the morning after, our proud parents pored over every column inch of their boys' success.

The whole basis of Ramsey's 4–3–3 system was that it emphasised the need for energy and teamwork. No one, it was patently obvious, could do it on his own. We had to rely on each other, and the other beauty was that, if the hearts of your team-mates were right, it was basically quite simple. If you were one of three midfield players and you had the ball, you were a forward. If you didn't have the ball, you were a defender, and if you couldn't win it back yourself, you generally received it from one of the central defenders or, in my case, most frequently Nobby Stiles. You went up together and you came back together, always making sure you were in position to receive the ball, either to relieve a team-mate under pressure or set up another attack.

Being the character he was, Ramsey could impose some of his philosophy quite brutally. A classic example is the famous – or maybe notorious – story of the little tutorial he gave Alan Ball.

It allegedly went along these lines:

'Alan, what happens when a man takes his dog for a walk?'

'The owner throws a stick and the dog runs after it and fetches it back and drops it at his master's feet.'

'Quite so, Alan. Now I want you to think of yourself as the dog, the stick as the ball, and the dog's owner as Bobby Charlton.'

Alan Ball was already a wonderful player and he would grow into one of the best creative midfield players in the history of English football, but he grinned cheerfully when he dined out on the story. The point was that it did more than illustrate the often awkward style of Ramsey. It was an integral part of his belief that we should play for each other in the ways that were most easily at our disposal.

When you thought of some aspects of Ramsey's coaching, it was possible to smile at the comment of one of the gridiron Green Bay Packers team when asked about the operating style of the legendary coach Vince Lombardi, author of the famous remark, 'Winning isn't everything. It's the only thing.' Said the

Green Bay player, 'The great thing about coach Lombardi is that he doesn't play favourites. He treats us all like dogs.'

Ramsey didn't treat us like dogs, but he did make it clear that as far as he was concerned we all had our separate roles in the making of the team – and not one was more important than another.

Indeed, for me, the greatest strength of 4–3–3 is its power to bring teams together, especially outstanding individuals who are often playing different systems for their clubs. In recent years, when such talented midfielders as Paul Scholes, David Beckham, Steven Gerrard and Frank Lampard have been successful in club football in England, I have been amazed that 4–3–3 was a way of playing almost totally shunned by Eriksson and his successor Steve McClaren.

Scholes, who in my opinion always showed the most natural instincts for a true midfielder, became so frustrated by being asked to play out of position on the left, in the service of Eriksson's mythic 'diamond' formation, that he decided to retire from the international game. Gerrard and Lampard seemed to dwindle from the level of their performances for Liverpool and Chelsea the moment they put on the England shirt, and I found myself asking, 'Why on earth don't they do it, why don't they play 4–3–3?'

The one heavy demand of the system is that it does turn midfield into the hardest area of the game, but if a team is to have an authentic and consistent rhythm, that is always going to be the case anyway. You need three highly mobile midfielders equipped with good engines. If you have this, the difficulties are made easy, as was proved in Madrid in a way that, I believe, has survived every tactical fad that has come in the years since then. If the midfield is mobile enough, and sufficiently creative, you give yourself the means of running the other team to death.

In some ways, I feel the victory over Spain was one of the most important matches in the history of English football – one to put alongside the shocking defeat by Hungary, which provoked my friend Geoffrey Green to write that Billy Wright responded to the challenge of Puskas with the urgency of a fire engine, but unfortunately one going in the wrong direction. The Hungarian defeat made the most intelligent people in English football think more deeply about the game than ever before. In Madrid, it was as though one of them, Alf Ramsey, who, remember, was also a victim out on the field when the Hungarians ran riot, had finally delivered the football nation from the fear that we could no longer hope for anything better than second best.

As a schoolboy, I was shocked to hear the Hungarian result. 'Six-three, at Wembley,' I thought. 'This is something that just cannot be ignored. They will have to do something about this. We cannot keep believing that our way is the only way.' Thirteen years later, it was part of my pleasure and exhilaration to contribute to a performance that offered the real promise that the day of ignominy, when Puskas and Hidegkuti appeared so superior in everything they did, might finally be consigned to history – and who knew, on the same field in the final of the World Cup.

No doubt Ramsey wouldn't have thanked me, or any of my team-mates, for such speculation. He would have said that it wasn't a case of the job being half over, it really hadn't truly begun. What we were doing was putting in the building blocks, establishing what we could achieve in certain ways. He was also no doubt eventually, if privately, aghast at the widespread aping in English football of the system he had devised as much as anything out of necessity. His torment over whether or not to play wingers would go on, at least on the face of it, through to the end of the World Cup group games, but the real point of Madrid was that he had established beyond any doubt that he had, at the very least, the players to work an alternative system.

This was the key, I'm sure, to all his thinking. The 4–3–3

system worked for England only because Ramsey had the players who could make it work. Many of his imitators in club football would not enjoy such riches, and the result would often be something between narrow and stodgy, and outright shambles. The game in Madrid was an example of how easily, if you indeed had the best quality of players, 4–3–3 could absorb changes in personnel.

Joe Baker, who scored our first goal (the other came from Roger Hunt) was injured and, under the new rules of non-competitive football, we were allowed a substitute. Norman Hunter, Leeds United's formidable defender, came on to replace Baker. It is hard to imagine quite such different players, Baker, the quick and waspish forward, Hunter, a supreme defender, but the change was virtually seamless. Suddenly, we had the power to interchange, to make minor alterations of position for a few individuals, and yet maintain perfectly the flow of the team.

All the way from Madrid to the opening World Cup game against Uruguay, the new confidence seemed to ooze from the team. In the next match in that run, which I didn't play in as Ramsey took a look at the possibilities of Burnley's Gordon Harris, Poland held us to a draw in a hard-fought game at Goodison Park, but the other seven, it is worth repeating, were all won with nineteen goals scored, including one by Nobby Stiles against West Germany, and just four conceded. Even that draw on Merseyside was not without a certain encouragement since it confirmed, after a recent draw with Wales at Villa Park, that in England we did our best work at Wembley, which was where it was likely we would play all our World Cup games.

Most encouraging of all was the sense that Ramsey had thought everything through. Just as every position was covered, so were the possibilities of tactical change and, should they happen, the decisions on which players were best capable of making them work. Maybe the most significant case study in the last run to the World Cup lay in Ramsey's identification of Martin Peters, West Ham's leggy twenty-two-year-old, as a potentially vital factor if he should indeed decide that he could not afford the luxury of wingers who had failed to give anything like a guarantee of the level of performance it would take to beat the world's best teams. There was no question that here was a player mobile enough, and clever enough, to slip perfectly into the 4–3–3 system.

Peters proved almost immediately that he could meet all of Ramsey's demands when he was awarded three caps in the last five games before World Cup zero hour. In the 2–0 win over Yugoslavia at Wembley, he ran with freedom and guile in attack and was always willing to get back when we didn't have the ball.

In his second game, in Helsinki, he scored the first of our three goals against Finland, and in the final game in Poland, he almost certainly won his place in the tournament with another display of willing legs and mature thinking.

The appearance of such outstanding young contenders so late in the race perhaps required certain old boys to offer reminders that they could still make the odd contribution. Into this category fell such as J. Greaves and R. Charlton. By now, Greaves was approaching his fiftieth cap and I was near to my seventieth, and although we were still the right side of thirty (Jimmy was twenty-six, I was twenty-eight) neither of us were inclined to take anything for granted as Ramsey drew closer to some of the most vital decisions of his career.

The greater pressure was undoubtedly on Greaves. A striker trades on his natural-born gift for finding the net, and to best accomplish his work he has to be at his best physically. Jimmy's misfortune was that he had been hit by a viral illness during the season, which had cost him games for both Spurs and England. We knew how carefully Ramsey had monitored the fitness of Johnny Haynes and it was natural for Greaves to feel that he was under the same microscope.

He had missed five England games when he came to play against Yugoslavia at Wembley in May. That was the last home game we played prior to the three-week break with our families before reporting back for the training camp among the pastoral charms of Lilleshall and the pre-World Cup tour – perhaps a good time to leave a lingering impression of our ability with the home audience and a press corps that was now analysing each game, and individual performance, with the acute eyes of jurymen.

Jimmy scored the first of our two unanswered goals in the ninth minute, heading home a cross from Terry Paine, and Ramsey had to be impressed with his general sharpness.

I scored the second and, of the forty-nine I would eventually claim for England, I have to say it was one of the best. Partly it flowed from arguably the best piece of advice Jimmy Murphy ever gave me. 'Always aim in the general direction of the goal,' he said. 'Don't try to pick a spot, because for one thing that gives the goalkeeper a chance to read your intentions.' On this occasion, I realised that the position of one of the Yugoslav full backs meant that, if I hit it right, his goalkeeper, Milutin Soskic, would see the shot very late, if at all. From twenty-five yards the ball rocketed into the net via the crossbar. Soskic did exceptionally well to get his hands to it because, as I had hoped, he could not have seen it until the last second.

Another big factor in the goal was the quality of the Wembley pitch. Throughout the season we played on all kinds of surfaces, many of them quite wretched, and it was always the ultimate luxury for a player of some skill to reach the oasis of the old Empire Stadium. You could trust the run of the ball and its bounce. Sometimes, I look out at the modern pitches, even in mid-winter, and my old footballer's eyes show me a picture of paradise. I recently saw Tom Finney at Old Trafford and we both laughed when I said, 'Tom, imagine what it would have been like playing almost every game on such a pitch.'

Greaves's determination to remind Ramsey of his ability to score outstanding goals for England, which he no doubt worried might have come under question after his lay-off and with the threat of Geoff Hurst rising to the surface, was fulfilled most impressively, however, on the less manicured field of the Ullevaal Stadium in Oslo when the trial process was resumed after the short time spent with our families following the completion of the Lilleshall training camp.

Greaves notched four goals in the 6–1 destruction of Norway and each one of them seemed to say something different about his unique scoring ability. It was as though Jimmy was saying to Alf, 'Yes, I know I've been out of things, I know the one area of the team you're probably worrying about is striking, but, really, could anyone do it better?'

Such a question would arise again, of course, but that night Greaves had written his version of the answer brilliantly across the northern sky.

His first goal came, as did the one against Yugoslavia, from his head, after some typically unselfish work by another forward, who might ultimately stand between him and a place in the World Cup team. My United team-mate John Connelly – who perhaps better than anyone represented Ramsey's work ethic – made his way down the flank, then crossed for Greaves to produce a header that would have been happily claimed by Nat Lofthouse, or any of the other fabled aerial specialists.

For his second, Greaves fought off challengers for half the length of the pitch, then beat the goalkeeper with the easiest of rapier thrusts. The third was classic Greaves, a smash-and-grab after Connelly had collided with the now distraught goalkeeper, and the rest of the Norwegian defence stood and watched. The final line in a personal statement that could scarcely have been more expressive came when Connelly and Paine combined to slice through the cover and Greaves finished off their work from a narrow angle.

Greaves could rest more easily on the flight to the next match in Copenhagen, the second one that year in which I didn't play as Ramsey again took the chance to review all his other available options. But Greaves must have known, as well as anyone, that with Ramsey there could never be a point when an individual player was totally secure. As I discovered at the Copacabana beachside, the manager had his own values and instincts, and they could not be so easily read.

In the matter of Jimmy Greaves, was Ramsey about to reveal his final hand so long after laying down the foundations of a team that might not have been instantly recognised by football men locked into more traditional values? It was one of the last, but certainly not the least intriguing, of the questions that accompanied Ramsey to the start line of the tournament that he knew would decide his reputation for the rest of his days in football.

As far as the dressing room was concerned, Ramsey had already passed the vital tests and implicit in this was the understanding that picking one talented player above another would always be the most difficult task in the game.

My team-mates went on to beat the Danes 2–0, but the most significant aspect of that leg of our tour was the relief we all felt in the fact that, before we landed in Copenhagen, it was confirmed that the twenty-two players on the trip would form England's World Cup squad.

The goalkeepers were Gordon Banks, who seemed to be growing a little more assured with each game, Ron Springett, the veteran of Chile, and Peter Bonetti, who would celebrate his elevation, and his first cap, with a clean sheet in the Danish match.

Of the four full backs – George Cohen, Jimmy Armfield, Ray Wilson and Gerry Byrne – Cohen and Wilson appeared to have made the positions their own. Armfield was a highly experienced player, quick and composed on the overlap, and Liverpool's Byrne was a fine, tough full back – as he proved when finishing the 1965 cup final against Leeds United with his arm in a sling – but the defensive qualities of Cohen and Wilson, and the degree of their understanding, had become quite phenomenal. Ramsey, the old full back, had been a fine passer of the ball but of all football men he knew that what you most wanted from the position was security. My friend Keith Newton, a talented full back from Blackburn who had fallen in the final pruning of the World Cup squad, once learned this at some cost after making a critical mistake on England duty.

The full extent of Ramsey's reprimand wasn't loud but I knew how cutting it was going to be when, as I walked away, I heard Alf begin it with the words, 'What the fucking hell did you think you were doing . . .'

Among the half backs, the men in possession were Nobby Stiles, Jack and Bobby Moore. Among the challengers was another veteran, Ron Flowers, but perhaps more menacingly Martin Peters, who might have been seen as Nobby's rival, and Norman Hunter, who had picked up four caps and in his ferocious tackling and underrated skills may, in a corner of Ramsey's mind, have been an alternative to the majestic but not overly quick Moore.

That may sound like a statement of some sacrilege but part of Ramsey's strength was his willingness to make decisions that might be unpopular but he believed fervently to be right.

After discarding Peter Thompson, who had been unlucky with injuries after making such a good impression in Brazil two years earlier, Ramsey still left himself with the pick of three wingers – Connelly, Paine and Callaghan. If 4–3–3 was still, surely, his strongest hand, the wingers had not yet been sent to the wall. Striking duties would be disputed by Greaves, Hurst and Hunt, and Ball, Eastham and I were the attacking midfield options.

For Ramsey, in so many ways the ultimate loner, this was the time when his best counsel could only be his own. It was not that he believed there were no other football men with valid opinions. Indeed, I was often impressed by the sight of leading club managers arriving at the team hotel to discuss with him their feelings about the strengths, and the best way to use, their players, and this was something Ramsey had initiated. Yet he knew better than anyone that, finally, it was his judgement that would have to shape his team.

Speaking for myself, I have to say that I never feared his judgement. If it went against me, I would have felt honour bound to accept it. You cannot admire a man only so long as he acts and speaks in your favour. I believed that then and I continued to believe it after I had played my last match for him.

However prickly he appeared to be when facing the wider world, and however uncomfortable he might be on the official occasions he found so irksome, I, along with many of my England team-mates, felt sure that I knew the real football man. I knew how painstaking he was and how keen that his players should never be faced with needless difficulty or confusion when they went on to the field.

He couldn't shield us from the inherent cruelty of the selection system, the need to make decisions that sometimes could seem harsh, even arbitrary, to the victims, but once selected we knew we would get every bit of support at his disposal. For one example, he always insisted we became familiar with those parts of the pitch on which we would most likely operate. It seemed no detail was too small for his attention.

As I noted the mood of the team in those final days before the World Cup began, when I listened to the kind of banter that generally comes only from players who are feeling good about themselves and their prospects, I couldn't help but make comparisons with other England teams I had known. The obvious one was with the squad that found itself so quickly divided in Chile four years earlier. Then, Jimmy Adamson had concluded that a World Cup squad who didn't feel as one was probably doomed. A lot of work had to go into solving this problem, Adamson declared. Perhaps there was just too much of it, he may have decided before electing to stay within the more manageable boundaries of the Burnley club he knew so well. Now, under Ramsey, it was clear this work had been done, and so much more besides.

Unquestionably, Alf Ramsey had laid the foundations of a team, and if it was true that this team was in some ways in his own image, it had certainly been given a life and a competitive personality of its own. The banner had been raised in Madrid and now I was confident it was about to fly victoriously at home.

16

ON THE BUS TO
ROEHAMPTON

AFTER THOSE TESTS on the fields of Helsinki, Oslo, Copenhagen and Chorzow, we were given twenty-four-hour passes to see our families before moving into our old headquarters at the Hendon Hall Hotel. When I said goodbye to Norma and the girls, I couldn't get it out of my head that the longer we were apart on this occasion, the closer my England team-mates and I would be to an achievement that could change all our lives. Nobody needed to tell me I wasn't going to war but still, in the context of our lives, it was a bittersweet parting that we understood might be the most momentous we would ever know.

That gave me fuel for deep thought as the team rode the bus again to the Roehampton training ground to apply what Alf Ramsey no doubt hoped were some final brush strokes to a tactical masterpiece.

My thoughts turned to his quirky ways and his sometimes distant moods, and I wondered if there was a time when any of us could say we truly knew him. Perhaps it was natural, though, at that advanced hour of all our work and ambitions, to dwell mostly on the quality and the nature of the players he had asked to share a moment of football history.

Had he, through all the trial and error, the lurches from hope to dismay and then back again, indeed put together the right ingredients? Making a mental inventory of our resources was encouraging work.

Since he is gone from us now, along with Bobby Moore, it is maybe inevitable at this distance to find myself first thinking, all over again, of Alan Ball. He was the boy among men and even now I can shut my eyes and hear his voice, high-pitched and optimistic, but what I remember most is that he never seemed out of place.

When he died so tragically, trying to control a fire in the garden of his home in Hampshire, there were some suggestions, along with all the magnificently earned tributes, that he could have made more of his life after the glory of 1966 and this was very hurtful to all those of us who came to think of him as our little brother.

That's what he was, our little brother. He was twenty-one-years-old. We saw him as a unique lad with a squeaky voice among hardened professionals, but one with an enormous heart and great talent, a boy you just wanted to look after because that's what he needed and certainly it was what he was worth.

Could he play a vital role in the next few weeks? You only had to be around him on the training pitch or in a match for the briefest time to know that he could. His enthusiasm and energy were constantly bubbling to the surface. He had two favourite subjects. One was his football. The other was his dad, Alan Ball Senior. His father was involved in football professionally and had plainly seen early, and nourished diligently, the talent that burst from his son.

Bally had many qualities as a footballer and among those I most admired was his willingness to take the responsibility of scoring goals. It is one thing to run relentlessly for ninety minutes but sometimes a midfielder has to do more than that, he has to break open the game by the force of his own decision and Alan was always willing to do that, apparently from an early age. He came to us in the England team not as some highly talented but still green apprentice, but as a professional who had already proved that he understood the game profoundly and also knew exactly how he could contribute to any team in any circumstances.

When I see him in my mind's eye all these years later, I still have an amazing picture of bursting life and dynamism and I think to myself, as I know all those who played with him do, 'Imagine it, coming to that great stage with all that passion and confidence at such an age.'

He was never afraid of asking for advice – or admitting that each day he called his dad. He told us about his daily conferences with his father and what was said when he knew he would be playing in the World Cup final. According to Alan it went something like this:

Father: 'Alan, why are you calling me today?'

Son: 'Because I've just been told I'm playing in the World Cup.'

Father: 'Well, son, it is quite clear what you have to do. You have to make it the best day of your life.'

He did, too. Throughout the tournament he ran with a consistency and a bite that was stunning, and when he lost his place for a couple of matches, you knew there was no question of him retreating from the battle. At training his freckled face blazed with redoubled determination. No, there was no doubt that with Alan Ball you knew precisely what you had, and ultimately Alf Ramsey could not have been more content with a football package that was small but most certainly complete.

He was the baby of the squad and in some ways he was loved for that, almost as a mascot, but this didn't blur for any of us the essential reasons why he was around, why we were glad to awake to an enthusiasm that stretched to the sleeping hour. On top of his passionate love for the game, his brilliant vision, his superior technique, his astonishing industry, he was a winner. It was something he announced every time he went on the field. I do not know precisely why he failed as a manager, any more than why I was never entirely comfortable in the job while Jack took to it so ferociously and successfully. It may well be that as a player, Alan Ball set for himself standards that, in changing days, another generation of footballers could not meet, with the result that he became extremely frustrated. There is no doubt that right to the end of his life he still yearned for those days when he could go out and do it for himself.

In 1966 England's good luck was that he realised he could fulfil so many of his ambitions in one extraordinary rush. This was maybe the key to what in the end was his most valuable contribution to a team who would not be strangers to moments of crisis until the target was finally achieved. It was absolute reliability. On a football field you could trust him with every last one of your hopes.

In choosing Alan Ball, as in the selection of George Cohen, Nobby Stiles, Jack and Martin Peters, I felt we had seen the real genius of Ramsey. He was able to examine all the attributes of a player, see his strengths and weaknesses – for example Ball was not big, and in the eyes of another manager this, along with his inexperience, could have counted against him decisively – and then project beyond all the pluses and the minuses to a picture of what he might do for his team, how he could help to make it whole and perfectly balanced.

It was the same with Jack, Nobby and George. Before Alf Ramsey, I suspect that none of them would have played for England and, looking back, it is stunning to think of what an injustice that would have been. There were more stylish players around, those whom you might imagine would have looked more instantly the part in an England shirt, but the England manager was plainly looking for deeper substance.

In one respect, George was the classic example of the Ramsey intuition. I hope he doesn't mind me saying it but when he was on the ball, the quality of his final delivery was not something that prompted huge optimism. He was apparently hurt, as quite a young player, when his team-mate Bobby Robson said that George had probably hit more photographers than Frank Sinatra.

But there was truth in that, and sometimes we laughed about it – not against George but at the incongruous fact that no one could get into such fantastic positions so regularly and yet somehow manage to miscue the final ball. He did everything right until the moment of breakdown. He would overlap perfectly so that the ball would be there for him, and then, having got to the dead-ball line in some lung-tearing effort, he would hit it ten yards over the bar. It was at such moments you laughed because it was better than crying.

Yet you always knew that any failures in technique were dwarfed by the qualities George could bring to any game at any level. Among the most important of them were tremendous fitness, speed and strength, a great ability to read the game and a knack of terrifying wingers. He wasn't dirty or cruel, but a winger, as I was when I met him several times in First Division games, knew that against him there was no way of avoiding a gruelling afternoon if you wanted to make a serious impact on the match. I saw wingers of ultimate ability – Francisco Gento springs to mind – who were plainly petrified simply by the sight of him pounding down the right flank. Were they tempted to test him with some of the best of their artistry? Almost invariably, they decided to save it for another day.

When it happened, George's emergence as England's right back seemed to many terribly harsh on the reigning captain, Jimmy Armfield. The Blackpool player was a true stylist, who had won forty-one caps, and Ramsey was certainly not against his defenders displaying a flourish or two on the ball. But I suspect Ramsey looked at the rivals and asked himself the vital question – which of them is most likely to scare a defender? The answer was plain. Jimmy Armfield had some wonderful qualities, but he wasn't a winger's nightmare.

Another factor was that no one absorbed more completely than George did, Ramsey's belief that players need always to be thinking of the situation of their colleagues. If Jack or Bobby Moore were ever drawn out of position, or Nobby committed to some forward foray, George was there to cover, as watchful as a hawk.

There were so many examples of superb professionalism in this team preparing for the supreme examination of their careers, but none of them surpassed the one presented by George Cohen.

Just seeing him on the bus, always amiable, always willing to lend a helping hand on or off the field, was enough to create a wave of well-being. This warm feeling among his northern team-mates was not affected in the slightest by his Londoner's reluctance to embrace the humour of Ken Dodd. When we went to see the Liverpool comedian, most of the lads were highly appreciative – Nobby had tears rolling down his cheeks from the opening line and there seemed a danger at one point that he might finish up rolling on the floor – but George watched stony-faced. 'What on earth did you northerners see funny in that?' he grumbled on the way home, but at no cost to his popularity.

Six months earlier, he had also escaped unscathed, this time from a training session mishap that left the manager groaning on the frosty pitch on the eve of the victory in Madrid. George collided with him so fiercely that an anxious group formed around Alf Ramsey's prone figure. When Alf eventually got to his feet, he said, icily, 'Cohen, if I had another fit full back around, you wouldn't be playing tonight.' But of course the threat was idle. George had long since become indispensable to Ramsey's idea of his best team.

Jack rose very quickly to the highest rank in the category of player the manager prized so highly. Alf's England player was one who, above all else, wanted to win, and on those trips across the Pennines to watch him with Leeds, my understanding of this drive in my brother deepened a little more each time I saw him. His image was of a giraffe let loose on a football pitch, but the more you analysed his performance, the more you saw the three qualities that lifted him above all rivals. His positional sense was brilliant, at times almost uncanny. He was magnificently dominant in the air, at both ends of the pitch. And in a Leeds team of some very strong personalities, no one was more influential in keeping people around him completely focused.

At every corner kick won by Leeds he was up there in the box, and when his team conceded one, you could almost put the mortgage on his long neck stretching furthest to knock the ball away.

On one drive back from Yorkshire in the spring of 1965, after seeing a particularly effective performance from him at Elland Road, when his newly promoted team were pushing so hard for what would have been an astonishing cup and league Double, I found myself speculating on his chances of making the England team.

They had improved, obviously, with the rise of Don Revie's team, but you had to worry that maybe it had come a little late. Jack would be thirty at his next birthday in a few weeks' time, and not many international careers started at such an advanced age. Maurice Norman of Spurs had the experience of twenty-three caps and had been virtually an automatic selection since Ramsey took over the team two years earlier, and Brian Labone, Everton's polished centre half, had been earning some enthusiastic reviews. But did either of them battle quite like Jack, had they fought their way to prominence over quite the same obstacles?

I was conscious, too, that my older brother had in many ways been obliged to operate in my shadow. While scouts led by Manchester United's legendary Joe Armstrong had besieged our house in Ashington looking for my signature when I was fifteen, Jack was seventeen before it was confirmed by Leeds that he had a future in the professional game, and it was only then that he realised his progress had also been noted by a posse of scouts from the big clubs. His first appearance for the Leeds league team came when John Charles, his idol, was moved to centre forward, and he confessed to being filled with apprehension over the extent of his responsibility. But Jack battled through and I was proud of him on that night I drove across the moors with my head full of his latest performance.

I laughed a little when I thought of how he was vilified for persecuting goalkeepers by plonking himself in front of them and then dismissing all cries that he should desist. Jack revelled in pointing out that there was nothing in the laws of football that said where you should or shouldn't stand. 'Why shouldn't I stand where I choose as long as I'm not doing anything illegal?' he demanded to know, and of course he was right, and the more so today when you consider how outrageous is the liberty granted to defenders to stop attackers in almost any grabbing, shirt-pulling way they choose.

I thought of how it was probably true that in many eyes he was the lesser of two brothers who played football, but I knew he had done things that I would never be able to do in my life. He had always followed his spirit in football and it seemed he was due some higher reward.

It was thus wonderful to hear a few days later that, finally, the call had come to him from England – he was to take on the Scots at Wembley seven years after I had played my first game against them at Hampden Park. Jack would play thirty-five times for England, losing just twice in a period when the team, astonishingly, conceded a meagre twenty-one goals. During that time we had other superb defenders, not least Gordon Banks, the world's best goalkeeper, but Jack's role was immense and filled me with great pride.

He was, I believed, another key source of Ramsey's certainty as we prepared for the opening of the World Cup, and as the tournament unfolded, and his influence grew, he handed some of his best advice to his kid brother. One day he took me aside after training.

'You know, I think it would be better for us if you tried to get in the box a little earlier,' he said, maybe suggesting that I wasn't displaying enough faith in the defenders.

'Well, if you're winning, what's the point in going forward and exposing yourself to the counter-attack?' I responded. Jack's point was that it was better to inflict all your skill and go for the kill, and he cited the young sensation, Franz Beckenbauer.

'You know when he comes into the box, playing his little one-twos, it's almost impossible to stop him doing it, and I think you should do more of that. You have the ability and you should exploit it more.'

It may seem like odd advice, given that I was most associated with flowing attack and spectacular goals, but something inside me said that maybe Jack was right. Maybe I could go forward more often, maybe I should try to banish some of the caution I felt deep down.

One thing is certain now, as I recall assessing our strengths all these years down the road: I see clearly that if we had lacked any one of the players riding the bus to Roehampton that absence might have been critical. We were a team whose interdependence was as vital as oxygen.

Bobby Moore had captained England when he was still a youth player and he had grown into the role as sure-footedly, as apparently effortlessly, as he performed on the field. He carried a huge burden of expectation but he could hardly have borne it less lightly. His particular friend was Jimmy Greaves, but there was never any question of a captain's clique. He had a word for everyone – never effusive but with a warmth that washed over you. Despite his youth, he didn't have to work on projecting authority. It was part of him. He asked about your family, if everything was all right with you, and then he went his way. Yet you knew he was always there, a strong but never overstated voice of command on the field and, off it, someone who made it easy for you to look up to him.

He was the natural captain, and this was despite the fact that it wasn't so easy to list the playing qualities that normally determine the top performers. He shared his best asset with Nobby Stiles – an innate positional sense that for both of them was as instinctive as breathing. He could sniff out trouble before it arrived, which was especially helpful in view of his lack of speed, his indifferent heading ability and the fact that his left foot wasn't really exceptional. Everything was redeemed and made superb by that anticipation. He could read the game so well that more often than not he got in front of an attacker to win the ball rather than waiting at the back, which would have been the natural course for someone without speed. Early on, that had a tendency to make team-mates shudder because it was such a dangerous thing to do, but soon enough you took his ability to play so audaciously for granted. The worry that if he made a mistake everything could be lost faded quickly because he didn't make a mistake. His judgement was so sensational that even when you are obliged to be less than complimentary about many of his skills, you still cannot talk about the world's greatest players without mentioning him.

If you tried to break it down, rather than just accept the glory of it, you entered the territory of racehorse trainer Sir Noel Murless, who said of Lester Piggott's ability to bring home winners, 'It's a mystery known only to Lester and the horses and God.' I don't know about God, but for Bobby it was a mystery he was happy to share with the ball.

When Ramsey made him captain on a permanent basis, after Armfield lost his place to Cohen, he had just eighteen caps, against my forty-nine, the thirty-three of Jimmy Greaves and

Ray Wilson's twenty-four, but I know I can speak for the rest of the senior pros when I say that not one of us had a questioning thought when he led us out at Wembley against Uruguay, for a 2–1 win, at the age of twenty-three.

A year earlier he had been given the honour, fleetingly, when Armfield was injured before the match against Czechoslovakia, another victory, and if there were any doubts then about the elevation of someone who had just up to that point eleven caps to his name, they had disappeared without trace a year later. He had led West Ham to a rare honour, the FA Cup, and been voted England's Footballer of the Year. It seemed obvious that he was equal to any challenge and it was only later that we learned that this was as true off the field as on it, when at such an early age, he had to fight testicular cancer.

What I'm sketching here is not a series of pen portraits of outstanding footballers but of men who would, I suspect, have proved their substance whatever they did. Something inside all of them made them reach out for some achievement that would separate them from the crowd.

The relentless competitive instinct of my friend Ray Wilson was the perfect complement to the equally determined George Cohen on the other side of the back four. This was a back-line that would have instilled confidence in any team at any time, and behind them was the perfect fail-safe system, the ultimate goalkeeper, Gordon Banks.

When Banks was establishing himself in the England team, Lev Yashin, goalkeeper of the USSR, was generally regarded as the world's best. Yet brilliant though he was, the big man dressed in black, who would become a good friend, didn't appear to me to be anything that Gordon Banks was not.

In time, the Leicester City goalkeeper, who moved on to some brilliant years with Stoke City, would be acknowledged as the best of his era and, possibly, in history, but right from the start you could see that he had extraordinary qualities. Whenever I played against him, he never offered the encouragement of ever seeming even briefly flustered, nor was anything even vaguely cosmetic about his work. Everything was completely functional until the moment he was required to produce something sublime. If he didn't have to dive, he wouldn't, but if he did, it was with total conviction.

I cannot begin to count the times when I played against him and found myself in a good position, in full flow, hitting the ball hard and accurately enough to think, 'Bloody hell, that couldn't be better.' Then I'd see Gordon make a save so easily it was embarrassing for someone who already had his arms half raised in celebration.

But the more I played with him, and practised against him, with England, the more I understood why it was he could make such phenomenal saves. It was because no goalkeeper can ever have worked harder at his trade. He practised so long, and with such physical commitment, sometimes you wondered quite how his body was able to take the punishment, and this was when his reputation had long been established. He broke your heart in practice and he restored it in the most critical of moments during a match. He was perhaps at his most amazing in another World Cup, in Mexico in 1970, when the ball flew about in the thin air of high altitude.

If the ball flew, so did he. He wasn't a flamboyant character, he never tried to make more of something than it was and this was true of some of the most memorable saves ever made. 'How,' I was once asked, 'is it possible for Gordon Banks to make such brilliant recoveries?' It was not the most difficult of questions. I said it was because he did it so many times away from the public gaze, hour upon hour and sometimes in the most difficult practice conditions. In Mexico the fields might have been made of concrete, but time and again he would throw himself down and then get up again all in one motion. If anyone commented on his bruises or his gashes, he would say simply, 'It's what I have to do if I'm to do my job properly.'

Inevitably, there was wear and tear and at one point he had to have a hip operation, but he never flagged in his belief that, if he was to be the best, he just had to do the work, however painful it might be at times. In Mexico, because of the atmosphere, we were encouraged to blast shots at him from every angle but so brilliantly did he adapt to the conditions that he began to carry an aura that became almost a twelfth man. Whatever happened, however we struggled, we could say there would always be Gordon Banks, and when we couldn't say that, inevitably we feared the worst consequences. English football would one day be required to face that dread, but on the bus to Roehampton it belonged far in the distance.

Down the years, Gordon has remained particularly close to Roger Hunt, and when I occasionally join them in a round of golf, I am invariably reminded of why this might be so. They practised widely different football disciplines, Banks the most defiant of defenders, Hunt a remorseless forward, running and harrying, but they might have been joined at the hip in their determination to extract every last morsel of all the talent they had been given.

When Banks lost the sight in his right eye following a car crash, he was nearing the end of his career, but it did nothing to lessen the shock of it. When I visited him in hospital, I couldn't help thinking, 'This would be hard for anyone, but, oh Jesus, Gordon Banks, for him to have his career ended by impaired vision, this goalkeeper who saw everything so early, it is hardly imaginable.' For a while, the accident seemed to change his nature a little. He became somewhat argumentative, a touch bitter about the fate that had befallen him at the end of a career that had brought so many honours and plaudits but, as was common in those days, no great material reward. Alan Ball made a similar point to me once when we sat together on a long flight. He complained of his wages at Everton. He made the age-old footballer's point that however packed the stadium, however popular the game you played, the reward in your pay packet remained the same – and it was dwarfed by the scale of pay received by other entertainers.

I told Alan what older players had in the past told me, but I did not dare say it to Gordon in the days after his accident, as he ruminated over the uncertain future that in those days faced all ageing footballers, whatever their achievements.

'You have everything before you,' I said to Alan. 'You're playing for England. Why are you worrying about money? If you've done well enough, if you've made your name because you've given the game everything you have, money will find you as did the other rewards, the only ones you were really interested in when you first started off, the playing of football and the satisfaction of winning.'

This was, of course, easier to say back then because it was a time when young footballers, without a moment of experience at the top of the game, did not have their financial security settled by the signing of one contract. Although later I did mention it to Gordon, I didn't really succeed in putting it across, and anyway for a while I suspect he would have rejected it with some contempt. Now, I believe, he is a lot more philosophical about the course of a great career, his gentle brand of South Yorkshire humour largely restored.

This is reassuring for all those of us who came to see him as the bedrock of our hopes when we pulled on the English shirt. There was always Banks, always that figure of endless resistance. Sometimes he brought boyhood days to mind, when I would spend so much time poring over pictures of great saves. They seemed to be the staple of the football photographer in those days, certainly far more than today. Those pictures still flicker in my mind's eye. Frank Swift, Bert Williams and then Bert Trautmann, my favourite for so long, come alive as they once again defy gravity and geometry and much else besides. Gordon Banks belongs in such a gallery, and if he was a typical goalkeeper in that he mostly set himself a little apart, inhabiting his separate planet with its special demands, there was no more warming sight than Banks at work as we strived so hard in 1966 to become the best team in the world.

Ray Wilson had that same quality of being able to concentrate utterly on the task he had set himself. He was a joy to play alongside because he was so consistent, and on the rare occasions when he made an error – as he did in the most important game of his life – he had the remarkable capacity to banish it instantly from his mind. You never saw him brood for a moment over something he could no longer rectify. He lived, as all great defenders must, from second to second. In his quiet way, he was as hard as Nobby or Jack in his refusal to yield an inch to the opposition, and he proved it throughout and in the aftermath of the meanest and most desperate game most of us would ever have to play.

When I was assigned to the left wing, we were able to develop the kind of understanding I had with Tony Dunne at United. It meant that when the opposition were on the ball, we were never in doubt about which of them to pick out. I went with the runner, who was usually the advancing full back, and Ray went for the man on the ball, the out-and-out winger, who was his speciality. He didn't have any self-doubt. He always knew how capable he was and the sharpness of his conviction was a powerful source of confidence throughout the team. If he had something he felt was worth saying, he would say it with some force. Otherwise, he just played quite ferociously. I never saw anyone embarrass him or, still less, make him question the fact that it was his right to win.

Even today when I think of Nobby Stiles, maybe after a visit to his home in Stretford, near Old Trafford to which he donated his heart as a boy growing up in the tough district of Collyhurst, one phrase inevitably comes to my lips – what a lad! What a unique little character, what a friend and what a competitor to have on your side. In my account of the Manchester United years, I devoted considerable space to his sublime clumsiness, which once provoked the sportswriter Hugh McIlvanney to say that, by comparison with Nobby, Inspector Clouseau was 'blessedly adroit'. Along the way, though, I hope I also conveyed that he was one of the most superb footballers I have ever known and that behind the laughter and the good heart was a seriousness of purpose that refused to shy away from any challenge.

Jack recalls, 'Once when I lost my concentration for a second and made a mistake, all I could see was this little face coming at me from about thirty yards, breathing smoke and fire, and I remember turning away and thinking, "Oh, bloody hell, I've upset Nobby Stiles." '

It didn't matter who you were, if you slipped from what Nobby regarded as a basic professional standard, you were due a fearsome dressing down. He wasn't a coach's player, he wasn't a Bobby Moore, but no one was more astute at the business of quashing danger. There wasn't a man alive he feared except one – his father Charlie, an undertaker who was no great football expert but loved the game enough to build a football pitch for the lads in the neighbourhood. Until then, their most regular playing field was an abandoned graveyard.

Once we were coming up the tunnel at Old Trafford after Nobby had lost his temper and been booked, and when we turned towards the dressing room, passed the point where the fans could get close to the players, we heard a summons such as you might hear from an angry headmaster in a school corridor. 'Norbert,' shouted Charlie Stiles, and Nobby went to him with his head down to receive a lecture about how he should behave while wearing the shirt of Manchester United. I didn't hear all of it but it was enough to remind me that my friend wasn't the only United player to be scared by Charlie Stiles.

I never had a relationship on the field with anyone quite like I had with Nobby. Although he wasn't without skill on the ball, he decided early on that his mission in life was to win the ball and give it to somebody who, he thought, might do something more with it than he could. Luckily for me, I was among the favoured recipients. He scored his one goal for England in the friendly against West Germany at Wembley, which kicked off our winning streak on the run-up to the World Cup, but he never had any great aspirations to get in the box. He saw football in two stages. The first one, in which he specialised, was winning the ball, and this was the result, more than anything, of reading the play and timing your tackles, and he knew that if he did his part properly, there was a very good chance we would win. For him, the game's second stage rested elsewhere. Nobby won the ball, often ferociously, and he made it clear that he did not expect his work to be wasted. He got it, you used it – or had a volley in your ear. What that meant was that whenever you received the ball from Nobby, you always felt a certain weight of responsibility. You thought, 'Hell, the little fellah had to spit blood to win this ball, I just can't waste it.'

One of my foremost responsibilities for both United and England was always to be free to receive the ball from Nobby. His was to defend, which he did like a tiger and with brilliant vision, and maintain a regular supply of possession. Also, just as Jack didn't know of any law that said he couldn't stand close to a goalkeeper, Nobby never read anywhere that it was illegal to frighten an opponent out of a game. During the coming tournament, this would land Nobby in some controversy, and when all hell broke lose, I could not help thinking that in this he was right at the heart of the English football tradition.

Getting under the skin of an opponent is, of course, a time-honoured tactic, something I learned early in my career when the Newcastle United veteran Jimmy Scoular needled me to the point where I came the closest I've ever come to striking someone on the football field. Fortunately, I resisted the temptation after he had dragged me back while I was in full flow against the team that had been such a huge part of my boyhood. As well as superb defensive instincts, Nobby had that capacity to inflame an opponent with his physical approach, and put him off his game, and if sometimes this spilled over into something a bit more serious, it was an aspect of the game English players – and fans – understood more readily than did their foreign counterparts.

Even today, Europeans regard some of the physicality of the English game as something that happens on another planet, although many of their own players are involved in it now. This was evident when Manchester United and Chelsea played the 2008 Champions League final and everyone agreed that only two English clubs could have produced a game of such physical intensity, despite the presence of such outstanding European players as Cristiano Ronaldo, Michael Ballack and Didier Drogba. 'Such a strong match,' said one observer from Spain. 'It could only have been made in England.' This toughness, I believe, plays a significant part in the enormous popularity of the Premiership across the world.

Why, you have to ask, does England's top league now command so much more interest than the Spanish, Italian or French Leagues? Is it because of something built into it down the years by the likes of Nobby Stiles? The games have an edge, a spice, and the players show a willingness to do battle physically, which is a fundamental part of a contact sport and has embraced a whole new audience.

Nobby, like Jack, always understood that part of the game. While it would never touch someone such as me so deeply, because, maybe, I was made for a different purpose, it had to be taken on by certain players if matches were to be won. Nobby was always at the head of this tough crew. In a physical game perhaps some people did get hurt on the way, but Nobby saw most clearly that it was life and it was football and in any successful team, someone would have to take on this role.

At the time when sweepers came into vogue, Stiles revealed the full range of his talent. He swept up for Bill Foulkes in the United team, and placing him in that position was one of the most inspired moves Matt Busby ever made. Busby will always be associated with the purest football values but he understood the need for iron and defensive security. He used to tell Nobby, 'Norrie, let him [the man he was marking] know you are there in the first five minutes and things will be a lot easier for the rest of the match.' If George Best, Denis Law and I received most of the plaudits during the 1960s, no one in the dressing room was unaware for a second of the value of having Foulkes's power and Nobby's radar working in tandem.

Bill Foulkes was an incredibly tough player but he was not a delicate one and he did make some mistakes. Nobby, however incongruous it sounds, was Bill's protector. He also covered the full backs and rushed at every opportunity to support the midfield – and, all the time, he was winning the ball. Jimmy Murphy, in praise of Stiles, told me, 'The hardest thing is winning the ball and the easiest is playing with it.'

That is another reason why I have never been embarrassed to list Nobby Stiles among the great players. When anyone questions the claim, I tell them, 'Well, if you think I was a great player, you have to include Nobby in that category, because on the field I could never repay the debt I owed him, at least in any way apart from love and my respect.'

Martin Peters was the newest boy on the bus, having played just three times for England when he came into the second game of the tournament. He didn't have much to say, at least when compared to Alan Ball, but he had confidence you couldn't miss, which made it much less surprising when he quickly became one of the cutting edges of the team, producing both vital tackles and goals.

There was much questioning of Alf Ramsey's assessment that he was a decade ahead of his time but you could see why Alf thought so. Peters' instinct was so sharp, and unpredictable, he was the most difficult player to avoid or to mark. It was as though he was connected to some separate system of thought that enabled him to drift into the action from nowhere, with a key interception or strike on goal the frequent result. Sometimes you might think he did it on a whim but the more you played with him the more you realised how deeply he understood the game and the rewards it offered the most subtle movement.

Occasionally, I see a player produce something that reminds me of the best of Martin Peters, and it makes me sit up in my seat and say, 'Where did he come from?' With that in mind, my best possible tribute to the youngest member of the West Ham axis that did so much to lift the hopes of the boys riding that bus, is that more than forty years on, I do not utter that phrase today nearly so often as I did when I played at his side. He was never a shouter but there were times when I fancied I could hear the working of his football brain.

Finally, as I looked down the bus I saw Alf Ramsey's last great conundrum, the one that would dominate the final stages of his campaign, at least in the public's mind. How did he turn three into two? How did he separate the virtues of Jimmy Greaves, the born goal scorer, Roger Hunt, who would run forever and with an absolute selflessness, and Geoff Hurst, the young, strong representative of the new breed of target men?

It was only sometime later that I learned that in the great debate over Greaves, Roger Hunt's place was also at risk. I had thought at the time that the issue was plainly between Hurst and Greaves, but later one of Ramsey's closest contacts in the media told me the manager had confided to him that Roger was even more vulnerable than Geoff Hurst, if Jimmy had been brought back.

Everyone knew Greaves's qualities, so often had they lit up the sky on behalf of Chelsea, Tottenham and England, and Hurst's powerful running, heading and excellent control were, in their way, just as visible.

Roger Hunt tended to work more in the shadows than the limelight. Of course he would score goals – 245 of them for Liverpool in 404 appearances and 18 for England in 34 – but he had developed his special talent with superb application down the years. Somewhere along the line he had acquired an extraordinary knack for making space for his team-mates as well as himself. If the goals came, well, he accepted them with the eagerness of any front man, but he seemed equally happy to supply a team-mate. Ramsey loved this quality of a supreme team man, and before the end of this tournament so would I, with a new depth after he contributed, apparently unnoticed, to one of the moments of my own career that would be most celebrated.

Today he is as he was back in 1966, one of the most un-assuming men I have ever known. Maybe one aspect of his game does need some emphasis if I am to avoid any risk of handing out the faint praise that often goes to life's natural toilers. Roger Hunt was so much more than a workhorse. Alf Ramsey could have picked up one of those almost wherever he turned. What the manager most valued was that along with inexhaustible energy Hunt also brought tremendous vision. There was always a point to his running. He worked with guile and had an eye for possibilities, for both himself and any team-mate who grasped quickly enough the purpose of a run. He rarely attempted to smash in a shot from thirty yards, but when he went into the box it was always because he had sniffed the possibility of a goal.

Sometimes it seemed that Geoff Hurst could receive the ball under pressure, hold it, and wait for reinforcements precisely as long as it took them to arrive. Ramsey saw him as such a fierce rival to Greaves because it was clear that, as well as his strength both in the air and on the ground, he had the touch and the persistence to make the fullest contribution to the 4–3–3 system. In some ways, Eric Cantona's rise at Old Trafford reminded me of one of Hurst's most significant assets, that ability to hold on to the ball with a combination of touch, two feet – Hurst's left was more than passable – and a willingness to take punishment.

Hurst had played just five games for England when the World Cup started but, like his club-mate Peters, he had displayed exemplary timing. So, it seemed to me, as we got off the bus and worked on the playing fields of the Bank of England, had Alf Ramsey.

He still had a few days to wrestle with decisions that, in the end, might shape everything in one direction or the other, but I could understand why there had not been any pause in his assurances that we were now so close to winning England's first World Cup. For me at least, riding the bus had brought into a wider but sharper focus a long-held view that England, without doubt, had the men and the means finally to win football's ultimate prize.

17

YOU ONLY LIVE TWICE

MONDAY, 11 JULY 1966 – the first day of the World Cup, a colossal day in my life. However confidently you project your hopes, questions always work away at the back of your mind. When the time comes, will you be ready? When you walk up that gloomy tunnel and hear the first roar of the expectant nation as you hit the bright light of the evening sunshine, will you still be a self-elected champion of the world?

When I parted the curtains, just a little so as not to disturb my still-sleeping room-mate Ray Wilson, and saw a glorious morning, I decided I would. I wanted breakfast and then for the action to come as soon as it might.

It was not as though I had not been well prepared for this moment. I had played sixty-eight times for England, seventeen times more than my next most experienced team-mate, Jimmy Greaves. I was a link between the old days of Finney and Nat Lofthouse and the arrival of Alan Ball and Martin Peters. I was somebody who had seen the best and the worst of English football, some of its genius and quite a bit of its stubborn and arrogant belief that it had nothing to learn from the rest of the world. Most of all, I felt that England's time, and maybe my own, had come.

When Scottish goalkeeper Tommy Younger raced down the field to congratulate me after I had volleyed home Finney's cross, he said that there would be many more goals and many more great days. Surely, I thought now, this one in London would be among them.

I couldn't have asked for more than this feeling of confidence and excitement back in those days when nothing was simple, not even the game that had so dominated my life. If I'd been one to make a prayer, as Nobby did when he went to mass, it would have been that, in the next three weeks, nothing I had learned and been given by the lads who died in Munich, by Billy Wright and Tom Finney, Matt Busby and Jimmy Murphy, my grandfather Tanner and the last of my patrons, Alf Ramsey, would go to waste.

I would have continued, asking that no one would be let down, no one would be able to say that someone who had been given so much did not, when it mattered most, show the nerve and the ability to pay some interest on all that he had received.

I didn't make a list of all those I might be playing for that day, but had I done so it would indeed have been vast. It would have stretched all the way back to Ashington and the North Hirst Primary School, where headmaster James Hamilton had dressed me in a new shining crimson team shirt, placed a miner's hat under my arm, to represent a ball, and sent me running into the classroom while he hummed the theme of 'Sports Report'. It would have included George Benson, the games master at Bedlington Grammar School, defying another head-master and driving me to the station so that I wouldn't be late joining England Schoolboys.

Of course my mother Cissie would have been on it, such a ferocious supporter of Jack and me, and my father Robert, working down the mine and taking his little horse to the shore-line to collect coal to augment our income, and talking about football not out of his great fascination for it – he was a boxer at heart – but out of what he considered a duty to his sons.

In football, you can never give guarantees and Ramsey knew

that when he told the nation that his team would deliver the World Cup. But on this bright morning, I believed that he knew what kind of team he had and that when he talked of winning he did it from a hard professional perspective. Two years earlier he had told us that Brazil would not be a factor and now he said that if Portugal, Germany and Argentina had to be respected, none of them had reason to believe they had the means to push us aside on our own soil.

I believed Alf, I agreed with every word he said, because I felt it myself. Alf could be distant, even elusive, but anyone who knew football also recognised that, about the game, no one could have been more focused, and possibly no one on earth was less inclined to say something he didn't mean or could not support from his own experience. So when I went down the stairs for breakfast I found myself thinking, 'We have a great record at Wembley and now we go overseas and beat almost everyone we play. So when we have the world here in England, and possibly at Wembley for every game, why the hell can't we win this World Cup?'

The night before, Ramsey had followed his custom of informing individually those who would be playing, this time in the opening game against Uruguay. The big news was that John Connelly, a traditional winger, had resisted, for one game at least, the challenge of Ramsey's man of the future, Martin Peters. Jimmy Greaves's latest flurry of goals, and clear evidence that he had recovered fully from the draining effects of hepatitis, had held in check the march of Geoff Hurst. Otherwise, it was all as expected: Banks, Cohen, Wilson, Stiles, Charlton J., Moore, Ball, Greaves, Charlton R., Hunt, Connelly.

The manager's selection routine, he told us, had grown from his belief that it was right that we should have plenty of time to gather ourselves and sleep on the task that faced us. It was not the easiest one that could have been put before us, Ramsey agreed, but if we were going to win this tournament, we could not allow ourselves to be intimidated by the notoriously efficient defence of Uruguay.

As a significant South American football nation, who stole away from Rio with the World Cup in 1950, inevitably Uruguay would have players of skill, notably Pedro Rocha and Julio Cesar Cortes, but we could be sure the limit of their ambition would be to frustrate us on the way, at the very best, to sneaking a goal on the counter-attack. As we tended not to concede goals – just one in our last five games – a little resolution and patience should enable us to make a positive start.

Ramsey was always attentive to detail before a game, he never left any of us unsure about what was expected of us individually, but nor did he burden us with excessive concern about the strength of the opposition. He knew the mentality of his team and, as far I was concerned, the set-up was perfect.

It did not go beyond the specifics of the jobs we had to do. Each player would receive a word or two, a nudge in one direction or another, depending on how Alf suspected the game would unfold. Against Uruguay the priorities were clear enough. We had to penetrate the tank traps of their defence without an unacceptable degree of risk at the back. A win would be good. A draw, with France and Mexico to come in the group games, would not seriously imperil our hopes, but a loss might just bring disaster.

It all seemed straightforward enough until you remembered that, in terms of defence, Uruguay were the South American equivalent of Italy. For both, protecting their goal was not so much a chore as an expression of national character. There were many things you could not do to Uruguayans and the plundering of an easy chance was one of them.

Ramsey also made it clear that he had picked a team for one game rather than the whole tournament. Peters and Hurst, wingers Terry Paine and Ian Callaghan and full back Jimmy Armfield had chances of playing that went beyond the possibility of injuries to their colleagues. As far as he was concerned, every player, whatever his reputation, still had everything to prove.

I followed my usual rituals, including taking the option of light morning training at a local ground. I wrote a few letters, as I had done in the company of Billy Wright before my first game against Scotland eight years earlier, and strolled into Hendon to post them. It was not an age of hysteria but I felt the beginnings of a buzz in the street and no shortage of well-wishers. 'Good luck, Bobby, you can do it,' they said and I was obliged to agree.

Three hours before kick-off time, 7.30 p.m., the correct period to allow for proper digestion, according to team doctor Alan Bass, I had poached eggs, my staple on match days.

When the bus neared the stadium you could see the England banners and flags and the optimistic faces, and for a little while we were hushed. It had been a long journey and now perhaps in a few hours' time we would have the first concrete evidence that we had been travelling in the right direction.

You could feel the tension building in the dressing room before the buzzer announced there were five minutes to go, then a minute, before we had to walk up the tunnel. Some players, Alan Ball inevitably among them, chattered, others slipped into their own thoughts. George Cohen, as always, went through his elaborate warming-up process.

Ray Wilson and I were in the first stages of a ritual that we would continue to follow as the World Cup wore on. As room-mates we packed our gear in the same bag, which Ray always carried. Twenty minutes before the start, after I'd had my rub-down, he handed me my boots, one at a time. He then passed me an ammonia inhaler – it had to be the same one with the top broken – which I used just once to clear my nostrils.

At the final buzzer we all shook hands and walked out to face both the nation, which expected nothing else but victory, and arguably, for the next ninety minutes at least, the most obdurate football team on earth.

From the first moments, as the blue shirts fell behind the ball in what seemed like a solid pack, it was plain that no one had told Uruguay that the English people, in the stadium and in their homes, had been primed for the biggest national party since the end of the Second World War.

Our problem was two-fold. If the Uruguayans were the most relentless spoilers who made it clear right from the start that they would do anything to stop us – grab, trip, elbow, whatever came to mind – they also carried the threat of brilliant skill. The following morning's headlines were so cruel that even the fervent Scotsman Sean Connery commiserated when he welcomed us to Pinewood studios the following day, but Ramsey defended us as robustly as ever, pointing out that an extremely talented team had failed to get even a sniff of a goal while we pounded against them with scarcely a pause. In fact, I counted just two Uruguayan opportunities, once when Banks was forced to turn a shot from Cortes around a post and then when Jack strained to his limits to squash a dangerous run by the winger Domingo Perez.

By comparison, we did have a few chances, most notably when their goalkeeper Ladislao Mazurkiewicz superbly saved Connelly's deflection of my screaming shot, and then later when a header from the winger dropped on top of the crossbar.

By the end, though, there was no point in kidding ourselves. The party mood had been put on pause. The cheers we had confidently anticipated had turned to boos when we left the field. You couldn't blame the fans. They had been primed for a great statement from their team at the start of the tournament they had come to believe we would win. Uruguay, apart from anything else, explained that perhaps it wasn't a formality. No matter how often we told each other, and ourselves, on the ride home that it was unlikely that any of our most serious rivals would have broken down the Uruguayans on this particular night, there was not much we could do to remove the numbness of anticlimax.

While still awash with adrenalin, it was not easy to rationalise our situation. However, despite the bleak headlines, we had hardly been dealt a fatal blow. Perhaps we had to quicken our game a little more at the front but with group games to come against Mexico, whom we had beaten by eight goals five years earlier, and a quite lightly regarded France, our place in the quarter-finals was surely not in serious jeopardy.

In fact, by the time we were mixing with Connery and Yul Brynner, George Segal and Robert Morley at Pinewood the following afternoon, we were identifying quite happily with the title of the film being shot, the James Bond adventure, *You Only Live Twice*. It was unlikely, we concluded, that either Mexico or France would pose any unanswerable questions against that claim.

We had gone to the studios at the instigation of the team doctor, Alan Bass. He had a contact there and Alf agreed that a visit would make a good break from the pressure that had been growing so strong in the days before the first match. We were given such a warm welcome that the manager, already a confirmed film buff, was moved to give a speech of thanks. There were some suppressed giggles from some of us when he thanked, particularly, 'Seen' Connery for his support but Alf sailed on, happy that we had found, for a few hours at least, some haven from the critics and the disappointed fans.

Our belief that all was far from lost was encouraged by Ramsey, and in support of that he had decided to ban us from reading the newspapers. It was perhaps a wise move because most of the headlines were saying that our challenge was virtually over before it had begun – a sharp divergence from his own belief that what had happened against Uruguay was really quite predictable when only one team had chased victory, and at no risk of a defeat, which might just have been something to worry about.

It did seem, however, that a large body of opinion had shifted back to the position taken by England's leading TV pundit when we had lost our last match. Nearly a year and twelve games earlier Austria had beaten us in a friendly at Wembley and Jimmy Hill had declared to the nation, 'We will not win the World Cup, but don't blame Alf Ramsey. No one could win with this lot.'

We had been defying that view with ever-increasing conviction right up to the moment of running into the pale-blue spider's web of Uruguay's defence.

Still, within twenty-four hours of the disappointment, our confidence was definitely on the rise again. Especially when we received that unexpected support from James Bond himself, the man who had single-handedly wrecked so many foreign conspiracies. Sean Connery said to us that he could not have been more certain that England would win the World Cup, and added, 'I'm honoured to meet you and I know everyone should put their trust in you.' A Scottish accent had never sounded so sweet in the ears of our manager.

18

UP AND RUNNING

I CANNOT SAY it was the best goal that I ever scored for England, and I wouldn't claim, as some do, that it finally convinced both the nation and team we could indeed win the World Cup, but about one thing I can be certain – I never felt more relieved, or elated, to see the ball smash into the back of the net.

The goal broke the resistance of our opponents, who, but for a certain shortfall of technical ability, might have been dressed in the blue of Uruguay rather than the plum-coloured shirts of Mexico, and I felt a surge of gratitude for the unsung hero of the thirty-sixth-minute strike. The man who made it possible was Roger Hunt.

I have already spoken of the unselfishness and the biting instinct he brought to his running and here, as the tension began to rise with every desperate Mexican tackle, every English move of promise that finished in futility, he provided a classic example.

The move started when Martin Peters, who was playing with great confidence after coming into the team for Alan Ball (the other victim of the Uruguayan impasse was John Connelly, who was replaced by Terry Paine), broke up a rare Mexican attack and passed quickly to Hunt, who immediately transferred the ball to me.

I was still in my own half but I had space and thought, as I do today when I see a player free of a marker in his own terri-tory, 'Why not carry the ball forward, take the game to the other team from whatever position you find?' Against Mexico, in a game that was proving as frustrating as we had feared when we saw our opponents retreat *en masse* at the first whistle, the need to address that question was pressing. I looked around and saw that Hunt had found me in a good pocket of space and so I ran forward as quickly as I could. In this first contribution to the move initiated by Peters and carried forward by Hunt, I was following, as I would be in the final moment of the passage of play, another piece of advice from my teacher Jimmy Murphy.

On so many Saturdays after the match, and even when I ceased to be a single lad with time on my hands at the digs, Jimmy had come into the dressing room and suggested I went round to the ground on Sunday morning to work with him. On some weekends in the early days, perhaps after a particularly hard match or a night out with Tommy Taylor or Shay Brennan, which often seemed to call for a Sunday morning lie-in, it was something of an effort. But I never declined and not once was there a session when I didn't learn something new. The morning usually ended with him taking me for a pint in the pub around the corner from the ground.

Now, in the rising thunder of Wembley, I remembered one of his insights. 'If you get the ball in space, move with it as quickly as you can over the first ten to twenty yards,' he told me. 'This serves two purposes. It will discourage a front player from chasing you and it will create a little confusion among the defenders.'

So I followed one of Murphy's many laws as the Mexicans retreated before me. 'There's no one around me,' I thought, 'so let's run and see what happens.'

No Mexican gave chase and, as I moved forward, I saw that Hunt was performing the football equivalent of an American running back blazing a trail for the man with the ball. He was darting backwards and forwards and I knew exactly what he was doing. He was drawing the Mexicans away from me, creating a diversion, and the more he did it, the more I was able to settle on the idea of testing the goalkeeper, Ignacio Calderon.

Roger had so preoccupied the Mexicans they failed to send in anyone to challenge me. Had they done so, at that distance from the goal, I would almost certainly have laid the ball off to Peters or Paine. Instead, as I swayed first to the left, then to the right, I was still asking, 'When is somebody going to come to me?'

But they didn't, they stayed back, still mesmerised by Hunt's decoy run, and as I progressed forward, once again Jimmy Murphy's voice was ringing in my ears. 'Just hit it in the general direction and put your faith in the flight of the ball.'

Further encouragement to fly the ball at Calderon's goal was the quality of the Wembley pitch. On a surface as smooth as silk I thought, 'My stride will decide when I shoot.' As it happened, I didn't have to break my rhythm and between twenty-five and thirty yards out, I did as Murphy had urged me – 'Blast it, Bobby, and let the goalie worry about where it's going to finish up.'

I didn't look up before I shot with my right foot but when I did raise my head, I saw that only a miraculous save would deny me. Calderon did well, he wasn't so far away, but I do like to think that no goalkeeper on earth would have stopped it.

This, many would say, was the moment England found their way into the World Cup – and regained the momentum that had gathered strongly in our build-up matches. Down on the field, I didn't see it at all in such broad terms as I trotted back for the restart. I was delighted that I had been able to cut through the Mexican defensive blanket but all I could really think was that the match was won – and that I had never been so fit in my life.

At the age of twenty-eight, and with a Wembley crowd cheering you on in the belief that the World Cup was suddenly within touching distance, this was something to say. It was maybe the loveliest, most exhilarating feeling I had ever had as a footballer.

I felt so full of running, as though I could do it all day. I said to myself, 'You know, right now you could probably run a ten-second hundred yards.' But then I thought for a moment, and added, 'No you couldn't. Maybe eleven seconds, though.'

When my shot swirled past Calderon, the overwhelming feeling was that we should enjoy the rest of the game to compensate for all the frustration and criticism that had swept over us at the end of the Uruguayan deadlock. Another strong sensation, which often came over me at Wembley, was one of freedom. The crowd, though you could hear them well enough, were set back from the pitch, which meant that when things weren't going so well they were less oppressive than in many other places on the football landscape, and if you had the energy and instinct, it seemed there was always plenty of space to find.

If someone had the patience to trawl through all the detail on the video of the Mexico match, they might find evidence of exactly how good I felt at that time. I reacted to the half-time whistle in a way that, looking back, seems a little bizarre.

As the teams came off the field I sprinted, for no apparent reason, forty or fifty yards. There was no point except maybe to express quite how uplifted I was. 'Feeling like this, playing so confidently for such high stakes under a manager and alongside players you trust, well, this is football paradise,' I thought. 'This is the way it always has to be. What is there to worry about? We're ready for France now.'

In fact, Ramsey was quick to put a check on the euphoria. We still had another half to play and were just one goal ahead. However spectacular it had been, the goal still counted as one, and if Mexico lacked a little of the iron of Uruguay, and quite a lot of their skill, they were not without some menace. When I came down from my spectacular view of the world, I noted that the Mexicans had a dangerous, clever striker in Enrique Borja, and in midfield and along the flanks Isidoro Diaz and Aaron Padilla had some good skills and excellent energy. They were not easily killed off and when the concluding stroke came, with fourteen minutes to go, it took quite a lot of work from Peters and me, and a typically easy strike from Greaves. Peters and I exchanged passes along the left before I fed the ball in to Greaves. Jimmy's shot was palmed out by Calderon, but Roger Hunt was there to follow up and the Mexican lights were switched off as decisively as if he'd flicked a switch.

Alf Ramsey made sure that we kept the victory in perspective. He said that we had played better than we had done against Uruguay, but still we had work to do, and if we hadn't beaten Mexico, we would have been exposed as false contenders for the most important prize in football. Even so, the hard edge of tension that had accompanied us home to Hendon Hall after the Uruguay game had almost completely disappeared, and a quick glance at the morning's back pages would be a lot more psychologically rewarding than if Ramsey had permitted us the doubtful privilege after that first goalless draw. At least, this was true beyond the concerns of a few players who may have felt they had not advanced their claims for a secure place in the team.

Terry Paine had, for example, less reason for satisfaction than Peters. Paine was skilful on the wing, and a tough player, but Peters had looked good both in defence and attack. Martin had been involved in both our goals and his reading of the game from a defensive position was acute and perfectly expressed when he made the interception that put in motion my opening strike. The burden on Paine's shoulders was carried less easily. Ramsey, everybody knew now, was balancing carefully the value of the width provided by a winger on top of his game and the impact of a worker of Ball's dynamic energy – and quality of touch on the ball. Paine had his moments against Mexico but it had to be doubtful if they had been numerous enough or sufficiently menacing.

It seemed most likely that if a now slightly subdued Ball was to get back into the team, it would be at the expense of one of the wingers rather than Peters, who could not have established his claims with any greater conviction.

Nobby had grown very fond of Ball. He loved the passion and natural buoyancy of his room-mate, which in so many ways, of course, mirrored his own, and he reported that Alan was taking his exclusion very hard – not on the surface, perhaps, and certainly not on the training ground, but there were moments when Nobby had seen, as never before, doubt in the eyes of the young player.

Nobby tells a revealing story of Ball's mood after he had a win on the horses when he was agonising over his chances of a recall. Apparently, Alan spread his winnings, a few fivers, on the hotel bedroom floor and performed a breezy little tap dance, finishing with the statement that Alf Ramsey could go to hell or something very much to that effect.

Of course, it was a front. Alan admired Ramsey deeply and was desperate to win back his approval. Before this could happen, though, he had to continue to slave away in training and show that he remained very much part of the squad. Unsurprisingly, he did this splendidly, maybe with a little reinforcement from Ball Senior in their daily phone conferences.

Ramsey's emphasis in training was on increasing the pace of our game. He'd noted that our stamina at Wembley was markedly superior to that of our early opposition, and he wanted it to develop even more during the course of the tournament. Harold Shepherdson and his assistant, the fighting-cock trainer of Leeds, Les Cocker, were given full rein in the matter of cracking the whip. There were also some specifics to attend to, most notably a certain weakness Ramsey had detected in the way we lined up to defend free kicks. This problem would recur at a most critical point of the tournament, by way of confirming the legitimacy of Ramsey's concern, but for the moment he decided that an hour's intense work at the training ground was sufficient to deal with it.

A television, serviced by two technicians, had been installed at our hotel so that we could watch other games live, and we were beginning to get a good sense of how the tournament was unfolding, and how some of our most threatening rivals were approaching their campaigns. Alf insisted that our selection of live games must be determined by our need to see upcoming opposition. Still, we were able to watch Mexico's goalless draw with Uruguay, although it was redundant to our research – and much less compelling than the battle between the physically battered holders Brazil and the highly-gifted Portugal at Goodison Park.

The Mexico–Uruguay stalemate was probably a more intriguing game than our own firing of blanks against the South Americans in the opening match, what with the return of the Mexicans' thirty-seven-year-old goalkeeper Antonio Carbajal, who was playing in a record fifth World Cup. Borja, the player who had so impressed me when he performed against us a few days earlier, strove hard to score the two goals his team needed to reach the quarter-finals, but inevitably the match paled against the bitter drama of events on Merseyside.

The process that reached a sickening conclusion with Pelé, the best of all time, hobbling out of the tournament he had already twice graced so magnificently, and would do again four years later in Mexico, started grimly in the same ground a week earlier against Bulgaria. If you had merely read the details of the scoreline – Brazil 2 (Pelé, Garrincha) Bulgaria 0 – you would have had every reason to believe that all was still well with the world champions. But the reality was much darker. By the time he blasted in Brazil's first goal in the thirteenth minute, from a free kick awarded against Dobromir Jetchev, who would spend most of his time apparently intent on halting the great man in his tracks, Pelé was already bruised and seething with anger. His face was a picture of grim satisfaction when he sent the ball hurtling past Georgi Naidenov. There was no Brazilian subtlety in this set-piece. It was a statement of raw power and the desire for instant revenge.

Later the referee, Kurt Tschenscher, had to separate Pelé and Jetchev and book the Bulgarian. Today, Jetchev would scarcely have survived the first exchanges before being dismissed from the field. Pelé said later, 'My legs ached as a result of Jetchev's constant tripping and kicking.' Shockingly, this was only the beginning of Pelé's ordeal. He was still recovering from his injuries when Brazil's campaign was thrust into crisis by a brilliant display from Hungary, England's conquerors at the same stage of the tournament four years earlier in Chile. But if Hungary had been impressive in Chile, beating us 2–1, they were quite luminous in the 3–1 win over Brazil. Ferenc Bene and Florian Albert, the players who were said to be in the process of reviving the Hungarian football legend created by Puskas's team, tormented the Brazilians, and not least Garrincha, who was, poignantly enough, playing his fiftieth and last game on a day when the best he could do was probe in the margins of a ruinous match.

The result meant that Brazil were playing for their World Cup lives against Portugal, and Pelé, despite being far from full fitness, was obliged to return to the battlefield. Goodison Park was all of that. It was also the site of an extremely sad day for football, a time when the culture of violence reached one of its most brutal expressions, and if we were not unfamiliar with ruthless, dangerous tackling in English football, and nasty gamesmanship, perhaps we were not quite prepared for the game to be so callously disfigured at the level of a World Cup.

Anyone who cared about football had to be saddened at the sight of Pelé being hacked out of the competition, and as I watched him being helped off the field while Portugal marched on to the 3–1 win that sent the champions home, I felt a certain smarting in my eyes. This, after all, was not just another highly talented footballer. He was the light of the game, its prized possession, its greatest example to kids in every corner of the world who were now seeing, on flickering black-and-white TV screens, their hero cut down.

I thought of the impression he had made on me that first time we met on the field at the Maracana, when he shouted, 'Goooo . . . aaaall,' the moment he drove the ball, and I felt a wave of nausea sweep over me.

What was most surprising, and depressing, was that it was Portugal, a team whose football spirit I had always admired, who were the perpetrators of this systematic outrage. They had a team full of character and wonderfully skilful players, including Eusebio, who scored two of the three goals that banished Brazil, Mario Coluna and the big striker Jose Torres, but it was clear they came on to the field not to produce the best of such talent but to commit sustained skulduggery.

It was at times like this that you feared for the future of football, because here was a nation who, in my experience, had always displayed exactly the right attitude when they played even the most vital games. Earlier that year, my young Manchester United team-mate George Best had produced a devastating performance in the European Cup to shatter Benfica's nine-year unbeaten record at the Estadio da Luz. Yet this team, whose players would form the majority of the Portugal side that waged the most unscrupulous war on Brazil a few months later, took no cynical action against their youthful torturer. At Goodison Park, though, a decision seemed to have been made that the only way they could beat Brazil was by kicking Pelé out of the game, which they did quite without shame.

Perhaps history gave the match a little edge, with the mother country envious of the football achievements of a former colony, but in terms of the true meaning of the game, on its global stage, this surely was among the ugliest of football travesties.

There were long-term implications. In Mexico four years later, with Pelé majestically revived, Brazil would achieve their most glorious World Cup triumph but when they came to travel to West Germany in 1974, the eight-year-old scars of Goodison were still so livid they sent a squad almost unrecognisable in its emphasis on physical strength rather than the highest skill. Pelé was not present, his international days were over, and you could only say it was a kind of blessing.

Back in Hendon Hall, the England players understood that, whatever the circumstances of their departure, and Ramsey's long-held doubts about their ability to go all the way, the most feared name in world football had been removed from the list of contenders.

It was not such a relief, though, when we considered the strength of the teams who were marching through to the quarter-finals. Argentina, under the commanding leadership of their tall captain Antonio Rattin and their notoriously combative coach Juan Carlos Lorenzo, showed that they could travel well by defeating a Spanish side who had hoped to be inspired by the brilliant Luis Suarez. If the Portuguese had been brutal, they had the power and quality of Eusebio, potentially the giant of the tournament following the departure of Pelé. The Hungarians were sparkling and both the West Germans and the USSR were displaying enough skill and discipline to worry anyone.

Before joining them, plus North Korea and Uruguay, in the quarter-finals, we had the formal business of disposing of France. This did not promise to be a dangerous challenge. Ian Callaghan would be England's final investment in a traditional wide man, taking over from Terry Paine, but Alan Ball would have to fret on the touchline again as the manager restricted himself to the one change. Geoff Hurst, who had made such a strong case for himself while winning his five caps, would also have to stretch out his patience a little more under the shadow of Greaves's scoring genius. For the rest of us, it was more of that which had, in the end, comfortably dispatched Mexico.

In our room the night before the match, before slipping into sleep, which came easily, Ray Wilson and I agreed, once again, that we had no pressing reasons to concern ourselves. The French had some skill, but it seemed unlikely that they would have the strength to give us any serious trouble.

No doubt Nobby Stiles and Jimmy Greaves were similarly relaxed. Nobby had become almost a symbol of the 'New England', tough, resilient and wonderfully sure about what he was doing, and Greaves's talent was unique, a threat to any of our most serious rivals if he could be supplied with enough opportunities. They, along with the rest of us, would pass by the French serenely enough.

Unfortunately, football, like life, is often a lot more treacherous than it appears.

19

CRISIS MANAGEMENT

To spectators, the French game may not have looked too menacing, and nor was it, even though our play lacked the drive and pace Alf Ramsey had been demanding in our training sessions. But long before it was over, and Roger Hunt had scored the second of his two unanswered goals that made a quarter-final place safe, our manager knew the match had left him his two most critical tests since taking over England.

First, he would have to fight for the international career of his – and my – beloved Nobby Stiles. Second, he would have to wrestle, against the widening backcloth of a national debate, with the possibility that a passing injury, a gash on the shin, to Jimmy Greaves had given him a chance to reinstate fully the system that had brought such a glow to the sky above Madrid eight months earlier. And if he did this with the success he anticipated, where would that leave the national folk hero Greaves? There could be no doubt it would result in him riding a great wave of public sympathy if he stayed on the sidelines after recovering from injury.

Greaves was absent through illness when the Wingless Wonders had been unveiled to such dramatic effect in the 2–0 win over Spain at the Bernabeu, and although he had restored himself with his burst of goals against Norway, it seemed to me that Ramsey still hankered strongly for the simplicities and industry that had overwhelmed the Spanish.

Greaves was a sublime finisher on his good days but they continued to be rare in World Cup games, and the pattern was threatening to become entrenched with his failure to score in any of the group matches. His overall record for England was superb, forty-four goals in fifty-seven internationals, but it fell away sharply when you looked solely at World Cup action, for which his record was one, against Argentina in Chile, in seven appearances.

It was also true that if Greaves wasn't scoring, his contribution to the kind of performance Ramsey was now demanding tended to be not much more than ornamental. Ramsey needed goals, desperately, but he also wanted the work-rate that dominated the opposition and ultimately made scoring more likely. This was the cue, surely, for Geoff Hurst, who had fought his way ahead of a player some believed was more naturally talented, Chelsea's Peter Osgood. Hurst brought the great advantage of being able to hold up the ball under the kind of pressure we had already encountered, and were likely to experience in a sharply intensified form against Argentina in the quarter-final game.

The fact that Ramsey had much on his mind was evident when we got back to the Hendon Hall Hotel, following our defeat of the French. After excluding the scorer Hunt from all criticism, he picked a series of holes in our performance. He pointed out that even though their player Roby Herbin became virtually a passenger after an early collision with Nobby, we never moved coherently enough to exploit the advantage properly. We had presumed too much of our superiority and the certainty of the victory. If this mood continued, we would pay the heaviest price against superior teams such as Argentina or Portugal.

We sat, uncomfortably, as Ramsey laid out his complaints – and no one more so than Nobby Stiles. The trouble was that while Ramsey was talking about a crisis in form, Nobby was confronting a crisis in his career.

Later, he said that he couldn't remember clearly the build-up of play that left the polished French player Jacky Simon in a heap while he received a lecture from the Peruvian referee Arturo Yamasaki – and a booking from a Fifa official in the stand.

What he was sure about, though, was that his intention was both to win the ball and to remind Simon that he could not dwell on his creative thoughts without the risk of some quick and hard attention. Now, I realise I may be in danger of being charged with a certain contradiction if, so soon after castigating the Bulgarians and the Portuguese for their assaults on Pelé, I rush to the defence of my friend Nobby. There is no doubt he made a tackle that was, from any viewpoint, shocking. It provoked the battling but always fair-minded George Cohen to think, 'Oh, Christ, Nobby, that looks bad.'

That was the reaction of the Fifa observer, some members of the Football Association hierarchy, and just about every Fleet Street headline writer – 'Stiles Horror Tackle Brings England Crisis' screamed one back page. By the morning, it was clear that immense pressure would be applied to Ramsey. The argument was that England should have no part in such tactics and Stiles should be banished from the World Cup. Nobby was distraught, close to tears, and I felt for him deeply.

This wasn't to close my eyes to violence in football. Like most attacking players who lived by speed and a certain amount of skill, I had been a victim of unscrupulous tactics and would be again in the future. A few years later, in a vicious collision with the Argentine club team Estudiantes my shin was cut to the bone, and all through my career I ran a gauntlet of heavy tackling and often worse. But what I knew most about Nobby was his honesty.

Yes, he knew that part of his role was to tackle hard and put players such as Simon, and me for that matter, on their guard against taking too many liberties. Nobby had a well-deserved reputation in English football for being a physical player – most First Division teams had at least two of them – yet in all the games I had played with him for United and England, I had never seen Nobby doing anything sneaky, vicious or vindictive. He would fight on equal terms, and if somebody wanted to foul him, he would return the compliment in at least equal measure, and he would protect his team-mates fiercely, but I don't believe he ever went on the field with the idea of injuring a fellow professional.

Unfortunately, in this case the tackle on Simon was, at the very least, extremely late, and as George Cohen said, it looked horrendous.

Later, Nobby explained, 'As I first recalled the build-up, we were attacking along the right with George Cohen on the ball and Simon, a very good player, tracking him. When the French goalkeeper, Marcel Aubour, gathered up the ball and threw it out to Simon, I was already on the move, watching the ball looping down and lining up my tackle. George remembers it differently. He said the ball reached Simon via a throw-in and that I came in so late the Frenchman just collapsed in a heap in front of the royal box.

'What I should say is that for certain my intention was to hit the ball – and him – just as he turned. It is not a foul if you go through the ball, hitting it with all the force you have, and that takes you through the player. That is a hard but legal tackle and it is what I intended to do.

'Unfortunately for Jacky Simon, and me, on this occasion he did not dwell on the ball. He moved it on first touch and I steamed into a man without the ball.'

Nobby wore a hang-dog expression as we worked at training under the supervision of Harold Shepherdson and Les Cocker. For once, Alf Ramsey was not around to put us under his microscope and, soon enough, word was out that he had been summoned to the Football Association offices at Lancaster Gate.

It could only mean one thing. The FA, in an effort to appease Fifa, was going to demand Nobby's head.

A great tide of criticism was rolling over my friend. The much-respected Joe Mercer, working as a TV panellist, said that Nobby had committed such a terrible tackle it shamed all of English football. Danny Blanchflower and Billy Wright agreed. His one public defender beyond the England camp was Jimmy Hill, who said that while no one could condone the tackle, it was wrong to pillory a lad who had fought so hard for his country and was plainly not malicious. Some time later, Nobby told me with great delight that he had met Simon at a five-a-side tournament and been assured that no permanent damage had resulted. The Frenchman had played on for two more years. He said to Nobby, as they shook hands, that it was the kind of incident that was always going to happen in a contact sport and there were absolutely no hard feelings.

A rather different message was emanating from Lancaster Gate, however. Apparently, Ramsey was told he had a duty to English football, and the image of the World Cup, to jettison one of his most consistently successful players. Later, Nobby was told of Ramsey's reply – 'Well, gentlemen, most certainly Nobby Stiles can be thrown off the team but I must tell you that I see him as a very important player for England, one who has done very well for the team since he was selected, and that if he goes, so do I. I should you tell that you will be looking for a new manager.'

If anything was guaranteed to send a surge of team spirit into every corner of the dressing room, surely it was this declaration of total commitment by a manager to the players he had hand-picked.

The effect was compounded on the morning before the quarter-final with Argentina. Nobby still didn't know his fate when Alf walked across to him on the training field. The exchange was brief and Ramseyesque. He didn't want any elaborate explanation from Nobby. He just asked, 'Did you mean it?'

Nobby said, 'No, Alf, I didn't. I mistimed the tackle.'

Then Alf uttered the few words that might just as well have been a battle cry. He said, 'You're playing tomorrow.' So would, Alf confirmed later that day, Alan Ball, again, and Geoff Hurst.

We had come almost full circle from the unveiling of the battle plan in Madrid. Against France, Callaghan, such a fine player with Liverpool, had failed to strengthen the case for an out-and-out winger that had been left undecided by the perform-ances of his predecessors, Connelly and Paine. Ball's sideline agonies were over. The iron guard of England's defence, which had worked through the group games without ever suggesting seriously that they were in danger of conceding a goal, was to remain the same for this most critical match, perhaps the most challenging of the whole tournament. The places of Joe Baker and George Eastham, from the team who had faced Spain in December 1965, went to two players who could be most clearly identified as creations of the Ramsey reign.

Looking back now, I have to suspect that Alf's feeling was that he had arrived at the eleven whom he believed most suited his purposes. Yes, there were still players out there eminently qualified to play international football. Some had made the case for the virtuoso Osgood over Hurst, and the passing inconven-ience of Greaves's injury persuaded others that England were critically weakened, while yet another group asked quite what it was that Peters did, was he a defender, an attacker – or a figment of the manager's imagination?

That question mark had been removed from Peters by all those who had played with him in the potentially difficult games against Mexico and France. We had seen the intelligent move-ment, the deceptive running, the sound tackles and the insightful passing.

Even today, some who like to review history and put their

own slant on it argue that Ramsey stumbled upon his final formula, a team that would play, unchanged, through the knockout phase. They say that one bright performance from the trio of wingers might have kept Ball in cotton wool, and that if Greaves had found his scoring touch early on, his injury would have been merely a temporary problem. My own belief is that in Madrid, Ramsey, like Villalonga, concluded that England indeed had the means to win the World Cup and, despite his last experiments in the group games, which he was always confident of surviving, he never strayed too far from the prototype revealed on that thrilling Spanish night.

With Nobby's crisis resolved – the extent of his punishment was a public warning from Fifa's disciplinary committee, which some thought, misguidedly, would neutralise his most vital qualities – our team spirit had become stronger than ever. When Alf stood shoulder to shoulder with Nobby, and declared that if the player he respected so much fell, he would go down with him, he exceeded the value of a thousand pep talks. In that one curt sentence, 'You're playing tomorrow,' he offered his version of Henry V on the eve of Agincourt. Well, at the time it seemed more than a little that way.

But however close knit we became at Hendon Hall, and however skilfully Ramsey had exploited the siege mentality that developed in the dressing room when Nobby's place in the World Cup was threatened, I still missed my family and looked forward to the daily ten-minute phone call home to Manchester. I missed my daughters Suzanne and Andrea very much and each day they asked, 'Daddy, when are you coming home?' I urged Norma to travel down to see all our games but she said it wasn't practical except for night games because of the arrangements she had to make for the care of the children.

Sometimes I am asked about the way players are accompanied to the big tournaments these days by wives and girlfriends, and what I think of the publicity that surrounded the WAGs of

England in the last World Cup in Germany. I have to say that I recognise the world has changed and that what the boys of '66 accepted as normal would never be countenanced by the modern footballer.

Occasionally, I permit myself a wry smile, along with a little disbelief, when I read of celebrity footballers hiring small armies of security men for their weddings – mostly to thwart photographers of publications other than the one that has agreed to meet much of the cost of the celebrations – and I think of the day Norma and I were married in St Gabriel's Church in North Manchester. Some United fans arrived wearing their scarves and waving their rattles, noisily offering us their best wishes. I would have preferred not to have that kind of attention on a day I always consider more precious than anything that happened on a football field. They were very good-hearted, though, and now I recall them as representatives of another age, another existence.

For many reasons, I have tried to keep family life and football life separate, and one of them is that, when I was still playing, Norma could adopt quite a bossy approach. She once asked Bill Shankly what he thought of the 4–3–3 system. Shankly, who was reputed to have taken his wife Nessie to a reserve match on their wedding anniversary, was, naturally, charmed.

However, when she came down for the Mexico match, she wasn't so keen to discuss the theory of the game. No, what she wanted to know was why I had failed to score against Uruguay. When I met her before the game, we could hardly talk for all the thousands of fans milling around the entrances, and so we took a walk around the stadium. We spoke of the girls, of how they were progressing, of events back home and some of my impressions of the tournament.

I told Norma that the goals would come, for both me and the team, and that I was still very confident of our prospects.

I added that while it was hard to be parted so for long, this was a great opportunity that could change our lives for the better.

Norma recognised this, and much more. So much hard work and dedication had gone into the task, and so many other good footballers had been disappointed along the road that stretched back to the appointment of Alf Ramsey three years earlier, that failure would be hard to bear.

'Bobby,' she said, 'don't let us down.' As we kissed goodbye, I assured her it was not my intention.

20

WHY ARE WE WAITING?

WE BEAT ARGENTINA, the team I had feared most in the tournament after seeing them demolish Brazil on their own soil two years earlier, but like my team-mates I was not awash with joy. It's hard to celebrate when you have a rank taste in your mouth.

Sometimes in football, as in life, you know straightaway that the best you can hope for is to get through a match, or a day, and still feel whole at the end of it. At least then you can say you have done the best that was possible and move on to something better, ideally something that will not always remind you that the line between the best and the worst, victory and defeat, can be shockingly fine. Occasionally, if that line is crossed, it can be by a distressingly wide margin. That is what happened the day we fought our way past Argentina, wiped the spit from our eyes and saw more clearly than ever before that the World Cup was within reach.

In the ten years since making my debut in senior football against Charlton Athletic, not once had I played in a game that so thoroughly debased the true meaning of football. On all my travels with Manchester United and England I had inevitably been involved in many matches that had fallen heavily from the ideal of how sport should be conducted. I had been kicked, obstructed, tripped and spat upon but never before had I experienced so much foul practice applied so intensely and so relentlessly.

Afterwards, Ramsey made himself a hostage to fate, the

244

consequences of which would emerge so dangerously four years later in the Mexican World Cup, when he dismissed the Argentines as 'animals', an insult that caused outrage throughout Latin America. Later, when the anger had dissipated, I felt an overriding sadness and regret that the team who had dragged football into the dirt, you could tell almost at first glance, clearly had the capacity to take it to the stars.

They had beautiful skill, displayed in sudden bursts of speed, breaking a rhythm that a second before might have lulled you towards a little nap. Technically, they could produce football that was nothing less than awesome, but on this day they were intent on delivering something quite different. Almost from the first whistle, they spat out their phlegm and their hate, induced by what I could only believe was a terrible inferiority complex. Why it should emerge so nakedly on a world stage when they had such lovely talent was a mystery that was beyond me.

In some ways, it remains so today. Despite Anglo–Argentine relations suffering a far more profound trauma with the war in the South Atlantic, and with the exception of that other eruption of football skulduggery when I played for United against Estudiantes after we won the European Cup in 1968, I have always been charmed by my visits to Argentina. Buenos Aires is a beautiful, elegant city. I love the snap of the place and find it easy to understand why it is the home of the tango. Off the field, I have never been treated there with anything less than warmth and courtesy.

I doubt I have ever admired anyone more in football, not even Pelé, than arguably Argentina's greatest football son, Alfredo di Stefano. Since I first saw him in the Bernabeu – by which time he had changed his nationality to Spanish after playing six times for his homeland and winning four caps for the outlawed Colombian football association during a stint with a Bogota club – I have always believed him to be a glorious example of the game's best qualities: strength, supreme skill, pride and wonderful competitive values.

It is an honour to proclaim him a friend and among my best memories is one of him showing me the city of his youth, pointing out where, as an impoverished kid, he would leap from a bridge on to a British-made train and then jump off when it passed the Boca Stadium. There he would climb over the barriers and the wire to see his favourite team, Boca Juniors.

I have played five-a-side football with one of the nation's most successful, if controversial, politicians, former president Carlos Menem, and found him to be quite useful on the ball, which is what you would expect of any of his countrymen. Even the captain of Argentina on that disgraceful day, Antonio Rattin, has displayed his charming side down the years. Rattin is a politician now and whenever we are together at some Fifa function he seeks me out and could not be friendlier.

However, all of this becomes a background blur when I think of Saturday, 23 July 1966.

Reliving that day again now, I feel all the old anger that was probably best expressed by Ray Wilson in the dressing room after the match. We were relieved to have survived the afternoon, physically intact and with the win that took us into the semi-final against Portugal, and most of us were grateful for the chance to sit on the benches and try to make sense of what had just happened. We were agitated, understandably. There had certainly been the potential for a pitched battle when the teams came off the field and entered the tunnel, accompanied by much yelling and gesticulating from each side, and more spitting from the Argentines. But Ramsey was emphatic that our win should not be further complicated or besmirched, and he was desperate to avoid the disciplinary consequences that would surely have followed if punches were thrown, not to mention any serious injuries that may have been sustained. He seemed to be enormously relieved when the last of his players was safely gathered into the dressing room and the big door was locked.

However, the manager's relief was extremely short-lived.

Suddenly, there was loud banging on the door and somebody said, 'Bloody hell, it's the Argies – they want to come in.'

That was when I noticed the expression on Ray Wilson's face, filled with anger and distaste, and the cold look in his eyes, like a fighter sitting on his stool, steeling himself for the bell. He just said, 'Let them.'

Jack was of the same mind and, although I have never believed in violence outside the boxing ring to which our father Robert was always so devoted, I understood the feelings of my team-mates. I have no doubt there would have been quite a scene had some of the lads got their way and opened up the doors, but Ramsey made sure they remained closed until some of the raw emotion had passed and the Argentines had left the stadium, dejected.

Earlier on the pitch we hadn't been paragons of innocence – I later learned that we had the heavier foul count against us. We had put in some hard tackles, for sure. The impeccably honest professional George Cohen later confessed that in one tackle on Luis Artime he had never come closer to crossing the line between acceptable force and something quite different. But we didn't make a joke of the laws, we didn't tug and needle and spit or play football in staccato bursts.

We hadn't reduced the game to a dreadful series of skirmishes – and we hadn't tried to take over the role of the German referee, Rudolf Kreitlein.

The official has been accused of being fussy to the point of becoming pedantic but he seemed sound enough to me in his assessment of the play and the difficulties he faced in controlling the game. In my opinion, there was no question that eventually his only option was to send off Rattin.

We will never know what would have happened if Rattin had committed himself to playing the superior football that was within his capability and that of so many of his team-mates, rather than trying to referee the game. When he wanted to display it, Rattin had natural authority and a superb precision to his passing. What I do know is that until his departure, and, when I think about it, for quite some time after that, I had some serious concern about our chances of overcoming the Argentines if they ever got round to concentrating entirely on the need to play the game.

To my mind, Argentina were the toughest hurdle between us and the World Cup. The worry may have been born on that day in 1964 when I saw them beat Brazil, and it was not diminished a few days before the quarter-final when we watched Argentina's group game with West Germany at Villa Park on the television in Hendon Hall.

Despite the presence of so many talented players, the game was goalless and very tense, especially after Argentina's Albrecht was sent off for kneeing Wolfgang Weber. The Germans probably had slightly the better of the exchanges, and Argentine full back Roberto Perfumo twice put the ball against his own woodwork, but there was something about the Argentines that sent a little chill into your blood. We learned a few days later that Fifa had issued Rattin's men with a warning about their future conduct.

When the game was over, Bobby Moore turned from the television and said, 'I know in my guts it's going to be hard – maybe brutal.'

If I had been an independent observer advising Argentina's belligerent coach Juan Carlos Lorenzo, I would have been quite specific in my warning and it would have gone beyond simply the need for polite behaviour. Argentina were paralysing themselves with an absolute failure to understand their true strengths, those qualities that should have had them announcing their potential as world champions, and stepping out beyond the shadows created by their Brazilian neighbours. As it was, they hid in those shadows, lurking not like champions but instead like would-be assassins. However, I was hardly an impartial witness.

For the sake of England's prospects, I could only hope the Argentines continued to be their own most formidable opponents.

When they came out against us, they certainly looked good in their slowly paced but almost mesmerising control. On the rare occasions they played the ball rather than the man, you could see their potential for explosive attack and quite startling powers of acceleration. As a midfielder, I was particularly apprehensive about the promise of Ermindo Onega. He had wonderful positional sense and a superb left foot. He gave them bite and balance and created the fear that he could be the author of a dramatic breakthrough.

Others who stood out were Silvio Marzolini and Roberto Ferreiro, for their tremendous composure under any kind of physical pressure, and Oscar Mas, a small, elusive wide man who could weave wonderful patterns on the left, then deliver something direct and telling. Dominating everyone, though – and this could so easily have been in the most positive way – was the big and enigmatic Rattin.

Later, I heard that he, his coach and team-mates were obsessed with a rumour that was doing the World Cup rounds. It was to the effect that the Fifa president, Sir Stanley Rous, a former referee, had let it be known that he expected match officials to allow the football to flow, something that would be made much more feasible if they cast a lenient eye on the more overtly physical approach of the European teams. This was apparently translated into a firm South American belief, and one that would linger down the years, that Brazil, for whom Pelé had been kicked out of the World Cup by Portugal, and Argentina and Uruguay, who both had two players sent off in the course of the tournament, by Yugoslav, German and English referees, were all victims of a European conspiracy. This theory became entrenched in the minds of the South Americans, I was told, when the wounded Pelé was quoted as saying, 'I firmly believe this rumour to be true.'

Whatever the reason, all semblance of self-control seemed to drain away from Rattin as half-time approached, and it happened that I provided, quite unwittingly, the flashpoint. Twice in a few minutes Rattin fouled me, on the second occasion stopping me with a blatant trip. I was close to Rattin when he was cautioned and I could see by the expression on his face that he was near to erupting, which he duly did when his team-mate Alberto Gonzalez followed him into the referee's book. At that point, it seemed Rattin lost all interest in the flow of the game. As a captain, he committed the cardinal sin of losing his head. The big man pursued the short and slightly built referee and appeared to be insisting that he change his decision to book Gonzalez. Kreitlein waved Rattin away, but the captain refused to go. Repeatedly, he pointed to his captain's armband, presumably in the belief that this gave him *carte blanche* to negotiate with the referee.

Kreitlein stopped play and told Rattin that he had to accept his decisions and get on with the game. The ultimatum had no effect. As the game proceeded, Rattin continued to rage at the referee. Later, the captain claimed that he was merely asking for an interpreter, as though this was routine procedure in the middle of a World Cup game heading for the abyss.

Finally, Kreitlein announced that he had had enough. He sent Rattin off. It seemed to me the natural end to the affair but the trouble was that Rattin wouldn't go. It took the Argentine captain eight minutes to acknowledge the authority of the referee and the situation was worsened by the fact that his team-mates were milling around the official, shouting their protests. When Kreitlein was joined by Ken Aston, the referees' liaison officer, and Harry Cavan, a Fifa commissioner from Northern Ireland, in the effort to persuade Rattin to leave the field, all three of them were surrounded by the Argentine team and their officials. As the chaos deepened, and 88,000 supporters began to sing, 'Why are we waiting?' it occurred to me that probably the best solution would be for Kreitlein to order a restart and then disqualify the Argentines if Rattin continued to refuse to leave the field and his team-mates to play the game. It was a logical thought right up to the moment I considered the possible effect on intercontinental football relations.

Alf Ramsey had more immediate worries as Alan Ball and Nobby Stiles lurked dangerously near to the scene of the dispute. He must have been grateful to Ray Wilson, who beckoned to his team-mates to move away and shouted, 'Keep out of it, let them get on with it.'

By now, Rattin was standing on the touchline and then he sat down, as if to say he was going to watch everything that followed as perhaps the least dispassionate spectator in the history of the game. Finally, and with what suddenly seemed like immense resignation and sadness, he walked away. As he did so, he reached out to touch a corner flag, and held the cloth between his fingers for a moment in a gesture so poignant that anyone who saw it would never forget.

I'm not quite sure what he was saying at that moment but the suspicion must be that he had come to grasp that the most thrilling adventure of his career was over – and by his own hand.

For his handicapped team-mates, there was just one imperative, as they later admitted. More than ever, they would concentrate their efforts on preventing us scoring. If a chance came for them to strike at us, at absolutely no cost to their defensive security, perhaps they would make a foray or two, but in the absence of their captain, they had apparently concluded that their one chance of reaching the semi-finals was to hang on for the draw and win the toss after extra time. It seems scarcely possible in this day of the heart-wrenching penalty shoot-out, that this was the chosen method for ending a deadlock in football's most important tournament.

If containment was their aim, it didn't put pay to our anxiety when they had the ball. In defence, they seemed more resolute than ever, and just as cynical. With fifteen minutes to go, the moment came that I had feared from Onega's first silky touch. He sent Mas away with a long and perfectly measured pass and I could hardly bear to look when the winger's shot flashed just wide of Gordon Banks's post. For a second I imagined my heart was doing the same as that of the nation – standing still.

Earlier, Albrecht, who had returned to the team after serving his suspension for the bad foul on Weber in the group game, barged Jack dangerously when he was in the air at a corner, and Hurst, who from the start had been subjected to ferocious buffeting, stopped Ferreiro with a high tackle as the Argentine attempted to make another smooth run out of the trenches of defence.

That mistimed tackle apart, however, Hurst's reaction to his first immersion in the stormiest of World Cup waters could only have impressed Ramsey. We were still struggling to break down a packed and skilful defence equipped with talented, overlapping full backs, but in Hunt and now Hurst, the manager could see that he had two front men who would never shirk a yard of work – or stop looking for the chance to set the other free.

Later, Hurst talked of his ordeal in the most graphic terms. He likened it to walking down a dark alley in a strange town. 'At any moment,' he said, 'for no reason you felt that you might be attacked from behind. Twice I was kicked in the ankle when I was nowhere near the ball and each time I swung round and there was a ring of blank faces.' Bobby Moore confirmed Hurst's report of a stream of sneak attacks, saying, 'They did tug your hair, spit at you, poke you in the eye and kick you when the ball was miles away and no one was looking.'

If you think I'm recalling these events from a detached distance, maybe I should report that I also found my way into Rudolf Kreitlein's list of offenders. I like to think that I committed a minor offence when set against the rest of the mayhem, but I suppose for the referee every dubious tackle, every voice of protest, was still another dire challenge to his authority.

In the end, the match, and the day, offered only one obtainable reward – survival, the ability to play on and redeem all that had happened. It was duly delivered twelve minutes from the end by Geoff Hurst, who moments earlier had been denied by a fine save from Antonio Roma.

This was the first of the vital goals made in West Ham and Hurst scored it with such authority that when Jimmy Greaves joined the touchline celebrations, he must have done so in an agony of mixed feelings. He was the most patriotic of Englishmen but he was also a superbly gifted footballer who, like all of us, had long seen these summer days as potentially the dazzling apex of his career.

In creating the chance so well, Martin Peters reminded everyone of Ramsey's insistence that this was a player of great presence and intuition. When he received the ball along the left from Ray Wilson, the briefest glance told him that his club team-mate was in perfect position to run at goal. The left-footed, outswinging cross that followed immediately drifted out of Roma's reach and into the path of Hurst. With great certainty, Hurst headed across Roma and into the net. This was both sweet execution and reward for the kind of running that Ramsey had made the foundation of our challenge.

On a different day, the manager's unbendingly cool response to both triumph and failure might just have weakened against a rush of relief and pleasure. As it was, he remained consumed by anger at the approach of Argentina.

At the end, as I swapped shirts with one of the lesser miscreants of the mayhem that had just passed, a furious Ramsey saw George Cohen about to exchange shirts with Gonzalez. This was the man whose booking had been the signal for the descent into anarchy. Ramsey intervened, grabbing at a sleeve of the shirt and telling Cohen that such a transaction was inappropriate with an 'animal'. At that moment you knew that whatever happened in the next few days, the stains left by this match would not be quickly cleaned away.

The manager ensured that this would be so when he pursued his animal theme in the post-match statement that flashed across the football world. 'We have still to produce our best football,' he declared. 'It will come against the right type of opposition, a team who come to play football and not act as animals.'

Officially, the repercussions were quite mild. Ramsey was reprimanded for his remarks by the Football Association after Fifa demanded he be disciplined. Argentina received the maximum possible fine of £85 and three players were suspended, Rattin for four matches, and Ferreiro and Onega for three, for, respectively, manhandling the referee and spitting in the face of a Fifa observer.

Although we had survived, it was difficult to feel much else but regret that the great tournament had fallen so low. At least, this was so until we heard that back home in Buenos Aires, the Argentines had been given the welcome of heroes at the airport, had been presented with a trophy that recognised them as the 'moral' winners of the World Cup and been driven to the presidential palace to receive the personal thanks of the head of state, General Ongania. Then, there was for us a new wave of bitterness at the behaviour of the Argentines – and satisfaction that we had beaten them.

Our short-term reward was not quite so spectacular. Ramsey praised us for our character and our refusal to be dragged down to the worst level of sportsmanship he had ever seen, and singled out Nobby Stiles for his refusal to rise to the baiting he had received after plainly being targeted in the wake of the Simon affair, but he did not soften his message that we were still short of the level it would take to win the trophy.

If Argentina had been an ordeal we had done well to survive, the semi-final against Portugal, the most talented team left in the tournament, had to be something sharply different. It had to be the night we showed we knew truly what it would take to be champions of the world.

21

SPLIT-SECOND DECISIONS

GEORGE COHEN HAS said that in the days between the journey into that football night with Argentina, and what seemed like the sunrise of our victory over Portugal, it was hard to hold eye contact with Jimmy Greaves. For George, it felt like an intrusion into impending grief because, like all of us I imagine, he had the strongest sense that the finest scorer of our generation, and possibly of any other, had finally slipped out of Alf Ramsey's reckoning.

The debate was, understandably, fanned by the press and it would rage through the country right up to the moment we walked out to meet West Germany in the final. Here, surely, was a classic sports story to intrigue and impassion any sports-orientated nation – an heroic yet happy-go-lucky figure, a man plainly born to play at the top of the game, drawn suddenly into the worst crisis of his career. Would he get the chance to show all his genius on the most important day in the nation's sporting history, or would he be denied by the cold calculations of an old pro who had long made it clear that he would put aside all emotion in the pursuit of final victory.

It was a football saga that had everything Fleet Street craved and they played it for all it was worth, with each morning's editions building up the drama. I shared George's assessment that the position of Greaves, the scoring assassin, had been

255

ambushed by Geoff Hurst in the trenches against Argentina, and then in the much more beautiful match against the Portuguese. The truth, a bitter one for Jimmy, was the issue was really settled by the time the manager allowed us a little champagne to celebrate our arrival in the final.

For me, the argument had become somewhat detached from the realities of our situation. If by then my confidence in Ramsey's judgement had become virtually unconditional, I have to confess that when I look back I do feel that perhaps I could have been more sensitive to the pain of a great player who had been my England team-mate for seven years and won fifty-four caps when he was injured against France. My reserve at the time was rooted in the trust I had developed in Ramsey's instincts and judgement on form and ability, and if it sounds like an easy stance for me to take, given my rarely interrupted run of seventy-two caps for England over eight years, I can only plead that under Ramsey I never believed my selection was automatic.

I know, too, that when he stood at the front of the bus on the way back from Roehampton and said, 'The team for tomorrow is . . .' I never heard mumblings of disbelief or outrage. No one ever said, 'Alf, can I have a word with you.' Of course I would have been disappointed if my name had not been included, but I do not think I would have felt outrage or betrayal. My uppermost thought would probably have been frustration that, in the opinion of a tough but extremely analytical football man, I had failed one of the many tests he had set all of us.

Most of all, I believed that without Ramsey we could never have been standing just one game away from the ultimate prize. He had made us winners and in this process, inevitably, there would be deep personal disappointments. That Jimmy Greaves should suffer one so acutely, and carry it down the years, is a sadness that I came to understand, maybe because of my own charmed position, only when the first anger had gone from Jimmy's wounds. Mostly Jimmy kept his feelings to himself behind what was often quite a bleak expression, but from time to time he did give the odd indication of his mood, usually by humming 'What's it all about, Alfie?' In the most exhilarating moments of the campaign, in particular the victory over Portugal and then the final triumph over the Germans, Greaves managed to put his own disappointment aside and hug team-mates, including me, who were playing out the action he so ached to join. Maybe if I had my time over again I would have understood more readily the wave of sympathy that hit George Cohen whenever he saw, and then quickly averted his eyes from, the fellow Londoner he admired so much.

As it was, I could only believe that Ramsey had picked the team he considered best equipped to win the next match, and that was it. For me at least, this outweighed the disbelief of so many others that England could contemplate going into a vital game without a forward of such refined talent.

However, before the last act of the Greaves drama – even on the morning the final headlines still speculated on the possibility of his sensational return – there was the essential business of beating Portugal, a team whose progress had not exactly been short of soulful self-examination. We had studied on our World Cup monitor the two sides of the team I had always admired – the brutal cynicism of their hacking down of Pelé and then the glorious restatement of their talent after going three goals down to the extraordinary runners and fighters of North Korea.

The North Korean impact on the tournament was sensational – they had beaten Italy before threatening to drain the life out of Portgual – but not entirely unheralded. Stan Ackerley, a Manchester lad who had played in United youth's team, was entitled to play for Australia and he had met the North Koreans in qualifying. He recalled looking out of his hotel bedroom at six in the morning and seeing them running in what seemed like a frenzy in the nearby hills. As the Portuguese were to discover at Goodison Park, the North Koreans we obviously highly committed challengers to the old football order.

Yet, although the North Koreans, and their hero Pak Doo Ik, had leaped out at the football establishment with great force, they could not overcome the strength and talent of Eusebio as they had the Italians. His reaction was immense. He scored four goals, two of them penalties, recovering the ball so quickly each time that he seemed like a man possessed. Inevitably, from Ramsey down, Eusebio dominated our pre-match discussions until, in the changing room before the semi-final, Ramsey stated his faith in Nobby Stiles. The man who plainly posed the biggest threat to all our work and all our hopes was placed in the personal care of my great friend. Nobby didn't blink when he got the orders, even though he admitted later to knowing that he had been handed the toughest challenge of his career – and the ultimate test of his ability to read points of danger.

The pressure was beginning to build on all of us now. Hendon Hall was so awash with visitors on the Sunday morning after the Argentina game, including English and Portuguese journalists, and families who had just come along to join in the World Cup excitement, that I told Ray Wilson I had to get away from all the attention. He agreed to join me at South Herts Golf Club, where we had already played a round on a rest day and been told by the members that we should consider it a convenient hideaway whenever we felt the need to get away.

Ray and I didn't say much as we sat watching the members come in from their rounds, laughing and joking and giving the impression that sport, at any level, might not necessarily be the most important thing in the world. Ray and I agreed it was timely therapy. Whether Nobby or Jimmy would have agreed is an entirely different matter.

The relief was fleeting. The following day we went to Selfridges to a do a little shopping, but it was impossible in the press of well-wishers. English reservation seemed to be sliding away a little more with each step we took towards the final.

On the eve of the Portugal game, we felt a little comfort when the West Germans survived the force of the USSR in the other semi-final at Goodison Park. We admired the team spirit of the Germans, and the talent of their prodigy Franz Beckenbauer, but it seemed to us that the Soviets had been developing through the tournament. Their football wasn't spectacular but in players such as Albert Shesternev, the captain, Igor Chislenko and the late-emerging Valeriy Porkujan they had some strong characters who might be most threatening when the pressure was at its highest.

Such theoretical musings were, however, swept into the background when I woke on the day of our game still with a stiff neck. Normally, it would not have been a cause for panic. During the course of a season the problem, which was created by some fibrositis in my left shoulder, erupted three or four times, but it was invariably swiftly cured by physiotherapy. On this occasion, though, it hadn't cleared so quickly, and I was tormented by the thought that at a time when I had never been less likely to take my fitness as anything other than the most wonderful of gifts, I might be kept out of one of the most important matches England had ever played.

The stiffness had appeared the day before and I'd had some treatment on Monday morning and later in the day consulted the team doctor. On Monday night I had piled up the pillows on my bed and prayed that I would wake up with complete freedom of movement. But I didn't and despite the number of times I told myself that everything would be clear by kick-off, it was impossible to push back the rising tension.

The fateful moment came at lunch-time when Ramsey appeared at my side. As always, he went straight to the point.

'How's your neck, Bobby, are you fit to play?' he asked.

In a split second it was as though all my previous England matches came flooding back before my eyes, all the striving to get to this place we occupied now. It didn't help that when I replied, I had to hold my head at an angle.

'I can feel it slightly,' I said, 'but I'm fine.'

After the longest and most agonising pause, Alf responded, 'All right, we'll keep the same side.'

He made a leap of faith and, looking back, so did I. I just refused to believe that a difficulty that had been encountered successfully on every other occasion would be insurmountable on the day when I needed to deliver the best of myself out on the field.

Mercifully, by kick-off time that was how I felt and the result, some say, was possibly my best performance in an England shirt. I scored both our goals and at every point of the game I felt that I was in command of myself in a team that understood its own power. By comparison, the Portuguese, for all their skill and Eusebio's potential to confound us, didn't seem to know quite what they were doing, at least until it was too late.

They were not the same team who had removed Pelé from the tournament. Two of their hardest defenders, Joao Morais and Vicente, villains in the Brazil game, were missing, and the statistics of goodwill would have been scarcely believable in any circumstances. In the shadow of the Argentina mayhem, they were nothing less than stunning. The first foul came after twenty-two minutes, when Martin Peters obstructed Eusebio, and in all there were a mere ten. Yet this did not detract from the competitiveness of the game.

If Portugal were on their most polite behaviour, they had clearly not signed a non-aggression pact. Nobby had been stewarding Eusebio magnificently but at the approach of half-time we were reminded again of the power and skill of the man from Mozambique.

One shot of his flew in and out of the arms of Banks, perhaps one of the ultimate testaments to how well a ball had been struck. Another whistled perilously close to a post. This was the Eusebio who was football's version of a Lion of Africa, proud and dangerous. His bursts of attacking zeal were a reflection of the fact that after half an hour we had taken the lead with a goal that bore all the hallmarks of Alf Ramsey's football. It was the result of both hard work and an implicit understanding of what your team-mates could do. Ray Wilson fed a ball into the box and Roger Hunt, having seen the possibilities and run as hard as ever to take advantage of them, turned the ball inside the defender Jose Carlos. It then seemed to me that the Portuguese goalkeeper, Jose Pereira, panicked somewhat, diving forward for the ball but failing to prevent it rolling into my path, fifteen yards out.

The temptation to blast it into a wide-open gap was huge but in those split seconds that can change so much if you make the wrong decision, I opted for a safer course. I knew I could trust the roll of the ball on the Wembley carpet and a message was hammering in my brain – just hit it straight, just ease it home. So that's what I did, with the side of my foot, and when it nestled into the back of the net, the thunder of the crowd reflected my own thoughts – we are nearly there, we cannot be turned back now.

The Portuguese, however, clearly did not share that belief. Their attitude to this game reminded me of why I liked them so much. There was no hint of passivity from them. In the first half, Pereira had been under considerable pressure but now the action was beginning to move steadily in the direction of Banks. The towering Jose Torres was locked in battle with Jack, and the wingers Jose Augusto and Antonio Simoes were stretching us wide, so much so that Cohen, Wilson and Moore were not slow to call back defensive recruits from midfield. Ball, who was now such an integral part of the team it seemed odd that he had been stood down for those two group games, Peters and I were repeatedly required to help out as Stiles battled on with all of his grit in the toughest contest of all, the decisive one with Eusebio. While Peters, particularly, was capable of tackling with the precision of a specialist defender and Ball was tigerish, my own contribution at this point was necessarily a matter of running, supporting and offering channels of relief when the ball was won from the clever touch of the Portuguese.

My tackling had always been the despair of Jimmy Murphy but he acknowledged that I did not shirk from any running on behalf of the defence. If I could run all day and from time to time I could score, it mostly left the hardest taskmaster I would ever know content enough.

My second goal of the game came with just ten minutes to go and again it was the fruit of Ramsey's insistence that players must work for each other and if a team simply relied on flashes of virtuosity, it was never going to win the big games, or be a consistent force. The flow of the move and the vital role of Geoff Hurst live in my mind for, I believe, one basic reason. All of it seemed to define the team that Ramsey had made.

The ball was moved out of defence to Alan Ball, then switched across the field to Cohen via Moore. We were operating on another basic Ramsey principle. You do not sit on a lead; you do not invite dangerous opponents into your parlour. As much as possible, without any concessions on the need to be strong always in defence, you prosecute the game as aggressively, and as honestly, as you can. Cohen sent a long ball down the right to Hurst, running so powerfully he outstripped the defender, Alexandre Baptista, and although the angle was acute, my inclination would probably have been to shoot. Instead, Hurst did something that, who knows, may have clinched the argument over his challenge to Jimmy Greaves.

I'd never forget it for what it said about the ideal of being unselfish on the football field. Hurst checked for a moment as Baptista resumed his attention, and held up play long enough for me to run free inside him. He rolled the ball perfectly into my stride and the moment I hit it I knew that it was going home. That we'd booked ourselves one last test in the old stadium seemed to be confirmed when Augusto ran over to me and offered his congratulations.

I thought that was the oddest of gestures, charming in its way, but he made it seem like the end of something, as though a conclusion had been reached. That would have been the last thing I would have suggested with ten minutes still to go. He'd done the same thing a few months earlier in the Estadio da Luz in Lisbon, near the end of United's 5–1 victory in a European Cup tie. Maybe Augusto was trying to encourage us to slow down. There was nothing resigned about the way he tore into the box two minutes later as Jack found himself obliged to knock away with his hand a ball that had been headed in by Torres from a cross by Simoes and was arcing dangerously under the bar.

Eusebio swept home the penalty for his eighth goal of the tournament – and the first we had conceded in seven games, which is a record that still stands today. The next eight minutes stretched into an age. Nobby was immense under the pressure, fighting to contain Eusebio, who seemed to be playing for his very life, and yet still squeezing enough time to make a superb tackle on Simoes as he ran cleanly and alone on Banks's goal.

If ever a team was reminded that in football you can never take anything for granted it was England as we stood transfixed by a moment of both beauty and terrible apprehension. Eusebio produced one last effort to save Portugal's World Cup, moving down the left with immense power and grace, and then coolly stroking the ball inside to Coluna.

The Portuguese captain sent in a blistering shot towards the angle of the crossbar and the post, and in that moment I experienced what the French call *petit mort* – a little death. But it would not have been a little anything. It would have been a blow the like of which I would never have experienced on a football field. Then there, again, was Banks, who never easily accepted the concession of a goal. Like every one of his breed I have known, he would put it down to some shocking conspiracy of fate. This was the Banks who worked at his trade so religiously, who never spared his body and would always go wherever was necessary. Quite brilliantly, he turned the ball away.

It was around then that I saw the shoulders of the great Eusebio sag a little and tears come to his eyes. At least, I thought, he need not carry away any regrets from this field. Nobby Stiles had produced some astonishing defensive work, which should have been turned into a classic teaching film, but in the end the spirit and talent of Eusebio was still visible. He hadn't claimed the night despite the hardness of his fight but before, or since, I never saw a man go down with such spirit and defiance.

Our opponents remained true to the form they had always displayed when I played against them, and when the final whistle blew at Wembley, there were hugs from all of the Portuguese players and this time there was no attempt by Alf to prevent us swapping shirts.

For a little while we were swimming in our triumph – swimming in adrenalin, probably – and when I called home as soon as I reached Hendon Hall, I had it confirmed that the win had touched every corner of the country. My mother-in-law, a naturally quiet person, had never sounded so excited, and then there was another notch to my emotion when I heard Norma's voice on the phone, saying, 'Well done, Bobby, no one could have done better.'

Along with the champagne, there were more photographers than I had ever seen at the hotel, and Ramsey's face did not have even the beginnings of a frown. 'Well done, gentlemen,' he said. 'You played very well. There is more work to be done before we win this thing, but you have just earned your chance – and you did it splendidly.'

Predictably, the press in England and abroad were rather more fulsome. A Swedish newspaper thought that my two goals might be enough to get me into the House of Lords – or perhaps to replace Admiral Nelson in Trafalgar Square. The Russian news agency Tass offered a surge of lyrical comment, saying, 'England gave their finest showing in the championship. The match came like a spring of clear water breaking through the wave of dirty football which has flooded recent matches.'

Perhaps, though, it was a Czech sports newspaper that homed in most acutely on the confidence that came with our ability to withstand Portugal's last, brilliant charge. 'The English backs are almost indestructible,' said the man from Prague.

It was a statement of most glorious fact. Each one of them, along with the trouble-shooting Nobby, had confirmed the oldest truth in football. A team that cannot trust its defence can never have more than one foot in the reality of winning football. As we prepared for the last test, and I awoke to a letter from a wine-importing company saying that my two goals had earned me a dozen bottles of the best port, I had the most tremendous sense that our stance was perfectly balanced.

It was not something I would have said to Jimmy Greaves. For within the team, the ending of the intriguing and emotional story that had so captivated the public's imagination was already known. That was why George Cohen had found it so hard to look into the face of a man we all admired. When he did, he could see that Jimmy Greaves was also in on the secret.

For me, too, there was to be some news that I could not quite have imagined when Geoff Hurst, the winner of the race to the last door that Alf Ramsey had kept open, rolled the ball into my path for the goal that finally carried England to a World Cup final.

22

A MAN-MARKING JOB

When Alf Ramsey approached me on the Friday to explain the part I was to be given in his last game plan, one that he knew would define the success or failure of everything he had believed in and worked for in all his years in football, I didn't expect any radical departure. Yet maybe something in his expression should have warned me that this was not going to be quite the normal exchange.

Always after his analysis of the opposition – and he had watched film of ten German games in the few days he had known they would provide our last obstacle – he had something to say about the emphasis of our game, maybe making an adjustment here or there, and instructing that particular attention be paid to the threat of a certain opponent. His words rarely weighed heavily on your mind because he didn't make any clutter in his pre-game talks. He knew you well enough – and you him. He would remind us, individually, of our special responsibilities. 'Anything that comes in high, that's for you,' he would tell my brother.

Bobby Moore, the supreme reader, would pick out anything low. Nobby would have his assignment changed in small details from game to game, but he would know what was expected – he was to attend to points of danger, win the ball and give it to somebody, quite often me.

For me, surely, it was very much the same as before. I had played well against Portugal and I had the freighted bottles of port to prove it. This final would be the day I followed, as never before, the edicts of Jimmy Murphy on behalf of my country.

I would run with all the freedom and exhilaration that had provoked my mad dashes at the half-time whistle in the game against Mexico. I would accelerate into available space, piling pressure on the opposing defence, and if there was a glimpse of goal I would shoot with power and conviction in the general direction of the net.

Of course, Alf might tell me to be mindful of certain aspects of the German game, which was essentially sound but did not seem, beyond the potentially brilliant innovation of the rising young Franz Beckenbauer and the quality of Wolfgang Overath, to present the kind of threat posed by Eusebio's Portugal.

No one, I knew, had the right to do what he pleased or go wherever the whim took him. Geoff Hurst wasn't in the team because he had a superior technique to Jimmy Greaves when it came to scoring goals. Greaves was at the top of his game in that department. He, like my United colleague Denis Law, could conjure goals from nothing. Once, against United, he scored so effortlessly it was like he was running us through with a rapier. Spurs beat us 5–1. They pulverised us, and Jimmy Greaves was so elusive around the box he might have been a ghost. No, Geoff was in because he did some of the things Ramsey considered absolutely basic to our team performance better, more naturally, than Jimmy.

He ran into hard positions and held up the ball under immense pressure. Everyone who faced Germany would have their own responsibilities – and their own accountability if we should lose.

However, as I saw it, we all had our natural talents. Bobby Moore couldn't run as I could, but he could do things beyond my powers. He could time a tackle so easily he might have been doing nothing more complicated than closing a door.

What I could do was strike home from midfield, exploiting the forward work of Hurst and Hunt, and linking with Ball, Peters and Stiles as we took the game to the Germans. Most of all I could run, as I had been doing since I first kicked a football, with such unreserved pleasure, at home many miles north of where I was on this day. Of course, there might be a new wrinkle or two. There usually was. No two sets of opponents are the same. Their strengths and their weaknesses are invariably different, and we all had to be mindful of that.

So, as far I was concerned, it was something of a formality when Alf Ramsey sat down beside me, until he started to speak.

'Bobby,' Alf said, 'I want you to do something for me. I want you to stick on Beckenbauer every minute of the match. This boy is the only German player who can beat us. They have some other good players but I can plan for every one of them except Beckenbauer.

'I don't know what he's going to do from one minute to the next – and I don't think he does. So I can't lay plans for him. I can't know when he's suddenly going to try to get behind our defenders. It means I have just one plan for him – and it's you. I want you to stay with him through the whole game, don't go anywhere else. He is your responsibility. I know he's young and can run, but then you can run. You have a good engine. If you do your job he will not do any damage, and I'm sure we will win the World Cup.'

None of this was what I'd had in mind when I came down from the exhilaration of beating Portugal and playing one of my most confident games for England, but after drawing in my breath I said, 'OK, I'll do that.'

When he'd gone, I thought, 'Well, here I am in a World Cup final, as I've dreamed about for so long, and when it comes I'm told to do a man-marking job – something that's always been done to me throughout my career.' That was my first thought but then I had second one. I thought of how much I trusted Alf in all his decisions, and so to what did this faith really amount?

Was it something I could give or withdraw according to how his decisions suited me? No, it couldn't work like that. That would be terrible hypocrisy. It would also deny what we had all been pursuing for so long, which was to make a team for one purpose only. It wasn't necessarily to light up the sky above Wembley or parade our skills for the sake of it. It was quite simply to win the World Cup. So I told myself, finally, 'If we win, everything is justified.'

I said that, and I believed it, because when Alf assessed the situation, it was hard to dispute his logic. There was never anything from him that could be said to be vague, airy fairy. He went through the key parts of the German team, ticking off the strengths and weaknesses of each player, and he kept coming back to the conclusion that if we were going to be truly hurt, it would be done by this tall twenty-year-old from Bavaria who had arrived at the top of the game so quickly and with such assurance.

If he hadn't yet been christened Der Kaiser, 'The Emperor', there was no question that he was already carrying himself with the bearing of a young prince. We had watched with particular apprehension his performances against Switzerland in a group game and then in the quarter-final against Uruguay, the team who had so frustrated us at the opening of the tournament. Looking back, it is not so hard to see how Ramsey had arrived at his decision. Beckenbauer wrecked the Uruguayan defence several times with brilliant forward breaks but that game had become distorted by the dismissal of two South Americans. It was against Switzerland that you could see most clearly his potential to surprise any defence, even one such as our own, which was going into the final with the single blemish of a penalty strike conceded against Portugal, arguably the World Cup's most potent attack.

Twice, the man I had been ordered to shadow had cut through the Swiss defence to score, and twice he had done it so effortlessly his performance was hailed as a masterpiece of attack from midfield.

As you looked at the ease and the delicacy of the one-twos he worked with his forwards and then the sudden acceleration, so smooth that he might have been a Mercedes overtaking on the autobahn, you realised a football brain much less acute than Alf Ramsey's would have inevitably registered concern. Overath and Siggi Held, Uwe Seeler and Helmut Haller, whom I had played against as a youth with Manchester United, had easily recognisable talent but it was harder to see them tearing you apart.

Overath was a fine passer of the ball, but he did it a lot and he was not so difficult to read. Held could be elusive and had some skill, Seeler was powerful and with a hard instinct for goal and Haller had energy, a good touch and confidence in himself. But none of them made you afraid, or carried the elements of mystery and surprise that did so much to form the aura of the man whom I had been told to put in my pocket for the most important ninety minutes England had ever played.

But if the mind said yes, something in my bones wanted to say no. I suppose the emotion carried me back to my beginnings, when I was the kid who was always picked first in the playground, and was so confident in my ability that I once earned a smack from Jack for telling him that he had made 'a bloody stupid' mistake in a game I had just seen him play on the Miners' Welfare Ground in Ashington. Once, I'd been lifted on to the shoulders of my team-mates at Bedlington Grammar when I scored the goals that beat the formidable St Aloysius of Newcastle.

Franz Beckenbauer was a beautiful young player, anyone could see that, but he was just a toddler when I was being courted by the top clubs in the First Division, and was probably still in short trousers when I was lining up with Tom Finney and Billy Wright at Hampden Park.

Yet there it was for this devotee of the Ramsey method. I had a job to do for England that I wouldn't have chosen for myself. If you respect a manager, any leader, you cannot say that you will go along with the best of him and reject the rest.

This, anyway, was what I kept telling myself before slipping off to sleep that night, perhaps a little weary from all this wrestling of the mind. I also had to tell myself two other things. One was that I didn't share the pain of Jimmy Greaves. I would be out on the field and not in a seat when they played the national anthems of England and Germany. The other was that, however I bridled at the restrictions that had been placed on my natural game, I had been given the chance to make a vital contribution to what would be the greatest victory in the history of English football.

I had had to remind myself of that repeatedly after Alf unveiled his plan, and the tension, in Hendon Hall and around the nation, notched up a little more with each new hour. The pressure was relieved by our work at Roehampton. Alf believed in detail, and also in the need to go about your business in a consistent way. So we worked on the training field as diligently as ever, and when it was over we played a little cricket. It was circumspect cricket – there were no beamers or bouncers and very few heroics in the slips – but it was relaxing, as was the stroll down the hill from Hendon Hall to the local cinema. Ideally, I suppose, on the eve of the final we might have heard one of Alf's heroes, John Wayne, declaring something along the lines that men must do what men must do. Instead, we saw *The Blue Max* and, although I can't speak for my team-mates, I don't imagine too many of them were closely following the plot-line about a German fighter pilot!

For me, my mind kept drifting back to all the games I had played for England and all of the experiences I had had. I thought of being in that other cinema with Jack back in Ashington when we were schoolboys, waiting for the newsreel film of our relative Jackie Milburn making his debut for England, and the usherette trying to shoo us away when she thought we were trying to sit through two showings of the film . . . about a ballerina. She almost got her way, as well, until some patrons told her that we were relatives of Wor Jackie. The queue for the cinema had wound down the street that night.

I thought of all of it, going back to that first game in Glasgow when Billy Wright took me under his wing and Tommy Finney laid on my first goal in international football. The head waiter at the Marine Hotel in Troon even made an appearance in my reverie, presenting me with the cannonballs of haggis I carried so proudly home.

I could see all the great players, Matthews and Finney, Lawton and Lofthouse and Mortensen, Haynes and Mannion, who never got remotely close to a World Cup final, and, of course, I thought again of the question that I had carried so heavily in the first years of my England career – how different would the campaigns in Sweden and Chile have been if my friends and heroes, Duncan Edwards, Roger Byrne and Tommy Taylor, had not died in the aircrash I survived?

Edwards would have been touching thirty now, a giant in his prime. When I thought of this, the sacrifice that Alf Ramsey had asked me to make didn't seem so great.

Thinking of a man I had met at Hendon Hall in the wake of our victory over Portugal had the same effect. This was Fritz Walter, captain of the West Germany team that had ambushed the great Hungarians in the 1954 World Cup final in Berne. On that day, Walter had had an experience that I would enjoy in a few hours' time, that of playing in the most important game in football alongside his brother.

Walter had played with his younger sibling, Ottmar, in a victory that shocked the football world. Even rumours that have emerged in recent years suggesting that the German performance may have been enhanced by drugs in those innocent days before there was even a nod in the direction of the need for testing, seem unlikely to diminish its place in the folklore of football.

Several times I sat and talked with Walter. The conversations re-enforced the sense I had always had, if at some times only subliminally, that my football life had in many ways been charmed, as though it was almost a miracle of good fortune.

Walter's football had been disrupted by the Second World War, and it was only an act of mercy by a Hungarian guard in a prisoner of war camp, who knew him to be a fine footballer, that prevented him being marched off to a Russian gulag where the life expectancy was no more than five years – or the time it took West Germany to be reinstated in international football.

A few years later, the Hungarian team who were beaten in the final were caught outside their country when the revolution of their compatriots provoked an invasion by Russia, and Walter took over their management for two years. He arranged games for them and organised sponsorship. Walter admired the Hungarians he had played against immensely, and he also believed he owed his life to one of their compatriots.

He had survived so much, including malaria contracted in the swampy ground of the POW camp, but he seemed to shrug it away as he wished me well – although not too well – when I faced his countrymen in a few days' time.

As Walter talked, I couldn't get it out of my head that this man had once in his life had the feeling I now craved for myself at Wembley that coming Saturday afternoon. He had been able to tell himself that he was a champion of the world. But when I thought of all he had been through, and also of how I had walked away from Munich with just a small bump on my head, I wondered whether maybe there were times when we might attach just a little too much importance to the winning of a single football match.

At least, it was a passing theory I had on that day. It had lost much of its strength when I woke on the morning of Saturday, 30 July 1966, and saw a sky of racing clouds that might bring sunshine or rain. Then I knew nothing had ever felt as important as the need to win the World Cup.

23

30 JULY 1966

THERE WAS ONLY the game now, waiting either to free us, or to smother us. Who really knew? Everything had been said and done, except getting hold of the trophy, or shrinking away, and although I slept well through the night and into the morning of the game, and then ate my usual hearty breakfast, I couldn't shake off an edginess that I had rarely known before. You could only accept so many good wishes, however sincerely meant, and shake so many hands.

Then you just had to go out and prove you were equal to the greatest challenge that ever faced you. You had to find out if you were right to believe in yourself so strongly and in the quality of the leadership you had received and the men who had been put in place around you.

Ray Wilson also wanted to escape the hotel. I told him that I needed to change a shirt I had bought in Golders Green a few days earlier, which was true, but more than a better-fitting garment I needed to breathe and gather up all my thoughts without constant distraction.

We got a lot of attention on the way to the high street, but it was much easier to avoid than back at Hendon Hall. There was plenty of space to move quickly away with a wave and smile that were maybe becoming a little too practised these last few days. Ray bought some new shoes for the evening banquet and I changed my shirt and bought some cuff links that I planned to give to my friend Jose Augusto, who would be coming with the Portuguese team to the banquet, along with the fourth-placed Soviet team. I never made the presentation because at some point the cuff links went missing, perhaps because every-thing that wasn't directly linked to the most important ninety minutes of my career was swept into the margins.

The details of the day had begun to blur against my need for the action to begin, for all the preparation and the antici-pation and the doubts and the hopes to stop. My mother Cissie made clear, as always, her passionate hopes for her sons before the game and my father Robert, who always liked to keep most of his thoughts to himself, wished us good luck and said that he knew we would do our best. I saw Norma briefly and she too said that she knew we could do it.

On the way to Wembley you could see that the nation was already wrapped up in the drama that was yet to begin. All the houses seemed to have a flag. The people on the pavements waved and smiled and you could only hope that you could maintain that mood.

We were held up in the tunnel while the Queen and the Duke of Edinburgh took their seats in the royal box. I was standing next to the German goalkeeper, Hans Tilkowski, and I looked into his face for a clue to his feelings. He was impas-sive, but I wondered whether inside he was boiling, as I was. I remember thinking, 'Are you a man of iron or just a hell of a good actor?'

Earlier, in the dressing room, all the rituals had been followed, although Ray and I had become a bit bored by our boot-handling, ammonia-sniffing routine. George Cohen was in his usual fever of preparation, a few beads of sweat on his fore-head, and the players had their massages in strict order of prece-dence, Jack going last. Bobby Moore was looking so serene he might have been preparing for a round at his local golf club. When Ray handed me my boots, it was one last chore before going out into the sun and the summer showers to tread the fine line between our greatest victory or most wounding defeat.

If any of us needed a heightened sense of quite what was at stake, how our lives, one way or another, were just an hour or two away from changing quite profoundly, it was provided by the sound of a solitary drum high in the stands, pounding quite distinctly through the general uproar. Was the drum calling us to arms, or passing a sentence?

Alf, like Tilkowski, covered his feelings well. He moved among us, shepherding our thoughts with just a word or two, but he managed to convey his confidence that we all knew what was expected of us, and that none of us had been given a job beyond our powers.

If Ramsey had forgotten to remind me that Franz Beckenbauer was my responsibility – which, of course, he didn't – it would not have been a disaster because the great young player and his coach Helmut Schoen reaffirmed my situation at the first whistle. Beckenbauer did this by standing next to me. When he did so, it brought everything home to me much more clearly than even the words of my manager had done. Ramsey and Schoen had made precisely the same decision. They had put defensive security above all else, and neutralised the two players they believed were potentially the most dangerous on the field. As Beckenbauer, who would become such a good and admired friend down the years, and I exchanged glances, I suddenly grasped that both of us were aware that we were the pawns in maybe the biggest gambits either of our coaches would ever make.

Only one of them could survive without bitter criticism, because whoever lost would be asked, possibly for the rest of his life, why it was he had so restricted the natural ambition of arguably his most creative player. The winner would be a genius and the loser would be a fool. And when I thought of the pressure on Ramsey in making this decision, and the likelihood of which one of the two managers would prove to be correct, I also remembered that Ramsey had gone against so much popular, and some professional, opinion in excluding Jimmy Greaves.

Here, surely, was a man prepared to make the hard decisions, someone who would work his way to them with only one consideration in mind, and it had nothing to do with being seen to be fair or just or wise. It was all about the business of winning.

When Beckenbauer lined up beside me, I couldn't help thinking that Schoen, a much-respected coach and a fine and jovial man, had put much of his place in the history of football in my hands. My normal rate of possession of the ball would drop considerably, but Ramsey made it clear that he was not concerned with this. My job would be accomplished, entirely to his satisfaction, if, when the Germans had the ball, Beckenbauer was not in a position to receive it.

And as the lone drum beat on, I realised, with a surge of excitement, that yes indeed I could perform this vital service. I could play an important part in winning England's first World Cup. It was a beautiful thought, one that outweighed the artistic limitations that had been placed upon me, but I could not allow it to gestate for too long. In fact, it had a shelf life of just thirteen minutes. It was then that Ray Wilson made his one mistake in the tournament, and one of the very few significant ones in his entire career.

Siggi Held sent in a long cross from the left to the far post. Gordon Banks said later that he had called it as his ball but Wilson may have mistaken it for a shout of warning, and consequently rose too early and headed it down rather than away. Helmut Haller shot quickly and the ball glanced off Bobby Moore and past Banks, who later claimed that he had been unsighted by Jack.

A terrible fact came to our attention with the German flags – in every post-war World Cup final, the first strike had been made by the winners. That was not something to dwell upon so early in the game, but as I went to the centre circle for the restart I was telling myself, 'The world hasn't ended but we have to score quickly,' and so we did, six minutes later.

I was focusing on containing the threat of Beckenbauer, of course, and when I edged the ball away from him into the path of Bobby Moore, it was plain that England's captain was reacting quite ferociously to the setback. Bobby, as was mentioned so many times it might have irritated a saint, was not the quickest mover, but he never made a single step on the field without knowing precisely where he was going and to what purpose, and rarely had he shown such authority as in this moment. He charged at the German lines before being brought down by Wolfgang Overath and even the award of the free kick only served to emphasise his urgency. I ran to his left to give the option of a short pass but Bobby had seen another possibility, one well practised on the training field of West Ham United. He dummied to pass the ball to me but he had only one target, a gap that had opened in the square German cover.

Geoff Hurst ran into the space with perfect timing to send the ball into the top left-hand corner of Tilkowski's goal.

I have studied the film many times and each time I see it I'm reminded that this was so much more than a piece of inspired opportunism. It was the result of a fine understanding between team-mates, and superb technique. All goals ultimately have the same value, but this one sent out a crucial message – we had slipped behind for a few minutes but we had not lost control of ourselves or the match.

Yet plainly this was a German team transformed from the one that had given us such relatively little concern when beating the Soviets at Goodison Park. Both teams had powerful phases throughout the match, and perhaps our strongest came fifteen minutes or so after Hurst's goal. We had the momentum, and so much of it was being provided by Alan Ball.

April 1968. I scored the only goal in the first leg of the European Championship qualifier with Spain. We were on the way to a semi-final against Yugoslavia…

which we lost. We finished third after this play-off with the USSR.

21 April 1970. Gordon Banks congratulates me on my 100th cap. I couldn't know then that I only had six more to come.

Chart toppers on the way to Mexico. Teenyboppers across the country were swooning… (see end of book for list of band members' names).

The preparations for the defence of our world crown were meticulous.

And the training at Roehampton thorough.

Mexico 1970 World Cup squad (see end of book for names).

ining in the Guadalajara heat
er the watchful eyes of team
tor Neil Phillips and Alf.

rget Bogota. All that
ters now is what we do
e.' Our captain's words on
ining the squad after his
ase from police custody.

Blending in naturally to my surroundings in Mexico.

2 June 1970. Taking on Romania in the first match of our defence of the World Cup.

England 1 Romania 0. Geoff Hurst started up where he left off the last World Cup.

7 June 1970. Pelé at the height of his powers.

it even the maestro…

…sometimes meets his match. Gordon Banks making what many regard as 'The Save'.

Try as we might, we couldn't break the Brazilians down, losing 1–0, in perhaps the best game I ever played in.

1 June 1970. Lining up to face Czechoslovakia. We needed a draw. We got a win thanks to an Allan Clarke penalty. l–r, Our Kid, Peters, Bell, Astle, Banks, me, Clarke, Cooper, Newton, Mullery, Moore.

14 June 1970. World Cup quarter-final. Beckenbauer and I meet again.

ubstituted with 20 minutes o go and England 2–1 up.

It was agony to watch. The Germans turned the game around and we were out of the World Cup. And my international career was over forever.

But what wonderful memories it had brought me…

We knew well enough his qualities of skill delivered at speed, his energy and a fine eye for picking out the weakness in a defence, but now we saw his assets produced at a higher level of force and consistency. Our little brother was growing up before our eyes – and the German back line was suffering.

The German sweeper, Willi Schulz, could afford to be nothing less than relentless and the much-respected Karl-Heinz Schnellinger, who was one of the first expensive German exports to the Italian game, which was famous, or maybe notorious, for producing its own breed of master defenders, would have the look of a fighter out on his feet long before the end. He still knew the right moves but the pressure applied by Alan Ball meant that they were progressively impossible to produce.

Although it was hardly necessary, towards the end of the game Nobby Stiles would produce further evidence of quite how intense Ball's state of mind was on that historic afternoon. Nobby had one of those awful moments that can overcome any player at a late stage of a game. He felt a terrible draining of energy after making a run down the right flank. When he paused in an attempt to gather the last of his running power, Alan Ball came flying by, saying, 'Move, you bastard, move.'

It was the kind of command Nobby had been delivering routinely down all the years of his career and now, quite remarkably, he was having it returned, and with some interest, by the youngest member of the team, who was playing the entire game at a constant and remarkable pitch.

Hunt and Hurst continued to apply strong pressure on the German defence and Martin Peters was making the subtle, blind runs with which we were now happily familiar.

Bobby Moore, having already established his authority with the command he displayed in scoring the first goal, was in quite majestic shape, every inch the leader ushering his troops into the battle lines, and if my contribution was not as spectacular as I would have liked, in my heart of hearts, I knew that Beckenbauer had been unable to trigger any of those one-twos that had come to haunt Ramsey on the build-up to the final.

Yet in all of this, there was no question about whose presence was most compelling in an English shirt. It was as though Ball had created his own power supply. As far as the opposing midfielder and defenders were concerned, his running was literally breathtaking and, vitally, there was not a single pause from him when the Germans, far from wilting, began to play themselves back into the game at the approach of half-time.

Haller, Held and Uwe Seeler were particularly menacing, and Lothar Emmerich had a half chance before the Germans made some of their most dangerous thrusts of the game. Jack was required to go to his limits in checking Held on the left, and from the resulting corner Overath fired in a shot, hard and low, which Banks could only block. This provided another chance, this time for Emmerich, much closer in, and I gulped my relief when Banks gathered it up. If this was a fight, we were suffering an extremely bad round, and almost at the bell for half-time Banks was required again to save us when he touched a vicious, dipping shot from Seeler over the bar.

There was no mad sprint to the dressing room this time. My legs felt good and strong still and Beckenbauer had been as near to anonymous as Ramsey had hoped, but it was clear enough that this was not a day to expend energy needlessly. If there was any small surplus, it had to be stored against the certainty that all of it, and more, would be demanded before this game was won or lost.

Ramsey moved around the dressing room spreading reassurance. The Germans, he said, had made a strong effort at the end of the half, but he was pleased with our performance. We were composed and showing that we knew what we were doing. The lessons had been learned, he implied, and he had every confidence in both our ability and our character. There was no hint of a tremor in his voice. You would not have guessed this was the most important game of his life. He seemed to be saying that he was calm and that we had every reason to be the same. Most vitally of all, he confirmed a long-held opinion. He said we were the better, stronger side.

Looking back at the game now, I see that as a World Cup final it might not have displayed the sheer virtuosity that Pelé, Tostao and Gerson would bring to the one that followed four years later. But, still, you could say, 'I was proud to play in that match because I don't believe any two good teams could have played more honestly or responded more bravely to the demand that they produce, on that given day, only the best of themselves.' That would still be true, I believe, if the second half had allowed one of the teams to make a mortal strike – if, for example, the couple of chances that fell to me when I was freed, for a few seconds, from the obligation to shadow Beckenbauer, had been dispatched as efficiently as I had come to expect from myself. But then as we walked back on to the field, with a summer shower falling through the sunshine and gathering tension edging towards a state of foreboding for the nation, we should really have guessed that whatever this game would come to bestow, it was unlikely to be a clean kill, or anything like a serene march to the finish line.

Yet, suddenly, and with just twelve minutes to go, that was the prospect that flashed brilliantly before our eyes. It was preceded by a spell of sparring, but this was not a day when even the briefest lull gave any real respite from some urgent intervention by Alan Ball. He won a corner on the right, scampered to take it and the ball reached Geoff Hurst on the ground. On this occasion, Hurst snatched at his shot, which struck Horst-Dieter Hottges in the middle of a thicket of players and flew up in the air. The race for its return was between two Englishmen, Peters and Jack, and to everyone's relief, Peters won and swept the ball through a gap between

Tilkowski and Schnellinger. And it really was *everyone's* relief. Jack confirmed after the game, 'No, I didn't feel cheated. I'm glad the bugger didn't come to me because I would have kicked it over the bar.'

But the ball was in the back of the net and at that moment I believed I had never seen anything so beautiful on a football field. Nobby Stiles was standing closest to me and I ran to him shouting, 'Nobby, Nobby, we've won, we've won, they can't beat us now. We've made it.'

It was the prettiest of thoughts but, of course, it wasn't true, although it might have been if, with four minutes to go, my shot had been more accurate after Alan Ball released Hunt with a superb pass and Hurst and I outnumbered the suddenly isolated Schulz.

The regret I felt at my failure to convert the chance went deep. I could only imagine the sweetness of a goal at that point, the feeling it would give, truly, that the journey was over. And even as I thought that, the Germans strived to turn my musings into nightmares. The main dangers to us now were Held and Seeler, attackers of both power and commitment, and their most gifted allies from midfield, Beckenbauer and Overath.

That Beckenbauer should escape me for one vital contribution had, of course, been my ultimate fear from the moment Ramsey had redefined my purpose, and as the Germans swarmed forward, and I fell back with Stiles and Peters to reinforce the back line, the final whistle seemed an age away. There was, in fact, just a minute of normal time left when the Swiss referee, Gottfried Dienst, sent a chill through all of us by deciding, incorrectly we felt, that Jack had fouled Held when getting up to head the ball away at the edge of our penalty area. Stiles, Peters, Hunt and I made the wall, from right to left, under the direction of Nobby, who had been given this responsibility in training.

The Germans called up the powerful Emmerich, who had

had a poor game and no doubt saw this as a gift of redemption. As he approached the ball, I prayed that he would blast it at the wall, which, on this day of all days, would surely be unyielding. His other option was to lob the ball over us and hope that maybe Seeler would get his head to it, a possibility lessened sharply by the presence of Jack and Gordon Banks. The tension was like an immovable knife in my ribs as Emmerich, shunning the obvious, shaped his kick into the defenders deployed behind us. The ball touched George Cohen and then, we claimed with noisy but unrewarded desperation, was controlled by Schnellinger's hand, before it bobbled out of a jumble of legs and allowed Weber to shoot home.

The final whistle of normal time sounded the moment after I restarted the game from the centre circle. It had happened, my worst fear, and as I stood there trying to absorb the pain and clear away my emotions in time for the start of extra time, Uwe Seeler walked over to me and said, 'Bobby, that's football.'

It was indeed. It was dreams made and snatched away. It was a referee's decision going the wrong way. It was that fine line that had been so vivid when I ran out from the protection of the tunnel more than ninety minutes previously. So what do you do? You play on, of course, you fight for what you believe belongs to you, and if anyone had forgotten this old truth, Ramsey was moving among us now with the reminder. He asked Bobby Moore, who was lying down on the pitch, to get back on his feet because it was imperative that the Germans did not get the idea that we were exhausted. At the final whistle Jack had also gone down. I would never forget the sight of my brother sitting there, after having spent so much of himself, with his head in his hands.

Ramsey made a short but extremely effective speech, which two years later would be echoed by my Manchester United manager, Sir Matt Busby, on this same pitch after a second-half goal by Benfica had forced us into extra time in the European Cup final.

Ramsey said that we had won the game once but it had been taken away from us. Now we had to go out and win it again. We had to make sense of all the work and all the sacrifices. We had to do something that would make us proud for the rest of our lives.

Bobby Moore was not a man easily impressed by words intended to be inspirational, but he would always insist that this was among Alf Ramsey's finest moments. He touched all the players. He reminded us of all that had been achieved in three years, how far we had come and, most of all, how it would be absolutely intolerable if the prize was allowed to slip away.

When Seeler made his philosophical remark about the unpredictable nature of football, my legs had never felt so heavy. Now, I could feel life and determination return. Naturally, Alan Ball's eyes were still aglow.

Almost immediately we had again the sense that Ramsey was right when he said that we were the stronger team and that, in his opinion, the Germans had given all they had and were now battling to put one step after another. Ball tested the theory a minute or so into extra time and it was not found wanting. Alan tore down the right flank and forced Tilkowski into a fine save as he tipped the shot over the bar. We were in charge of the tempo of the game, and five minutes later I put in a left-footed shot that Tilkowski could only turn against a post. Still there was no killing thrust from Beckenbauer, and as we began to lap menacingly around the now hard-pressed Schulz and his co-defenders, I had the strongest feeling that the breakthrough couldn't be far away. When it came, after a hundred minutes of play, it was shaped by three of the players in whom Ramsey had placed so much faith when he faced his most difficult decisions of this World Cup.

Stiles, whose neck Ramsey had saved in the face of pressure

from both Fifa and the FA in the wake of the French match, sent a perfect ball down the right. It was collected by Ball, who had been recalled for the duel with Argentina, and placed at the feet of Hurst, the man Ramsey had selected from under the shadow of the Greaves legend. It is impossible to believe that anyone who saw the action of the following seconds, English or German, and had an interest in football, will ever forget it.

Hurst controlled the ball, turned and smashed it against the underside of the bar, from where it landed, I will always believe, over the line. At the flashpoint, my reaction was entirely the same as that of the in-rushing Roger Hunt, the most honest of players, who instead of trying to slam the ball back into the net, instantly turned away with his arms raised. My own feeling was so strong I found myself behaving as I had when Peters had shot us into the lead. I was ecstatic as I raced to embrace a team-mate, anyone who was wearing the shirt of, as I believed, the new world champions. But then, out of the corner of my eye, I saw the referee running to the linesman from Azerbaijan, Tofik Bakhramov. Many years later, as a result of this moment of drama a statue was built in his honour outside the main stadium in Baku.

We waited an age for their conversation to finish and for the referee to point to the centre circle, but when he did it was as though we had gone beyond the point where even the mysteries of football could touch us again this day. Surely we had been taken to our limits and, just as surely, we had survived.

It remained only for Bobby Moore, defying Jack's desire for him to boot the ball high into the stand – no footballer had ever been less susceptible to such a classic request from the old, hard school of defence – to send a beautiful pass to Hurst, who was dredging up still more resolve as he gathered the ball and drove it fiercely into the roof the net.

At the same time, the man of the match, Alan Ball, was helping to split the German defence with still another astonishing run.

24

YOU WANTED TO WIN
IT MORE

ONLY LATER COULD I begin to shape in my mind anything like a clear record of the excitement, relief and joy that gripped me and my team-mates in the minutes and hours after the game.

It was wonderful to be reunited with Norma at the Royal Garden Hotel on Kensington High Street, where we had been moved for the post-game celebrations, and to see the pride of my mother Cissie and father Robert, and to catch everyone's excitement when we walked out on to the balcony to show off the Jules Rimet trophy and wave to the crowd. It was then maybe I saw the first clear indication that Alf Ramsey had finally relaxed in the knowledge that he had achieved all that he had set out to do. As the waves of cheers crashed in, he began to smile in a way that resembled a young, gratified boy more than an old pro who had realised how many things could go wrong. And even as all this was happening, inevitably I suppose, so many flashpoints of the game and its aftermath kept coming back to me. I remember thinking that each one had to be stored away and kept for ever.

One of them was Jack and me on the lap of honour, feeling suddenly so knackered, and my brother putting his arm around my shoulders and saying, 'Well, what about that, kiddo?'

'Our lives will never be the same again, I don't suppose,' I replied.

The enormity of what had happened struck me powerfully at that moment, and now when I look back, I see that I was right to feel that way because the yardstick we had just set has still to be met by the players who have come after us, and so many still ask the question, 'Will it ever happen again?'

It was so exhilarating because we had such a strong sense that what we had done was very rare and flew far beyond the experience of the vast majority of footballers, some of them of the highest talent. I remembered the tremendous feeling we'd had at Manchester United when we won the FA Cup at Wembley three years earlier, but also how Nobby Stiles was filled with such anguish when he failed to make the team after a bout of injury had put his place in question. He had fought such a desperate fight to get over the injury and he believed he had done so before the team sheet was put up. But you play for the cup every year. The glory of it is wonderful but brief. Other teams and other players quickly take your place. I said to Jack that when you win the World Cup, you have a foot in history, you have faced the best players in the world and you have beaten them.

Jack really didn't need any embellishment of our triumph. He had a great thirst for celebration and he did it so enthusiastically that we lost him for a while. He woke up, famously, the following morning after sleeping it off in somebody's garden.

After getting through the official banqueting – with wives being entertained separately, according to FA convention, which is impossible to imagine today – we encountered chaos in the hotel. Wherever you turned, there was a crush of people, and we felt the need to escape. Nobby and his wife Kay headed off to Danny La Rue's club with Alan Ball, John Connelly and Geoff Hurst and their wives. Bobby Moore had an invitation from the Playboy Club, so Norma and I joined him along with the Easthams and the Wilsons. First, though, we had to escape from the lift, which, not surprisingly in view of the hordes of people jamming into it and ignoring the alarm bells, became stuck. This particularly alarmed Norma and certainly wasn't what I had in mind for a night of celebration, but eventually we forced open the doors and inched our way back into the happy tumult.

On our way to the Playboy Club, sweeping by Hyde Park Corner and driving up Park Lane, where horns were tooting and one of the poshest thoroughfares in London was showing at least some of the gaiety of an Ashington street party, I felt as though we might have been a thousand miles from the training fields of Lilleshall. There, I learned later, the warden who had been pressed into chaplain duties, had found the strain of watching the game on television so great he had walked out of his house.

Here, though, among the bright lights of the West End were the rewards for the work we had put in, and the ambition and the willingness to accept that Alf Ramsey had worked out a way for England to win the World Cup. But it is not so easy putting aside the kind of drama we had come through that day, and although we certainly enjoyed ourselves, returning to the hotel at 4 a.m., I had no great urge to drink the night away. It had happened a few times in my youth, when lads were expected to take a drink, but I never liked the feeling that followed and on this night my strongest instinct was to be aware of everything and savour all of it. That wasn't the response of most of my team-mates but it was how I was and how I wanted to be, and had I been challenged about it I would have said, 'I'm feeling good, possibly as good as I have ever felt, and I know it's going to last a long time.'

In a perfect world there would have been no questions about the win. I said at the start of my England story – and it is something I will always believe – that the day of the final was the greatest expression of my football life, because it was about a team coming together and getting a very difficult job done, but there is no point in suggesting that some aspects of the game and what followed will ever be free of controversy, however ancient.

Even today when I go to Germany I am asked about Geoff Hurst's second goal and it does get under my skin, as the Germans know well enough. The incident is brought out as though it is not the supreme moment in the history of English football but some grim and haunting skeleton. When it happens, it irritates me more than good manners will allow me to say.

My main point is that with modern technology, television companies can freeze frames to support any argument they decide to put forth. One shot can convince you the ball was over the line, another that it was not. I can only say that I believed it was a goal. The Germans will never concur and if they persist in casting doubt, I find myself saying, finally, 'Well, if that goal hadn't been given, do you think you still would have beaten us?'

Over the years I have reviewed the game, and all the feelings it generates, with Franz Beckenbauer. We became friends almost from the day we were thrown together at Wembley, and our mutual respect did not suffer when, four years later in Mexico, we were once again pitted against each other in another big match.

He confirmed my first instinct that whichever coach lost his gamble in restricting us to marking roles would pay a heavy price in reputation. Schoen was savaged in the German media and Franz confessed that he was initially shocked when he was given his assignment.

Perhaps the deepest conversation we had about the final came in the Bayern Munich boardroom a few years ago. I was doing a series for Sky television and the first programme revisited 1966. We watched the entire 120 minutes of action together, me for the first time, and touched on everything – our own deadlocked duel, the outstanding performances and, of course, the goal, and when the showing was over, I turned to him and said, 'Franz, I just want you to give me your honest opinion. I want to know your feelings at the end of the game. Did you think England deserved to win or did you deserve to collect the World Cup?' He thought for a little before replying.

'Yes,' he said, 'I have to say England were the best team. I had a sense when the match happened, and I still feel it now, that you wanted to win it more, you were all more determined, while, deep down, we were just glad to be there.'

You can torture such a matter for only so long, but I was glad to hear Franz say that he felt the English team had the stronger desire. That certainly was my feeling. The Germans pushed us to our limits, but the more they pushed the harder we responded. I had never seen such commitment on the football field, and when it was over, when Franz and I shook hands, I knew in my heart that we had deserved to come out on top.

That feeling was quite sublime and it would always loom largest of anything in my memory. Certainly, it was more significant than the feeling of some of the lads that we had not been treated generously by the Football Association. Our bonus totalling £22,000 was rumoured to be much less than the Germans would receive for losing. We had agreed with Bobby Moore's proposal that instead of a system based on the number of appearances each player made, the money would be divided evenly through the twenty-two-man squad but other than that I could not get too involved in the issue. I knew, for example, George Cohen felt strongly that we were being given less than our due, especially when you considered the revenue the FA had made from the tournament. Looking back from a time when the current England team can negotiate huge personal bonuses, there is no question that George had a point. Maybe I was a little naïve, a little too trusting in the future, but my attitude with England was the same as it was with Manchester United.

I didn't bang on any doors, I waited for the club to decide what I was worth, and if that sounds too meek, too passive, I can only say, again, that it was how I was. I suppose, the fact that I was able to play football for a living, travel the world, and have a salary much better than I could have hoped for if I had joined so many of my north-eastern contemporaries down the pit or in a shipyard, outweighed every other consideration. And that included any even vaguely focused desire to be rewarded in line with the money I was generating with my team-mates when we filled a big stadium to the rafters.

If I was nagged by anything after the final, it was the fact that I lost my composure a little bit in extra time when I had the chance to make the score 4-2 before Hurst did so with his last charge.

When the ball came to me about twenty yards out, I thought, 'Now let's get this done, Bobby, because another goal will kill them off.' Unfortunately, I snatched at the shot, scuffed the ball on a surface made greasy by the rain showers, and felt some agony when I saw that I hadn't given Hans Tilkowski anything to do. Alf, unsurprisingly, had noted this and my earlier mistake and when he mentioned them in the dressing room afterwards – the old, tough pro right to the end of the mission – I was certainly not hurt or downcast by this flash of criticism, and I refrained from asking him if he had seen much of Beckenbauer out there. I knew this had been an outstanding team perform-ance, and that I had not been without recognition from the manager when I scored my goals against Mexico and Portugal. I could tell myself that the misses were made against the back-ground of an afternoon when mostly I had had to subdue my natural instincts for the benefit of the team.

I knew it was just another aspect of Alf, and that ever since he had taken charge of the team, he had been as demanding as he could be generous. Many times I had breathed a sigh of relief that I had not made a critical mistake, which could produce a quite withering reaction. I saw it happen on that occasion when he gave Keith Newton, a fine player, a merciless dressing down that made you want to be anywhere but within earshot. And then there was that theory that Jimmy Armfield might have been playing in the World Cup final but for one mistake made against Scotland, which had lingered powerfully in Ramsey's mind.

Certainly, I didn't feel the manager was indebted to me because I had submitted to his tactical demands. I was just happy to be playing, to be part of the great day. It always irritated me when I heard players complaining that they were being played out of position. As I saw it, you were a footballer and you played football at every opportunity that came. You didn't have some big debate about what might suit you best. When Manchester United asked to me play on the wing for several years, and then England followed suit, I wasn't overjoyed but I was glad of the success that came to me out on the left, although I would have always chosen for myself a place in the middle.

Yes, of course, on the day of the World Cup final I would have preferred to run free and, possibly, make the impact that had come in earlier matches. But if that was my instinct as a player, if I always wanted to go where I liked and get the ball whenever I could, I like to think I never lost sight of the fact that I was part of a team. Infinitely worse than not being able to indulge each whim as it came to me, would have been not to play, not to have had any of those sensations that flooded over me when I saw Geoff Hurst's final shot rocketing home.

So a sharp word from the man who had done so much to make England world champions, and had put so much trust in me, was never likely to draw blood – not when we had got home and everything we had pursued for so long had come to fruition.

It was not as though I had never before suffered criticism – or been afraid of it. When I worked with Bobby Moore, Jack and Nobby, and under Ramsey, I felt proud to be part of something that was really one long process of improvement. Around such people you were never liable to believe that you were beyond questioning, and this was particularly true for me, because I always realised, for example, that in one way I was quite different from Bobby Moore. I looked at Bobby and I thought, 'Oh yes, you know what's going on.'

Bobby was a thinker. He wanted to know everything he could about the game. As a boy, he trailed after his mentor at West Ham, the brilliant coach of the future, Malcolm Allison, bombarding him with questions. I wasn't a thinker. I was instinctive. Give me the ball and I will see what I can do with it. Sometimes I did things that brought praise showering down on my head. Other times it was criticism, sometimes from my teammates, sometimes from Alf. This wasn't a problem for me. I respected their views, and I knew that when the manager had something to say that was hard and perhaps not what you wanted most to hear, especially when emotion and adrenalin were swirling around, there was nothing vindictive in any of it. It was just the way he was and the way he would always be. Alf never promised you a place in his team. He simply let you know what you had to do, and sometimes even more importantly, what not to do, if you were to win one and then keep it.

Franz Beckenbauer sometimes sounds less philosophical than I tried to be when he recalls the time Helmut Schoen issued him with instructions identical to mine from Alf. He remembers the uproar across Germany, the headlines that declared the coach was disarming his forwards by denying them their most creative support. 'Schoen kept saying to me, "Stick on Charlton, stick on Charlton," ' Beckenbauer reports with a sigh.

For myself, I can only be grateful that football history so long ago pronounced Alf Ramsey the winner.

I'm sure my younger brother Gordon echoes that sentiment. He was serving in the Merchant Navy in the Indian Ocean at the time and managed to hear a radio commentary right up to the end of normal time, at which point he had to go down into the engine room. Eventually, the captain came running down and shouted above the hissing pipes and the noise of the ship's engine, 'We've won, we've won.'

I don't think Gordon's joy, and that of the nation, was too seriously tempered by the fact that I had been required to play out of position. We had won and Alf Ramsey always knew that it would be the only thing that mattered.

25

SETTING SUNS

EVEN NOW, NINE years after his death and nearly half a century from the peak of his glory, football historians still debate the meaning of Alf Ramsey in much less than flattering terms. This angers me to my core and offends the deepest beliefs I formed in my playing career for both England and Manchester United, because for me the man who was knighted so swiftly in the wake of '66 laid down an achievement that will always be the model of how to draw the best from the leading players of our national sport.

There are various charges against his football legacy, maybe the most serious being the claim that somehow he put back all levels of English football with an emphasis on defence and for a while expunged the idea of the glory of great wingers, such as Finney, Matthews, Cliff Jones and George Best, who had brought such spectacle to the top flight of English club football for so long. He did nothing of the sort. What he did was operate on the soundest football principle of all. He elected to play his best team, choosing the players he believed could make the most effective contribution to a winning unit, and in the context of the team of '66 it seems to me that there is simply no questioning he was absolutely right. He played three wingers, all good ones by any standard, John Connelly, Ian Callaghan and Terry Paine, in the opening phase of the World Cup finals and there is no doubt in my mind that if he believed they had shown the ability to undermine seriously the world-class defences of Argentina in the quarter-final and West Germany in the final, he would not have hesitated to play them. Instead, he picked two players who, while not being orthodox wingers, had convinced him they could make a major impact on team performance.

He selected Alan Ball, in almost everyone's view the outstanding player of the World Cup final, and Martin Peters, who scored a goal and was always a highly relevant figure. His third controversial choice, the one whose selection some still say was a blow against adventurous, attacking play, was Geoff Hurst, and he scored three goals.

The idea that Alf Ramsey retarded English football is monstrously malformed. He gave English football pride and an unprecedented belief that we could compete in the wider football world. It was not his fault if he had imitators who didn't begin to understand that his decisions had nothing to do with any tactical vogue, or any new personal brainwave about how to play the game, but rather his understanding of what the players he had at his disposal could offer and how best they could be brought together.

The enthusiasm for football created by England's success was not a problem but a huge incentive. It was an invitation to other football men to develop their own ideas in a new climate of confidence, and the best young ones, such as Brian Clough, Malcolm Allison and Dave Sexton, did exactly that. To blame Ramsey for the dull work and conclusions of less inspired figures is both unfair and, in my opinion, scandalously ignorant of the realites of football at the highest level.

I'm not saying Alf was perfect or that, when his winning team began to break up, he did not, perhaps in his anxiety, put more emphasis on preventing the other team playing. Indeed, you may think he had already done that when he told me to mark Franz Beckenbauer so tightly. But when he asked me to compromise my own way of playing, he didn't outrage my sense of what football should be. His logic, however painful it might have been for me to admit, was quite impeccable. In my experience, the decisions Alf Ramsey took were only ever based on a very hard calculation of how he could best use his resources.

Of course he made mistakes and miscalculations, like every man, and four years down the road from the euphoria of victory over West Germany some of them would both haunt him and hamper his team when the world title had to be defended in Mexico. But when you come to balance what he did, against what he didn't do, to my mind he certainly enjoys a vast balance of credit.

Always, he made one thing clear. He wanted to be judged by performance in the World Cup. European Championships were important, and if you didn't hone your team in friendly games against serious opposition, in all kinds of conditions, how could you possibly be prepared for the ultimate test of a World Cup? Nothing else mattered, he said, if it wasn't geared to learning something new about the players who made your team and how strong they remained when the next big challenge came into sight.

Certainly it is hard not to compare the thoroughness of Ramsey's preparation with so much that followed him down the years. All his players, however senior, had the sense that, each time they wore the England shirt, against any opposition, they were resubmitting themselves for judgement against the most exacting standards.

For anyone who played through the Ramsey years, the first lesson was that if you failed to be part of a team, if you didn't dovetail your strengths with those of the men around you, it didn't matter how much football talent you possessed, you would not be picked. For those of us from that era, it was particularly difficult to understand the process of team development that led Sven-Goran Eriksson into a debate with his players about their best midfield formation on the eve of the 2004 European Championship finals in Portugal; or, two years later, the decision to select for the World Cup teenager Theo Walcott, who had yet to play a first-team game for Arsenal and had had no chance of developing an understanding with his England team-mates.

By way of comparison, you could only recall all over again the agonies that went into the selection of Geoff Hurst over Jimmy Greaves, and how the opinions of the critics, the affections of the nation and the celebrity of a brilliant player became secondary to the need to field a team that functioned most effectively. My understanding of Ramsey's authority in all matters, from the sweep of the team plan to the most minor details of organisation and discipline, was enhanced by my occasional, and generally feeble, attempts to represent the dressing room. Ramsey simply didn't do debate – or speculation on the possibility of an untried boy doing something in World Cup finals he had not been asked to do in club football.

In the end, eight years after his supreme achievement, Ramsey would be punished, and by no one less fervently than himself, because he was unable to reproduce the level of team performances he had always sought and always demanded.

Maybe this emphasis on measuring himself only against the best opposition was partly the result of his experiences on two of the most traumatic days of his distinguished international playing career, the shocking defeats of England by the part-timers of America in the 1950 World Cup and against Hungary three years later, in front of his own people at Wembley.

The humiliation suffered at the feet of Puskas and Hidegkuti, I know, was something he could never quite forget. Maybe it was one of the key forces that drove his desire to see that English footballers would never again be so exposed, and so ill-equipped to deal with opponents who had, by slavish hard work as well as brilliance, reached another dimension of the game. In a one-off unguarded moment, this least romantic of men admitted that he had dreamed of the day an England side would surpass the achievements of the team that so tormented eleven of their predecessors on a grey afternoon at Wembley.

Perhaps another consequence of that painful experience was Ramsey's insistence on seeing the World Cup not just as the supreme test of a nation's football but also the only proper measuring stick for the work of an England coach. As a player, I have to admit, I felt rather the same way when the European Championship of 1968 ended anti-climactically, at least for the world champions, with us finishing in third place after beating the Soviet Union in Rome in a play-off for that honour. I'm sure Ramsey would have liked to gain another prize – if for no other reasons than it would have confirmed a winning habit for those players who were resisting the challenge for their places by emerging candidates, and given those who formed the first wave of a new England an early taste of how it was to be winners on the international stage. But the truth was, for Ramsey, the World Cup was the essential challenge. To make a team that he could rely on with unwavering confidence would always take a four-year cycle of building or rebuilding. Anything in between was valuable in arriving at the final combination: no more, no less.

That would have to wait until Mexico in 1970, he was forced to conclude, after Yugoslavia, the team who had so clouded my early days as an England player and almost certainly cost me the chance of an appearance in the 1958 World Cup, had beaten us by the only goal in the semi-final in Florence.

It was a classic Yugoslav performance. They were hard as nails in the tackle but capable of moments of fine and even delicate skill. The winner came from the celebrated left winger of Red Star Belgrade, Dragan Dzajic, and was so beautifully taken that it seemed odd it should come in a match that also featured an

alarming kick on Alan Ball by the hard man, Dobrivoje Trivic.
That move elicited a hard response from Norman Hunter, who
abandoned the niceties when he stopped their playmaker, Ivica
Osim. But despite his actions, it was not Norman who ended
up receiving censure. Alan Mullery became the first Englishman
to be sent off in a full international when he retaliated against
the ruthless Trivic. Ramsey did not enhance his reputation as a
diplomat when he dismissed the limping Osim as a clown. Ball
was also limping. The swelling of his ankle was so substantial
he said he was afraid to take off his sock.

With this result, we'd come almost full circle from the opening
of the qualifying campaign, the home international loss to
Scotland at Wembley so soon after our triumph over West
Germany – a result that one Scottish sportswriter claimed had
rendered the World Cup 'meaningless'.

However, we did play well in Rome three days after falling
to the Yugoslavs, when we beat the Soviet team we had admired,
and even to a degree feared, two years earlier in England. Geoff
Hurst and I scored the goals in front of a vast crowd in the
Olympic Stadium, and received some polite applause as a decent
warm-up act for the finalists, Italy and our conquerors
Yugoslavia, who again showed both toughness and skill. This
time it was not quite enough, as the home team narrowly won
(after a replay) the first of their European titles. Polite was not
quite the word, though, for the way the fans treated Nobby
Stiles. Not for the last time in his life, he was elected the hate
figure on a foreign field. A few months later we arrived at
Buenos Aires airport with Manchester United for our World
Club championship game against Estudiantes and were greeted
with a banner that read: 'Nobby Stiles, El Bandito – the Bandit'.
This view of Nobby was no doubt a consequence of his
combative role in the 1966 triumph which had left so many
open wounds in the Argentine football psyche.

In Rome, Nobby was booed every time he touched the ball

– or a Russian player – but he simply shrugged his shoulders, and played as hard as he had when he had faced Amancio, the Real Madrid winger, a few months earlier at the Bernabeu. That was when United won the European Cup semi-final that carried us to Wembley and our victory over Benfica. Amancio had kicked Stiles away from the view of the referee and my friend worried that he might not finish the game, which would have been a critical blow to the team in those pre-substitute days. So he made what he considered an illegal but quite moral decision. He whacked Amancio, who was causing us a lot of trouble, out of the vision of the referee but in full view of the soaring terraces. The crowd reaction he faced later in the Olympic Stadium seemed like mild disapproval in comparison, and as far as Nobby was concerned, it was something that just had to be endured.

No one in the world could have persuaded him that he had misbehaved in the Bernabeu because, as he saw it, he was merely righting a wrong, adjusting the balance of a game that had been distorted by Amancio's original crime. Certainly, the brilliant Spanish player's influence tailed off quite dramatically after Nobby's response to his earlier ambush.

Perhaps fortunately, Nobby was missing from both legs of what amounted to the quarter-final of the European Championship, when England narrowly overcame Spain, the reigning champions, 1–0 in April at Wembley, and 2–1 in May in Madrid, which set up our encounter with Yugoslavia. In both those matches, Amancio showed that when he concentrated entirely on playing football, he was one of the best in the world game.

By that summer match in Rome it was plain, certainly to me, that Nobby's time in the England team was running down quickly under the challenge of Tottenham's strong and talented midfielder Alan Mullery. Indeed, Nobby played in Rome only because of Mullery's sending-off.

Nobby would play just three more games for England, and

although he made the plane for Mexico, there was a belief – which Nobby did not dispute – that the loyalty Ramsey had displayed so openly in the furore that followed the Jacky Simon incident in the World Cup had again been expressed. I don't believe it was out of pure sentimentality, because Ramsey was too much of a professional for that, but perhaps because of an extreme reluctance to part with a player he trusted so much. It was as though the mere presence of Nobby – and Jack for that matter, who played just one game in the 1970 World Cup, the final group game against Czechoslovakia – was some kind of last investment in what he considered outstanding professional attitudes. Maybe Nobby or Jack might respond to a crisis on the field, while in the background they would work to maintain the spirit of '66.

Back in Rome, Nobby's situation was one that inevitably comes to almost every footballer – dreading the day when he would no longer be able play. In Nobby's case, he was in the middle of a fight to save his career in the face of worsening knee problems, which had already required surgery. Again, I had to give thanks for my own good fortune. Six years older than Nobby, I carried one small scar, the result of a flying tackle that had had no worse effect than keeping me out of a few games. Nobby, as Wilf McGuinness had done before him, would fight on against the odds, conscious that they were growing against him with each match he played. I could see that he had no other option because he hated the idea of no longer being part of something that had so inspired him throughout his life. He loved the game and he loved the people he played both with and against, however hard he traded kicks and blows with those in the latter category.

My abiding memory of him after that third-place play-off game is of how he led a young Russian player, who had been standing alone and uncertain about what to do and where to go, through the crowd of the after-match banquet to the bar.

It reminded me that however hard Nobby fought on the field, however much he saw the opposition as the enemy, when the final whistle came he had a truly kind nature – he fought, and then he celebrated the fight with his opponent whenever he could.

If Nobby was hanging on, along with Jack, who had now seen the strong, younger Everton centre half Brian Labone play nine times in his place, so was Roger Hunt. Roger was the first of the boys of '66 to be dropped, ironically for Jimmy Greaves in the home defeat by Scotland at Wembley. We had already lost George Cohen. His place was being disputed by Keith Newton of Blackburn Rovers and Tommy Wright of Everton. George's career ended suddenly when he injured his knee in a collision with the Stoke City winger Harry Burrows.

Whatever the new men did, you knew that George was irreplaceable in terms of the fighting spirit that evolved on the way to winning the World Cup. He has shown that spirit throughout his life, battling back from reverses in business and three bouts of cancer. When the boys of '66 meet to share our memories and feelings for those who have left us, Ramsey, Moore and Ball, he is always the same, always bright and proud to have been part of something we like to think will never be forgotten.

Cohen and Stiles, Hunt and Jack were never challengers for the title of most elegant footballer who ever played for England, but when you thought of them together, and understood that their days in the team were either gone or going, you suddenly realised that the new blood that was beginning to flow into the side had to pump very strongly indeed to provide adequate compensation.

This is meant as no insult to the men whose job was to fill such boots, and replace such hearts, but merely to return again to the genius of the football man who some will tell you, if you allow them, had a detrimental effect on English football.

I doubt that any of the quartet who were slipping away from

the heart of the side, and who could no longer be sure that they were not playing their last international games, would have been automatic England selections under any other manager. But Ramsey had always made it clear that his search was not solely for players upon whom natural gifts had been lavished. More than anything, he wanted players – and men – of substance.

In this vital respect, each of the players on whom the international sun was now setting had the consistency, and the competitive glow, of diamonds.

26

THE SANEST MAN IN
A CRAZY WORLD

IN APRIL 1970 I captained my country in what was my 100th cap, against Northern Ireland, in the build-up to Mexico and when a few days later we drew at Hampden Park in front of a crowd of 137,000, in a game in which I wasn't playing, it meant we had gone through the 1969–70 season so far undefeated. This might just explain why Alf Ramsey was surprisingly enthusiastic about the idea of Scottish music producer Bill Martin producing the first England song – 'Back Home'.

Some might say it was not one of the great musical classics but the public warmed to its patriotic lyrics, shooting it to number one in the hit parade, and certainly there were plenty of laughs when we were fitted out in evening dress before appearing on *Top of the Pops*. I felt able to take on the demeanour of an old hand, having had some success on the old Hughie Green *Double Your Money* quiz show when I still a youngster at Manchester United. My chosen subject had been popular music.

'We'll give all we've got to give for the folks back home' was a line from our chart-topping smash and it certainly reflected the mood of the squad as we gathered once again to take on the world. It has often been argued that that group of players that headed to Mexico was better than the one that had won the World Cup four years earlier. When I hear such conjecture, it is not enough for me merely to disagree. I also have to say it is nonsense because the record keeps taking me back to the fact that one squad won and the other lost. This remains true however many factors you feed into the equation, including some that were beyond the control of the manager and the players when we arrived in Mexico City early in May 1970 to prepare for our first group game against Romania in Guadalajara.

We couldn't have known that our captain Bobby Moore would be swept up in an absurd but potentially ruinous controversy, or that on the morning of what might have proved to be one of the greatest of his – and England's – days, Gordon Banks found himself still troubled by a stomach bug. The illness struck despite the defences that had been painstakingly put in place by our team doctor Neil Phillips, a fact some claim is mysterious, and even sinister. These were unexpected blows, but they did not, at least in my mind, blur the line between what was a proven winning squad and one that had its opportunities, along with some bad luck, but in the end couldn't take them – and this even though we were, indisputably, strong in those positions that had been filled by new men.

With George Cohen out of football and Ray Wilson, who had played his last game for England in that consolation match in Rome, so affected by injury that he had lost his place in the Everton team and been given a free transfer to Oldham Athletic, we might have been terribly exposed at full back, a position that had been such a source of strength in 1966. However, we had grown quickly and strongly at that broken place with Keith Newton and Tommy Wright competing on the right and Terry Cooper, the former winger who had emerged brilliantly on the left side of the Leeds United defence, making Ray's position his own.

Francis Lee, a key figure in the rise of Manchester City, and his club-mate Colin Bell, had brought new strength and attacking options. Lee was quick, dynamic and filled with self-confidence, and Bell, who had been nicknamed 'Nijinsky' – after the great racehorse, not the dancer – by his coach Malcolm Allison, seemed as if he could run forever with tremendous power. If Nobby had been marginalised there was no question that his successor, Alan Mullery, had brought an aggressive playing personality, and plenty of punch, all of his own. And there was still, of course, Norman Hunter of Leeds United, who remained a defender of great ability behind his ferocious image. I used to wonder sometimes if Norman ever sat back and reviewed all the footballing gifts with which he's been blessed and still harboured a regret that he was born around the same time as Bobby Moore, the man who had been keeping him out of the team for half a decade now. Roger Hunt was another missing stalwart but here again Ramsey was not without options, in the extravagantly gifted Chelsea favourite Peter Osgood, the fine, cool Leeds United finisher Allan Clarke and my young, free-scoring United colleague Brian Kidd.

No, there wasn't a question about the quality of the new men, only the doubt that every coach has to confront about how effectively he could integrate new faces with an old guard. In this case, the old guard was formed by Banks, who was now at the peak of his career, Bobby Moore, Martin Peters, Alan Ball, Geoff Hurst and me, as well as Jack and Nobby, fulfilling their watching brief on the sidelines. And soon another familiar face would appear. Jimmy Greaves, who had accepted the offer of sponsorship as a competitor in the Mexico road rally, was driving down winding roads and over mountains, and maybe reflecting all over again on how it might have been.

If I had repeated my inventory of our strengths, this time on the plane flying halfway across the world rather than on the bus carrying the boys to Roehampton, from most angles my conclusions would have been similarly encouraging.

There would, though, have been one significant difference that I can never discount when thinking about the two campaigns. In England, Alf Ramsey was perfectly in tune with his environment, happy that he could protect his players from all distractions and pressures. He was the master of every challenge to his authority, as he proved when putting down, with unwavering contempt, the one threat to his leadership when it was suggested that Nobby Stiles should be dismissed from the squad. In Mexico, it was different. In Mexico, Alf Ramsey wasn't the master of his environment – he was at war with it.

He didn't warm to the Mexicans and they, in their pride and sense that he rather despised them, responded in similarly hostile fashion. That perception may have been a consequence of the frequent rehashing in the Mexican press of his charge that their fellow Latin Americans, the Argentines of '66, were 'animals'.

It didn't help that a year earlier, when we played games in Mexico City, Montevideo and Rio, Alf had taken on the Mexican press in full-frontal argument. Mexican reporters were thrown out when they came into our dressing room after a 0–0 draw, and when he finally spoke to them, in a very frigid atmosphere, he said, 'Yes, I do have something to say. There was a band playing outside our hotel at five o'clock this morning. We were promised a motorcycle escort to the ground. It never arrived. When our players went out to inspect the pitch, they were abused and jeered by the crowd. I would have thought the Mexican public would have been delighted to welcome England. But we are delighted to be in Mexico and the Mexican people are wonderful.'

That last pleasantry did nothing to soothe wounded feelings, and nor did his decision, reached after we had been carried to the stadium in a rickety bus without air conditioning, to import our own luxurious coach for the World Cup, a shining vehicle that would be shipped to Miami and driven down in the tyre tracks left by Jimmy Greaves. There were other public-relations disasters, not least when Mexican customs inspectors rejected food brought into the country on Alf's orders. Meats and even fish fingers were burned for the lack of import licences, the fire being stoked enthusiastically by the Mexican press.

This was doubly unfortunate because not only did it help to create an antagonistic background for our defence of the World Cup – we were certainly the least popular football team in all of Mexico – it worked against Alf's determination to make the preparation perfect for his players.

Neil Phillips had been asked to explore every means of maintaining our health against the risk presented by a dramatic change of climate and altitude, and he had consulted all the leading experts in tropical and sports medicine. Each day we were given tablets to guard against infection and dehydration, and cream to rub into our heads to prevent damage from the broiling sun. The result was that in the weeks of build-up and competition we suffered just one case of a player laid low by a bug. That one occasion changed everything and was a crushing blow to every member of our party, but it was no reflection on what was undoubtedly meticulous planning.

Alf paid particular attention to the problem of altitude. Before our first competitive game, we stayed on the high plateau of Mexico City and then flew to Bogota and Quito in the Andes – the third and second highest capital cities in the world – for warm-up games against Colombia and Ecuador. So when we went down to Guadalajara, at a mere 5,200 feet – where the public had been courted relentlessly by our group rivals Brazil, the superstars of Latin America – we were conditioned and ready to run as hard as was necessary to remain champions of the world. I could not have failed to remember the time, eleven years earlier, when we lost 2–1 to an inferior Mexican team and I sat down in the dressing room, gasping for air and wondering why it was we had been brought to this altitude, and this climate, with such little help and care.

Alf, in his professionalism, had produced a good plan, and it may have proved a brilliant one but for the misfortunes that befell us and, maybe, for the fact that he had so enraged the locals.

What certainly didn't lend a helping hand to Alf's preparation was Bobby Moore and me, bored in our Bogota hotel after training for a 4–0 win over Colombia, deciding to take a stroll across the hotel lobby to a jewellery shop named Green Fire.

It wasn't really a shop, more a kiosk beside the hotel reception desk, and I had the idea that I might buy a piece of jewellery for Norma. I would have made a wider investigation of shopping possibilities if we hadn't been warned to be careful about leaving the hotel because there was so much random violence and thievery on the streets of Bogota. We'd been advised that if we did go out on to pavements that were packed with pedlars and, we were told, pickpockets, it should never be with fewer than three companions.

I saw a very attractive necklace and asked the price, suspecting that, in such a big hotel in such a place, it would probably be out of my range. A girl shop assistant unlocked a cabinet to show me the necklace and then confirmed that, at around £6,000, it was way beyond my means. Bobby and I did a little more window shopping, but it was mostly a matter of boggling at the price tags of the items in the window, and commenting, 'That ring is worth more than my house!' and 'Unbelievable!'

We drifted away, speculating on quite who could afford such prices and how they earned their money. It certainly wasn't by playing World Cup football. We didn't have anywhere to go, or anything to do, so we sat down on one of the sofas dotted about the lobby of the hotel.

Suddenly, the shop assistant appeared. Speaking in a way that seemed strange and agitated, she asked Bobby to stand up, which he did with a mystified look on his face, and then started rummaging around in the cushions of the sofa. We were baffled as the girl spoke in Spanish, but then a man, whom we presumed was the manager of the shop, appeared and announced that a bracelet was missing. He too searched the sofa.

Among all the emerald rings and necklaces I hadn't seen a bracelet, and my first thought was that this was some kind of joke. But there was little humour on the faces of our accusers, so I said, 'Hey, this is serious, get our manager, get the police, get whoever . . .'

The man walked away and within minutes was back with the hotel manager and Alf Ramsey, who asked, 'What on earth is going on here?' Alf took us away from the scene and told us that we should not say anything at this point. A few days later, Norma called me to say that the English press were reporting that there was evidence, based on the experiences of other visitors to Colombia, that Bobby and I had almost certainly been drawn into a classic scam aimed at extorting money from innocent victims reluctant to get involved in lengthy police and court procedures. That made some sense of what, right from the start, I considered a stupid, bizarre incident. The other school of thought was that Moore, the captain of England, was targeted precisely as part of a wider conspiracy to discredit the world champions, who had been so insulting to Argentina, the second most important South American football nation.

On the other hand, I wondered whether when those two rushed up to us and made their charge against Bobby – I was never accused of anything – they were not aware of who and what he was and what a huge furore they were in the process of creating. Surely they wouldn't have deliberately targeted a person of such stature and great integrity?

Bobby was taken away from the hotel by police while FA officials overcame their bemusement and started making calls to the British embassy. Diplomatic action seemed to be succeeding when Bobby was released to play in the match – and he produced his usual level of immaculate control so coolly it was almost impossible to believe that he had been thrust into an international incident.

When he was also allowed to fly on to Quito and take part in the 2–0 win over Ecuador, it seemed that the whole affair had lapsed into a swiftly passing farce. I was confident enough to buy a small and quite modestly priced piece of jewellery for Norma in a Quito shop, but not before making sure that I had a team-mate with me.

The transaction was quick and routine and Norma still has the small stone. Whenever I see it I recall that, as I bought it, I imagined I was putting a seal on an affair that could have shattered both Bobby Moore's career and most of our hopes of winning a second straight World Cup.

Optimism certainly seemed to be the prevailing mood when we returned to Bogota for a stop-over at the same hotel where the problem had first occurred. If going back to that hotel, of all places, now seems to be an odd decision, especially when you couple it with not trying to find a way of by-passing Bogota altogether on the return to Mexico City, there was little apprehension as Alf led us to the cinema to watch the classic western *Shenandoah*.

Ramsey had looked nervous at the airport that morning in Quito, where the 9,350 feet altitude had proved an ideal, although at the time extremely painful, conditioning exercise, but when Bobby went unmolested on our arrival in Bogota, even the manager, whose face had been filled with such anger and indignation when he first arrived at the scene of the mythical crime, seemed much more relaxed. This remained so right up to the moment his eyes were taken off the cinema screen by the news that in the darkened theatre a police officer had tapped Bobby Moore on the shoulder and led him away for further questioning.

Once again, Ramsey was outraged – he would say later that these were the worst days of his international career – but most of the rest of us believed that the nightmare would end that morning and Bobby would appear at the airport, imperturbable as ever, the sanest man in a crazy world.

When Bobby was still absent at the airport, I said to Ramsey, 'Look, I want to help all I can.' I suggested I stay behind and reiterate my statement to the police that I was with Bobby at every moment in the jewellery shop and there was no way he could be guilty of this ridiculous charge. Quite brusquely, Alf said, 'You must get on that plane, Bobby, there's no way you're staying. We'll let the politicians and the diplomats settle this.'

So we got on the plane without our captain, who made everything so easy – on and off the field – and I had an empty feeling. As our plane started its descent into Panama City, a stop on the way to Mexico City, we flew into a violent storm. The turbulence would normally have left me white-knuckled but not on this occasion. I just couldn't stop thinking about the way Bobby Moore had been treated, perhaps more than anyone else on the plane, because I was there with him and I saw everything. I also imagined the unimaginable, going into the World Cup without a man who so often appeared to be not so much a captain as the supreme example of what every player needed to bring to a big game – composure, strength and an unerring sense of where to be and what to do. What I felt most as the plane shook and bucked its way to the Panama runway was rage at the injustice and my own inability to influence events as a prime witness.

The only thing I could be sure of was my duty, along with other senior players, to help maintain the spirit of a squad increasingly anxious for news from Bogota. I could do that, at least, and also know that back in the British embassy, where he had been placed under house arrest, Bobby Moore would be unshakeable in his belief that nothing would be served by screaming and shouting. No doubt he enjoyed Jimmy Greaves's visits to the embassy, but at no cost to his awareness of the need to remain calm.

Even Bobby's coolness under pressure had to come under some strain, however, as the days dragged by with the knowledge that he was missing vital preparation with his team-mates. A week had passed, and we had moved from Mexico City to Guadalajara, when we heard that the case against Bobby had collapsed, partly because his two accusers had apparently gone to earth.

When he arrived back with us, his impact was huge and instant. By now Jeff Astle, the prolific West Bromwich Albion striker, had found his bearings again after his own ordeal. A poor flyer, he had taken a couple of swift drinks at the outset of our flight from Bogota to Mexico City and their interaction with a tranquilliser had left him in a poor state when we got off the plane at the end of the journey. The Mexican press saw through our attempts to conceal his condition at the airport and were quick to produce a few more disparaging headlines, the least surprising, maybe, saying that the reigning world champions were really just a gang of drunks and thieves.

Our freed captain told us that all he wanted to do was get back to the business of defending the World Cup. 'Forget Bogota,' he said. 'All that matters now is what we do here.' We would be doing it without six of the players who had set off with us from Heathrow – Peter Thompson, who for a second time in four years was receiving the hard news that he had failed to make the final cut, Peter Shilton, Bob McNab, Ralph Coates, David Sadler and Brian Kidd. The departure of four of these excellent players – Thompson and Sadler accepted Alf's offer to stay with the squad – was another reminder of how fine the margins were between a place on the world stage and a place in the audience.

Shortly before the game against Romania, as the Mexican fans feting the Brazilians continued to make clear their dislike of the English, noisily and at all times of the day and night outside our hotel in Guadalajara, we did have some warming evidence that we were maybe not the absolute pariahs of world football. It was an invitation to Bobby Moore and me from the Brazilian players. They wanted us to talk to them about the effects on the players of our success in 1966 – and the scrapping of the maximum wage in the English game in 1961. We went along to talk to Pelé and the great emerging triumvirate of Gerson, a superb left-sided midfielder, Tostao, a sublime forward, and Rivelino. By today's standards, we could report a mere snail's pace of progress in the lot of leading players, but it was a very pleasant visit to the overwhelming favourites to succeed us as champions, and, maybe, we liked to think, a nice touch of respect for what we had achieved at that time when the world's greatest football nation were literally being kicked out of the tournament they had annexed so brilliantly for eight years.

We worked well during training in the last days before facing Romania. Our leader had been restored. We had some tough, feisty and very talented players. Suddenly, it was not so hard to regain the feeling that belongs to champions, the idea that it would take a hell of a performance, or maybe some very odd circumstances, to knock us off our throne.

27

HEAT OF BATTLE

MEXICO WILL ALWAYS haunt me. The passion of it, the dark
magic and the magnificent, heart-touching skies, the brooding
volcanoes and the smouldering, angry, happy people who lived
in their shadows. I know that if I returned to Mexico City now,
at the age of seventy, I would probably spend most of my time
gasping for breath in the baking sun and the high altitude. Yet
I would also remember moments, in 1970, when I was inspired,
hopeful, my legs feeling so young and strong I might have been
a boy running in the wind-scored sand dunes of the North East.
However, for the majority of the time I wasn't quite sure whether
we were heading for another great triumph or some bitter
disappointment.

Jalisco Stadium, Guadalajara, 7 June – the place and date were
foremost in all our minds. Brazil, champions-elect in the opinion
of most neutrals, would be our opponents – and the litmus test
of our progress as a team through all the convulsions that had
come since we set foot in Latin America. Here, potentially, was
the match of the tournament, even though it might not be
decisive to the progress of either team. Better than that, it might
just possibly be one for the football ages.

We were not in a 'group of death' because Romania were
still decades away from the point where they could threaten any
team in the world, as they did in the United States twenty-four
years later, and Czechoslovakia were no longer the force that

reached the final in Chile eight years earlier. However Group Three did oblige us to play the one team in the tournament capable of producing supernatural football.

The Brazilians were hungry to re-assert their World Cup dominance after their dismissal in England – and to take revenge on their European torturers. Ramsey had been dismissive of their chances in '66, because he saw a team dwindling in every area of the field except the one occupied by Pelé, but he wasn't so inclined to discount them now.

They'd had plenty of turmoil with the sacking of their controversial coach Joao Saldanha and his replacement by the more orthodox Mario Zagallo, an unspectacular but effective winger in the winning teams of 1958 and 1962. But it seemed that they had come through the storm and, far from being left broken by the experience, found some of their old certainties. It always helps when you believe in a new generation of outstanding players.

Tostao, having flown to Mexico after an operation in Houston, Texas, for a career-threatening detached retina, now seemed to be seeing everything that much quicker than everyone else on the field except Pelé. Jairzinho was displaying a direct power that made the loss of Garrincha a little easier for the football nation that celebrates its heroes like no other. Carlos Alberto was a captain beginning to rival Bobby Moore in his conviction.

We would know far more about ourselves as a team after this test, and if we had long abandoned any idea that in Mexico we might carry a certain aura as reigning champions, at last we had the chance to win some measure of respect. Love, no doubt, was out of the question, but respect, well, it would wash over us very nicely after all the jeers and the abuse and the horrible blare of the car horns.

How we played Brazil might just send the right message to all our lesser rivals, and show that we remained legitimate contenders.

First, though, there was Romania and if their football didn't bring a chill to our hearts, their tackling certainly did. Naturally, the Mexican fans cheered even their most outrageous assaults, and the team in general. Tommy Wright, a second-half substitute for Keith Newton, and Francis Lee, in particular, did extremely well to remain disciplined. Defender Mihai Mocanu was the chief assassin and after retiring Newton to the bench he quickly added the replacement Wright to his list of victims. After the game, Lee shook his head and said, 'He must have created a new tackle. He left identical footprints on my knees.'

Ironically, the Romanians were missing their most creative player, Nicolae Dobrin, who had suffered sunstroke despite the massive efforts of the state sports system to support their team with medical assistance. It was on hearing about the Romanian preparations that Ramsey had urged Neil Phillips to take a crash course in tropical medicine and altitude conditioning. From his own playing experiences, he was all too aware of the difficulties presented by extreme climates and had been worrying about the great leaps in altitude we would have to make in Mexico.

The lone doctor had reason to be satisfied with the first result of his impressive effort to keep us healthy. Newton had left the match early, and was eventually followed by Francis Lee, who was replaced by Peter Osgood, but they had not been drained by the sun or the thin air – just that routine kicking by Mr Mocanu. In fact, the temperature was less fierce than we had feared when we first heard about the decision to play games in the heat of high noon – for the benefit of European TV audiences. We were also helped by a cooling rain shower in the second half, but no one could be complacent about a future for football in which it seemed obvious that the considerations of profit would be increasingly influential. The timing of the matches had not been made any less shocking for this one day's reprieve from the burning sun.

Before he left the field, Lee had a glancing role in the only goal, a cross from Alan Ball touching his head before reaching the scorer, Geoff Hurst, in the sixty-fourth minute. Earlier, Lee had sent a header against the crossbar, and he looked lively, and powerful, enough to trouble the rather more formidable opposition now waiting around the corner. As the tournament wore on, however, it became clear that the conditions were not helping either Lee or Martin Peters, both of whom based their games on their ability to run at defences and, in Lee's case particularly, with a sudden explosiveness.

In any circumstances the physicality and conditions of the opening game would have been a trial but coming after the constant harassment from the fans around our hotel, it was a serious test of already worn-down nerve ends. The Hilton Hotel, where we were staying, was on a small island in the centre of the city. Each night, a parade of cars circled the hotel, blasting their horns. Some mornings we were told that only extra security had managed to keep out fans trying to get into the hotel in the small hours, with quite what intention it was not too pretty to think about. One report was that some of them had, in fact, managed to get on to our floor before they were contained and ejected.

Ramsey was not slow to employ the tactics that are common to coaches who feel that their teams are developing a sense of persecution and perhaps an unfair stacking of the odds. Twenty-six years later at the European Championship, Terry Venables, another Dagenham man, employed a similar approach when his England team received a lot of media criticism after a drinking spree in Hong Kong and some misbehaviour on the flight home. The coach gathers his team into a circle and announces that they are under attack and thus have to fight harder than ever before to survive. This redoubles the need for everyone to work for each other, and there was no doubt our siege mentality had been given impetus the moment Bobby Moore was rounded up by police in the cinema in Bogota.

That feeling moved up a notch each time a player stirred in his sleep and heard the symphony of car horns and cries against England. But although Ramsey was prepared to try to turn the situation to our advantage, he was deeply worried about the level of antagonism we faced at every turn. At one point he considered moving the team to a new hotel, somewhere less accessible to the mob, but instead, the decision was to show that we were not so easily intimidated.

The Brazilians, playing on the same pitch the day following our Romanian encounter, recovered from a slow start, and an early goal from Czechoslovakia's Ladislav Petras, with some brilliant individual performances, notably from Gerson and Tostao. Jairzinho scored two goals in a 4–1 win.

Watching from the stands, we had to be impressed by this latest cycle of Brazilian virtuosity. There was something more, however. If they still showed thrilling quality, and could slip easily into dream-like passages of sublime play, they had added – perhaps under the influence of the old functional winger Zagallo – a degree of tactical sharpness, especially around set-pieces, that gave our entire squad, from Ramsey down, some new areas of concern.

This Brazilian team had not only kept pace with the game but was threatening to define a whole new dimension of it. For many of us, the free kick converted by Rivelino was most disturbing. We had heard about his ability to do extraordinary things with the dead ball and his 'banana kick' was already a key part of his fast-rising reputation, and here he and Jairzinho were showing themselves brilliantly equipped to make practice on the training field come to life in the heat of match conditions.

Jairzinho forced his way on to the left side of the Czech wall, and Rivelino appeared to drive straight at his team-mate. As Jairzinho flung himself away, the Czech goalkeeper, Ivo Viktor, could only brush the ball faintly with his fingers as it flew into the net. I turned to Martin Peters, who was sitting next to me, and the look on his face perfectly reflected my own feelings. Here was the reality of our next opponents. They so often made a fantasy of football, but they were clearly just as happy to deliver a killer blow as basic as a left hook. Later, Alf Ramsey was heard to say, 'My Christ, these people can play football – and we will certainly have to do something about their free kicks.'

On the training field the following morning, Bobby Moore gave his theory on how to make sure the Rivelino goal that shattered the Czechs would not happen to us. The captain's proposal was that if anyone tried to muscle into our wall, he would stand behind him – and then hold firm when Rivelino shot into a hole that had been suddenly filled.

It was a good idea – and it worked perfectly when Rivelino and Jairzinho attempted a repeat of the move against the Czechs. This time Moore was in the path of another beautifully struck ball and, of course, he controlled it and brought it away. He kept producing that kind of polished defence, in one highly pressurised situation after another, throughout the game.

Moore had attended to a vital detail, superbly, and Alf Ramsey, once again, showed that he had grasped the broadest picture. We couldn't sit back against these Brazilians because that would be like inviting in the sea. While never forgetting the ability of Pelé, for instance, to change everything in a flicker of an eyelid, we would be ourselves and we would make a match of it, uncontaminated by any hint of fear or resignation.

That much, unquestionably, we achieved. It was a great match and was always going to be settled by one roll of the ball, one little bit of fate. If I could go back through all the games I played for England and wish again for one of the defeats to be transferred to the win column, it would be this one, because if we had won it, I do not believe anyone could have stopped us. Defeat did not cost us progress in the tournament, no more than it would have done Brazil, but long before the end of the game we felt as though we were playing for very high stakes.

The Brazilians were without Gerson, their left-footed midfield playmaker, injured against Czechoslovakia, but their game still lapped around us with a beautiful rhythm, eliciting from Moore his sensational performance and from Gordon Banks his sensational save, the best I ever saw, or at least the one that made you feel it was the best in a game where one goal was probably always going to be decisive. The detail of it is familiar to all who saw it when it happened and to all those students of football who came after the fact. Most saw the save, and see it now on film, as a supreme example of goalkeeping talent, the kind of show of nerve and strength that separates the very best goalkeepers from the rest. I saw that clearly enough but when Banks dived low to his right and somehow scooped the ball over the bar, after Pelé had risen above Tommy Wright to head down Jairzinho's cross, I remembered all the relentless work Gordon had done in practice, all the times he dived on to flinty ground and moved a little closer to the inevitable hip operation, not out of his need for the roar of the crowd but the peace he felt in knowing that when the great challenges came, he would not fail because he had never, even once, neglected his work.

The sight of Banks recovering his ground so astonishingly, and twisting his body backwards to make the save after being drawn to the near post by Jairzinho's run, had a remarkable effect on me. At thirty-two, I was made to feel young again. My legs were so light, despite the scorching heat, I felt I could run for ever, and when I looked around I could see that my team-mates were affected in the same way.

When I had a chance, I shot hard but then cursed the playing surface as the ball rose over the bar. After the Banks save, our feeling was that we had become impregnable. All that was necessary now was one moment of precision in front of goal. Agonisingly, it didn't come. Franny Lee had one chance but, from close in, he could only head straight at the Brazilian goalkeeper Felix. Martin Peters had an opportunity earlier, after a typically subtle run, but his header went too high. A shot by Alan Ball flew off the crossbar. Finally, the ball fell to Jeff Astle, who had replaced Lee. Astle was brilliant in the air, less so on the ground, and his left-footed shot flew wide.

By now I was on the bench, having been replaced by Colin Bell after sixty-four minutes, and I could only put my head in my hands. Two minutes before I left the field, we had all been reminded of the key element in the genius of Pelé. After Tostao had drawn out our defence, Pelé realised the moment he received the ball that our cover had been stretched to its limits. He might have tried for goal himself but he was also aware that Jairzinho was making a perfectly timed run after working himself free on the right. Pelé made the simple, square pass into the path of Jairzinho and Brazil were ahead. We couldn't get back that goal, we couldn't get the draw that was, I will always believe, the least we deserved, but we could continue to show that we were authentic world champions.

It was a superb match and there was no question that we provided the hardest opposition Brazil faced in the tournament. We had the best goalkeeper in the world and when, at the end, Pelé and Moore exchanged jerseys, it was entirely appropriate. When I thought of what our captain had come through, and how he had handled it, and the lift he gave us all when he returned to the squad, I could only marvel at the quality of his performance that day in Guadalajara. He was a giant in a game that I will always rate among the best, if not the best, I ever played in.

The practical result was that we needed just a point against Czechoslovakia to progress to the quarter-finals. Allan Clarke, playing in his first international, gave us the win from the penalty spot after coolly volunteering to take the kick. It was not a distinguished performance and I felt no great elation when I was congratulated on winning my 105th England cap and equalling Billy Wright's record. I suppose we were all coming down from the mountain top where we had found Pelé, Tostao and Jairzinho, so we were happy enough to have avoided disaster against the Czechs.

We had to return to the high ground soon enough, against Franz Beckenbauer and his fellow Germans in Leon in three days' time. After Brazil, the prospect did not seem so daunting.

28

CLOSING OF THE STORY

IT WAS ODD, and worrying, to train on the eve of an important match without Gordon Banks. The ritual was familiar but we were missing that vital certainty.

Feeling a little off colour, Banks had been sent to his bed by Alf Ramsey after consultation with Neil Phillips. That's a mere precaution, we told ourselves, and if the nag of concern at the absence of our most reassuring presence should surface too strongly, we could always fall back on the fact that we were not exactly stripped of goalkeeping strength. If we feared the loss of the best, the rest was far from dire.

Peter Bonetti had been christened 'The Cat' at Stamford Bridge for good, and not ironic, reasons, and no one knew better than I did the strength and nerve of Alex Stepney, whose tremendous save against Eusebio had preserved Manchester United's life in the European Cup final two years earlier.

However, in our bones we had come to believe that Banks was irreplaceable. He was unique, everyone knew that, and not least Pelé. He was our rock and our talisman, someone upon whom we had come to rely at our most critical moments. So when he reported he felt well enough to take part in a light session of ball work on the morning of the match, you could almost taste our relief. It seemed that he had come through a small bout of sickness, as Keith Newton and I had after sharing a room with him in Guadalajara. We had both fully recovered by the time we reached Leon and surely Gordon would follow suit.

But if a sense of reprieve washed over us during the hot, tense morning, the same was true of the horror when it was clear he was suffering a relapse in the team meeting just before we left for the nearby stadium. He left the room to be sick.

By the end of the meeting it was plain that he wouldn't be taking the field. Alf Ramsey retained his composure when he announced that Bonetti, who had been warned the night before that he might have to play, would be in goal, but it was no great task to guess what was going through his mind. It was going through all our minds. 'Not Banks down, anybody but Banks.'

Some bizarre theories followed in the wake of the shock. The strangest was that the CIA, in the interests of a sense of well-being in politically volatile Latin America, had been plotting our downfall and that Banks was their prime target.

It was rather more likely, I thought, that Gordon had slipped up over the rule against iced drinks, but none of the speculation mattered as we shook hands with Bonetti and wished him good luck. Perhaps privately some may have hoped that his forthcoming performance would not add fuel to the suggestions that he was a bit distracted by the attention being paid by the media to his wife, Frances, and the three other wives who had come out to Mexico, those of Bobby Moore, Martin Peters and Geoff Hurst.

Norma and I had discussed the possibility of her coming to Mexico but we decided against it. We agreed that my mind could be on only the challenge ahead of me, almost certainly for the last time. If Norma had been in Mexico, I would have worried about her welfare in a foreign country with such a different culture from our own, and this would have been heightened by the fact that I knew Alf Ramsey would have been unhappy if there had been more than the most fleeting contact between us in the long and demanding weeks. Trying to win the World Cup, we decided, was quite enough of a job for anyone at any one time, and I was surprised when we arrived at our accommodation in Leon to see Frau Franz Beckenbauer, along with the wives of other German players, at the swimming pool.

Even today, in a world that has changed so much, I cannot say that I think of my attitude then as old fashioned or out of touch with realities of life beyond the touchline. Football was my life, and the means by which I could support my family, and for a few weeks so much depended on absolute concentration on the task in front of me and my team-mates.

Peter Bonetti was a great lad and a fine goalkeeper – he had conceded just one goal in his previous appearances, all winning, for England, and just a few months earlier he had performed heroically in Chelsea's FA Cup victory over Leeds – but if I am honest, it pained me to think that on this most vital of days he might have things on his mind other than the challenge of replacing the greatest goalkeeper in the world.

For more than an hour of the match, however, it seemed that we had all been fretting over something that had been rendered a non-issue by the force of our performance and our growing contempt for the latest German reliance on man-for-man marking. Again, although this time unilaterally, Helmut Schoen had put Beckenbauer against me.

The great player seemed more perturbed by the arrangement than I did. He was not able to develop his game in the early stages and his body language suggested that, once again, he was frustrated by the limitations placed on his ability to influence the game. Despite my advanced age, and the heat, I had rarely felt better out on the field, and certainly never in this tournament. Geoff Hurst, once again, was running with great force and, behind him, Alan Mullery was full of life and bite, and our full backs, Terry Cooper and Keith Newton, looked confident in their ability to take the game to the opposition.

It seemed inevitable that we would score, and we did after thirty-two minutes. In view of his impact, and his show of self-belief, it was fitting that the goal was scored by Mullery. He started and finished the movement, which confirmed our clear edge, finding Newton on the right and then bearing down on Sepp Maier's goal with a perfectly judged run to meet the return pass and send the ball high into the net.

The rhythm of our game was everything Ramsey had hoped for in the team meeting that had been overshadowed by our anxiety over Banks. It showed that against Brazil we had not been reaching beyond ourselves but simply fulfilling some of our potential. At half-time, Ramsey's face looked more relaxed than at any time since the misadventure in Bogota. He had encouraging words for everyone. The job was being done entirely to his satisfaction.

I was enjoying myself in a way that was not possible the first time I encountered the Germans in a World Cup match. If I'd had worries about my ability to flourish, at my age, in the heat and the altitude, they were gone now, along with the shackling duties I had carried into the final four years earlier. Maybe it was my reward for once subduing all my natural instincts in the team cause. Franz Beckenbauer was chasing me this day, and without the tight reciprocal responsibilities that had previously been placed on me. As long as I was having an influential effect, Beckenbauer's attacking ability was left in the margins as we restated our right to be world champions.

Martin Peters had not been as influential in Mexico as he was at Wembley, but five minutes into the second half he demonstrated again the most precious of his qualities. After Newton crossed to the far post and Maier failed to gather in the ball, the 'Ghost' was there to force it home. We were 2–0 up and cruising, and at that moment I could not have been persuaded that I was in the last minutes of my international career, and the story, give or take a few regrets that would probably last forever, was about to end.

But I suppose you are rarely given notice of when precisely the best of your hopes start to unravel. Looking back, it is easy to see when the process began. It was seven minutes after Peters had, in all our minds, put us into the semi-final against Italy, who at the time were slaughtering Mexico 4–1 in Toluca. That was the moment Schoen played his last card. He sent on his quick and aggressive right winger Jurgen Grabowski against Cooper, who, he might have guessed, was tiring after a superb performance. Apart from shutting down Reinhard Libuda, Terry had brilliantly maintained his initial threat to the German defence along their right side. But Grabowski came out running hard and quickly proved that his coach had been right. For the first time, the Germans looked capable of hurting us as Cooper struggled to contain his new and faster opponent.

It was then I saw some activity on the touchline that told me Ramsey was about to make what some will always say was the most controversial and damaging decision of his England career. Colin Bell was warming up on the touchline and this, I knew right away, meant that the manager was about to continue his practice of protecting me from the worst effects of the conditions. I didn't want to leave the field, I was part of the game and I was not suffering, but I did recognise the manager had to look at the wider picture. I was thirty-two, I had done a lot of running, and in three days' time we had to play a semi-final at an altitude 1,500 feet higher than we were at present in the Azteca Stadium in Mexico City.

So I prepared to leave, hoping that Grabowski would not be allowed to do any significant damage and our momentum would be maintained. I saw no big reason why this should not be so. Colin Bell, like Norman Hunter, who would come on for Peters in the eightieth minute, was a strong, good player who would grant the Germans few, if any, liberties. Yet I did feel a certain unease, partly because my legs felt so good and also we had achieved such a good balance in our performance. Sickeningly, this worry was compounded before I left the field. Beckenbauer went forward, and for some reason I will never know, but maybe it was because I was momentarily distracted by what was happening on our bench, I left him to do so, and he scored.

Franny Lee blocked his first shot, but he recovered it instantly and when Mullery challenged him, he was able to get the ball on his right foot and send it under the diving Bonetti. As I left the pitch I recalled one of Ramsey's more insistent instructions before the game. 'If Beckenbauer gets to the box,' he said, 'don't let him work the ball on to his right foot.' Yet still I didn't have any clear sense that my international career was over, that I was walking off the field in an England shirt for the last time. If there were certain fears, there was still at that stage an overall sense that we were the stronger team, and that the stirrings of concern would in the end remain no more than that. But as I watched the drama begin to unfold, these stirrings grew in force and as the Germans threw themselves forward with Beckenbauer at the heart of it all, I began to worry that our fears over the absence of Banks were about to be confirmed.

The great debate ever since has been whether Ramsey was right to replace me and I know that it haunted the manager until the end of his days, but the most important factor of our defeat, I will always believe, was that when the Germans made what appeared likely to be their last charge in that World Cup, Gordon Banks was journeying between his bed and his bathroom. The Germans needed to score three goals in the last quarter of the match and the fact was that even the best teams did not score three goals against Banks in the course of a whole game. The point had been underlined by the save against Pelé and now, as Jack became so anxious he was forced to leave the touchline and stand behind the main stand in dread of hearing the cheers from a partisan crowd that would announce the Germans had scored again, the absence of Banks was in the forefront of our thoughts.

Jack's worst fears came to fruition when his Leeds team-mate, Norman Hunter, was sent on the field. Jack was still depressed from his team's failures in the last strides of the FA Cup and the championship and he was convinced that it was not a year when anything good might happen to a player from Elland Road.

I sat on the bench sharing his agony. The unavoidable truth was that Banks would not have conceded the Beckenbauer goal. It was a soft goal. Bonetti mistimed his dive and that brought the usual consequences when the last line of resistance is perceived to be vulnerable – a degree of panic in a defence that had previously looked so serene.

There, so eloquent in its absence, was the value of a goalkeeper such as Banks. He made the difference between victory and defeat, reinforced confidence and warded off doubts, because you knew that if the worst happened and you broke down, there was every chance you would be rescued.

So sadly for a man who had enjoyed such a fine career, it was now clear that no one was more in need of rescue than Peter Bonetti.

There was just one chance that impending disaster might be averted and it arrived with Colin Bell's first contribution. He ran powerfully along the right before turning in a cross for Hurst to head for the far post. Franny Lee later admitted that he might have prodded Geoff's header home had he not checked his run because he was so mesmerised by the flight of the ball, convinced that it would hit the post and roll into his path.

The rest was a complete reversal of more than two-thirds of the match – it was their attack against our defence, and twice more our defence cracked. On both occasions, in the eighty-second minute and the nineteenth of extra time, there was good reason to believe that Banks would have seen us through the crisis, first when Uwe Seeler's backheader drifted over Bonetti and then when Gerd Muller got behind Brian Labone and volleyed home the winner.

There is nothing so bleak as losing a game you know you should have won, and if our sense of this needed any further emphasis it surely came when we returned to our base and Stepney went to see Banks in his sickroom. He was watching a delayed transmission. Gordon was jubilant. We were winning 2–0 at the time.

I had arranged for some drinks to be served at the swimming pool to mark my record 106th cap and after a phone call home and commiserations from Norma, I changed into my swimming trunks and went down to join my team-mates. It was, with the blessing of Alf Ramsey, supposed to be the happiest of affairs, and in my mind not just a celebration of my good fortune in being selected more times for England than any of my country-men, but also, for the second time in my long international career, being part of a team that had proved it was capable of facing any opposition. I had certain points to make, including gratitude for all the friendship and loyalty I had received, but most of all I wanted to express my pride that we had managed to overcome so many difficulties to remain competitive in an atmosphere that at times couldn't have been more hostile.

However, on the way to the pool I decided it was not a time for speeches but to share a little solidarity, perhaps unspoken, against the pain of such unexpected defeat.

We had a few drinks but it was impossible to imagine that anyone could turn this into anything other than a wake. Even-tually, Alf appeared, subdued and with a rather faraway look on his face. My friend Ken Jones, football writer on the *Daily Mirror*, had earlier found the manager disconsolate in his chalet. He was sipping, apparently quite without pleasure, champagne and every so often he would sigh and say, 'Of all the players to lose, why was it Gordon Banks?' Ken had the feeling that it was a question the conqueror of 1966 would take to his grave.

The party was dead even though it meandered on for a while.

You felt for Peter Bonetti and wanted to console him but quite how did you do that?

You couldn't say it was just another match, but maybe you could make the point that if every win had a hero, every defeat had to have its villain, and that in football it was not individuals but teams who lost games. That, anyway, was how it would be seen in a more perfect world.

Alf didn't saying anything that night about my future with England – that would come in a coded message when he came to sit beside me somewhere over the Atlantic on the flight home – but when I went back to my room and started to pack, I didn't need telling that it was over.

It was strange to think how tentative I had been at the start of something that had become such a central part of my life, how Billy Wright had to persuade me that one day, when the shadow of Munich had receded a little, wearing the England shirt would not be a new and difficult burden but the highest privilege of my career. Now I realised how right he had been because knowing that I would never be called to my country's colours again brought pain that was very sharp.

I thought of all the times it might have been over, cut short by injury or maybe if Alf Ramsey had decided that he wanted certain qualities that I did not possess, as he did in the case of Jimmy Greaves. I considered, too, all the places where I might have said farewell to my time as an international.

Rather than in this room in Mexico, it might have been in some grey hotel building in Belgrade, where I suffered my first crisis – and effectively missed the 1958 World Cup – after a thrashing by Yugoslavia and a superb performance by Dragoslav Sekularac, who would later become a friend. I thought of all the places, and the great stadiums including the Maracana and the Bernabeu, to which England had taken me. And then, with fierce disappointment, I went back to my hopes of just a few hours earlier. I thought of how we were going to beat Germany and Italy and then, for perhaps the supreme moment of my career and a climax beyond most dreams, including my own, compete again with Pelé and his Brazilians.

It reminded me, if I needed it, how football can destroy dreams just as rapidly as it creates them. If you were very lucky, though, you would be able to do what I was doing. You could pack away your travelling clothes along with your memories, and you could tell yourself that for four years at the prime of your life you had been a champion of the world. I had so wanted that to last for another four years.

On the plane Alf said to me, 'I just want to say thank you for all you have done for England – and for everything you have done on this trip. I'm sorry we lost – and I'm sorry it happened the way it did.' He didn't tell me my England career was over, but then there was really no need. I would be thirty-six when the next World Cup came around in West Germany, too old for Alf, too old for anybody. I played my last game for Manchester United at the age of thirty-five in Verona in Italy. My United colleagues gave me a beautiful clock. Alf was handing me something just as valuable in its way, his thanks after putting so much trust in me down the years.

I would never blame him for what happened in Leon. He was looking after me, as he had throughout that tournament. He was trying to keep me fresh for the semi-final, and if I was reluctant to leave the field in Leon because I felt I could continue to be relevant at the heart of the game, who was to say that I might not have felt jaded, or just a notch off my best game, when the next challenge came?

There was another question. Why did I feel so miserable, even bitter, that the end had come so suddenly in a game in which I played well? When I returned to the bench and watched us slip, step by unstoppable step, out of the last World Cup I would know as a player, it was suddenly like watching some terrible accident over which you had no control.

I had passed Billy Wright's record, I had memories that could have lasted me several lifetimes. So why? It was because I was greedy. From around the day I saw the stingray and played for the first time in the Maracana, I had – I knew now – never wanted it to end.

EPILOGUE

WHEN I WAS still young and reading Ernest Hemingway's *Death in the Afternoon* in the aftermath of my visit to the Plaza de Toros in Mexico City, I came across a line, near the end of his account of the lives of bullfighters and the meaning of what they did, that I never imagined one day reaching out to borrow. But I do now. Hemingway wrote, 'If I could have made this enough of a book, it would have had everything in it.'

Mine would have every player I've ever admired and, yes, loved, and it would have at least a little of the flavour of almost every country on earth and how it had been touched by the game that has been my life and given me the passport to see so many places and feel so many things that as a boy I could not have dreamed of knowing.

It would have me going to an exquisite little house and garden in Japan with a young man with whom I was working on the development of the game in that country before the World Cup of 2002 and being told by his mother, 'You're the first European I have ever seen.'

In Japan, it would also have me learning to sleep on a pillow made of a block of wood, and watching fighting dogs. When they are put in the cage, they do not savage each other but strive for a victory, which is signalled when the beaten opponent makes a strange whimpering sound of defeat and walks away.

It would have me in football camps in Africa, Australia and

the Andes, and in Arabia and China and, when I come to think of it, almost everywhere anyone cares to mention.

Not always, I have to admit, would it have me moving effortlessly from one culture to another. Perhaps I should also include the time when, while covering the second World Cup to be played in Mexico, in 1986, I stopped, with a TV crew, at an old colonial fort in the hills outside Monterey, where England were based before going up to Mexico City and colliding with Maradona's 'Hand of God'. It was in that twilight time of early evening, the views were thrilling and the waiter brought cold beer out on to the terrace. The following day, when I was boasting of our discovery, I was told, 'Congratulations, Senor Charlton, you have been to a clinic for venereal disease – one of the best in all of Mexico.'

In telling the story of my England years, I have tried to explain my feelings, and what I have always wanted for our national game, and also to express the privilege I felt at being part of the Ramsey epoch. In my opinion, an example of leadership and teamwork was given to English football then, that even today, in the new era of Fabio Capello, is as fresh and as valid as when the manager gathered his players together and issued that famous rallying call, 'Gentlemen, we will win the World Cup.'

You may think such words would sound bizarre on the lips of Capello if – so soon after our exclusion from a brilliant European Championship – he happened to say them to Wayne Rooney, Steven Gerrard and Rio Ferdinand. It will not be so if he can give them some of the belief that Sir Alf Ramsey passed on to Bobby Moore, Nobby Stiles, Geoff Hurst, Jack and me all those years ago. And, still less if he gives them a way of playing that makes them feel free and confident and not burdened by tactics that sometimes, since the years of Ramsey, seem to have been picked out of a football version of a lucky dip.

So much has changed since I first played under Walter

Winterbottom when his England team was subject, outrageously, to the suggestions, and the vetoes, of Football Association councillors, but certain attitudes lingered on long after they should have withered and died.

As recently as the eighties, when as a new director of Manchester United I was invited to attend meetings of the FA council, perhaps, I imagined, to try to pass on some of my experience in inter-national football, I was reminded of the old ways. I was given some background papers to read before the meeting, which I did in the council room some time before the FA elders arrived. The lighting was not so good so I went to a big window near the committee table to do my reading. Eventually, an elderly person entered the room, came up to me and, without introduction, said, 'You can't sit there – you'll have to go to the back of the room.' It was quite empty but for the two of us.

Perhaps those days have gone now. Maybe the presence of a former player such as Sir Trevor Brooking at the FA tells us that the value of experience of the real world of football has begun to count. It must, anyway, be a solemn hope, and one reinforced, I have to say, by my experiences in campaigning for the World Cup to return to England in 2006. The biggest stumbling block was something described as the 'gentleman's agreement', the alleged promise made by FA chairman Sir Bert Millichip that in exchange for German support of England's bid for the European Championship of 1996, we would defer to them when they sought the World Cup. There was much controversy over the German claim, and much doubt about its authenticity, but I was repeatedly told by members of the German federation, including my friend Franz Beckenbauer, that the promise had been made.

I can only say that I felt indignant at the possibility that anyone should presume to barter away the football rights of the country that gave the game to the world. I fought for England's chances in 2006 and covered a large part of the globe doing so, and if anyone thinks I can help in the pursuit of 2018, and still make any kind of sense, I will do all I can all over again, if only because I believe so much that our national game – as opposed to the wealth and power of the Premiership – is in desperate need of some new inspiration and support.

I hope, fervently, that Fabio Capello can lay down new foundations and that in ten years time we might just be able to invite the world to see first hand our love of the game – and a national team in which, once again, we can invest some pride.

One enemy of the kind of spirit and focus displayed by Ramsey's team is the force of today's celebrity and power of the leading players. We have seen so many examples of the distortion it can bring to the simple pleasure of playing football for a living, but if I have one great hope for this generation of stars, and the ones that follow, it is that somehow the joy and satisfaction I knew as an England player can be rekindled. It is possible, I believe, and evidence was provided by Spain when they won the European Championship in 2008. Their players came from many of the leading clubs, all of them wealthy beyond the imagination of England's boys of '66, yet still they displayed a passion for the game that surely warmed the hearts of not just football lovers across the Continent but of so many old players. If Spain, why not England?

Many old, and not so old, players fill my thoughts. Sometimes I think it is expected of me to draw up a team of those whom I think would have best represented England and the World, but I enjoy doing it, anyway. These are selected from all the teams I have played with and against, and watched, since I first appeared in international football at Hampden Park in 1958.

For the World XI, I have chosen, in 4–3–3 formation or, perhaps, whatever came into their minds: Bert Trautmann, Djalma Santos, John Charles, Franz Beckenbauer, Paolo Maldini, Michel Platini, Alfredo di Stefano, Johan Cruyff, George Best, Diego Maradona, Pelé.

The opposing Englishmen would be: Gordon Banks, Jimmy Armfield, Billy Wright, Bobby Moore, Ray Wilson, Bryan Robson, Johnny Haynes, Duncan Edwards, Stanley Matthews, Jimmy Greaves, Tom Finney.

Trautmann is selected over Peter Schmeichel, to me the first choice by far of modern goalkeepers, and Lev Yashin of the USSR, despite the fact that, because of his circumstances as a former Luftwaffe paratrooper who won the Iron Cross on the Eastern Front and finished the Second World War in a POW camp near Manchester, he never played international football. He had the most astonishing power, reflexes and positional sense I have ever seen. And this is before we discuss his courage, which enabled him to make some crucial saves for Manchester City in an FA Cup final while suffering from a broken neck. Once I was about to celebrate a goal when he seemed to turn himself around in mid-air to catch the ball cleanly. I can still hear myself saying, 'How could anyone do that?'

I first saw Djalma Santos play for Brazil in Sweden in 1958, and then again when they defended the World Cup in Chile in 1962. In Sweden, I saw a wonderfully controlled player, quick and hard, and always with plenty of time to pass the ball. In Chile, I said, 'Well, I don't expect ever to see a better right back.' And nor did I.

John Charles was a fabulous player and a fabulous man, qualities that made him 'King John' of Juventus, where they knew about talent, but perhaps never before had they seen so completely how it was possible to combine it with humility. Once he played for me when I was asked to help organise a charity match in Stockholm. He had filled out considerably in the brief time of his retirement, and the announcer felt it necessary to explain who he was and what he meant. Just when he was saying that John Charles was a credit to the game, the great man smiled sheepishly as he bent down to pick up something that had fallen from his shorts. It was a packet of Benson and Hedges.

I put Beckenbauer beside John because of all the riches that would create in midfield – and because he was so fast and read the game so beautifully. John would handle everything in the air, Franz everything on the ground, and he would turn defence into attack instantly.

Paolo Maldini never seemed to make a mistake. Often there are question marks against the great Italian players, but I never saw cynicism in Maldini – only tremendous character and impeccable technique.

Michel Platini was not a great athlete but he was a great player and, as I've said, the most precise passer of the ball I ever saw. Off the field, as president of Uefa, I sometimes think he wants to change the world in a day, but on the pitch his timing was always perfect.

Di Stefano, from the first time I saw him, filled all my football senses. He made goals and he scored them. He cut swathes through any defence as he ran hard and unstoppably through the middle of the field. If I ever wanted to present the ultimate picture of potential on a football field, it would be of di Stefano engaging a defence that also had to cope with Best, Maradona and Pelé.

Johan Cruyff was a genius who could visualise things others couldn't. He could see through defences as though they weren't even there. Once I asked Michel Platini who was the best player he ever saw, and his reply was instant. 'The Dutchman,' he said.

George Best is part of my life, and if there is anything left to say about him and the pain and joy he brought, it is only that, in playing with him at Old Trafford in the prime of his career, I never ceased to be surprised by the scale of his genius.

During the World Cup of 1986, I interviewed Maradona for the BBC. He was not the most popular footballer in England back then but he was bright and alive and you could almost see sparks flying out of him. No one ever attacked a defence with such concentrated, brilliant fury.

Pelé, about whom I have already said so much, is in so many ways beyond analysis. He is football, its strength and range and life, and whenever I see him, as I often do, I still feel a thrill of pride that I know him and played against him. I felt the same way about Ferenc Puskas, the most haunting of omissions from my World XI.

When I picked my England team, I might just have gone back to Wembley 1966, but as Alf Ramsey told Jack, he didn't necessarily pick the most talented players but those he felt would most likely work together. So I have gone with those who, I think, would achieve the best possible balance between the competing demands that face every coach.

Gordon Banks picks himself. Jimmy Armfield is preferred to George Cohen, not because I believe he could have performed any better than my World Cup team-mate, and according to Ramsey's instincts almost certainly not, but simply because he was a superbly rounded player of skill, and one of the first, and best, overlapping full backs football has seen.

Billy Wright had great balance and read the game so well, and with Bobby Moore beside him, he would have all the help and guidance that any defender under serious pressure could wish for. Ray Wilson is in because he was one of the most resolute defenders I ever played with or against. He was the kind of player you always knew would grow with the pressure.

Bryan Robson had a wonderful heart and a marvellous instinct to find an opposition weak spot. Haynes, the great thwarted general, would have operated brilliantly in this perfect scenario surrounded by players superbly equipped to respond to all his promptings. Duncan Edwards, I always felt, was going to be the best player in the world, and I still suspect that but for Munich he might have been.

I cannot say any more about Matthews or Finney, who thrilled me as a boy and, in Finney's case, helped so much to make me a football man.

Jimmy Greaves? Yes, he makes it to my World Cup final in the skies. If I agreed with Alf Ramsey that he had more effective options when he came to pick his team in 1966 and that, in the way the team had been created, Geoff Hurst and Roger Hunt had stronger claims, it was never at the cost of my understanding that Jimmy Greaves was a great player of his own age or any other.

One of my many good fortunes is that I played with arguably the two greatest strikers in the history of British football – Denis Law and Jimmy Greaves. They lived to score goals. They lived to strike.

You may have noticed that all the roads I have travelled as an England player have led me forward or back to Sir Alf Ramsey.

There is a good reason for this because, for me, he will always be the heart of English football that still beats down the years. He gave it strength and purpose and led it back into the wide world of the international game. If the lessons he taught are ignored, it is, I still believe so long after his triumph, to the detriment of the England team.

Even more saddening for me than his failure to qualify for the 1974 World Cup was the way he was allowed to leave, without significant honour or influence, to live with his ultimately fading memories.

When his team gathered in the church to mourn his death on a bright spring morning in 1999, I was asked, with George Cohen, to speak. I told some of the old stories of a tough and intransigent man, and I got a few laughs, but what I most wanted to say, in the best way I could, was that I would never stop being grateful for who he was and what he did.

He knew football and he knew men. What he did, for me and my team-mates, was enable us to beat all of our fears and our doubts – and the world.

ENGLAND STATISTICS

compiled by Jack Rollin

BOBBY CHARLTON

11 October 1937	Born Ashington, Northumberland
6 June 1953	Joined Manchester United groundstaff
4 October 1954	Turned Professional
6 October 1956	League debut v Charlton Athletic (scoring twice)
May 1966	FWA Footballer of the Year
June 1966	European Footballer of the Year
1969	Awarded OBE
May 1973	Appointed manager Preston North End
1974	Awarded CBE; PFA Merit Award
May 1974	Player-manager of Preston North End
1975–76	Waterford United player (played 31, scored 18)
1982	Wigan Athletic director and caretaker manager
1984	Director of Manchester United
1994	Knighted

Bobby Charlton won 106 caps for his country, a career that spanned from 19 April 1958 to 14 June 1970.

On winning his 106th cap, he became the most capped England player of all time. He has subsequently been overtaken by Bobby Moore (108) and Peter Shilton (125).

His England figures break down as follows: 14 World Cup finals matches, 2 European Championship matches, 1 European Nations Cup match, 32 Home International Championship matches (6 of which also doubled as European Championship qualifiers). The remainder were a mix of World Cup and European Championship qualifiers, friendlies and tour matches.

He also played 4 times for England Schoolboys, once for England Youth
and 6 times for the England Under-23s. He made 8 appearances for
the English Football League.

He scored a record 49 goals for his country and found the net on his debut
for the full England team, the Under-23s, England Youth and England
Schoolboys.

ENGLAND

1957–58

1 HC 19 April Scotland Hampden Park W 4–0 *
Bobby's debut goal for England, 62nd-minute volley from Tom Finney
centre

2 F 7 May Portugal Wembley W 2–1 **
Jim Langley hits post with penalty; Bobby scores with left-foot shot from
20 yards

3 T 11 May Yugoslavia Belgrade L 0–5
Poor England display, not fitting for Billy Wright's world-record 55th
consecutive cap

1958–59

4 HC 4 October N Ireland Windsor Park D 3–3 **
Seventh England game without a win; Tom Finney's 30th goal; two
vintage goals from Bobby

5 F 22 October USSR Wembley W 5–0 *
Nat Lofthouse's 30th England goal; Walter Winterbottom's 100th game
in charge; Johnny Haynes hat-trick

6 HC 26 November Wales Villa Park D 2–2
England without Johnny Haynes (injured); Peter Broadbent scores both
goals

7 HC 11 April Scotland Wembley W 1–0 *
Billy Wright becomes first player to reach 100 caps; Bobby scores with
acrobatic header

8 F 6 May Italy Wembley D 2–2 *
England leading 2–0, Ron Flowers goes off for facial repairs, returns to
find scores level!

9   T   13 May   Brazil   Maracana (Rio) L 0–2
Brazilian goalkeeper Gilmar keeps record 18th clean sheet; England
twice hit woodwork
10   T   17 May   Peru   Lima   L 1–4
England destroyed by Juan Seminario's hat-trick on his last international
appearance
11   T   24 May   Mexico   Mexico City   L 1–2
England fade after scoring first, and use two substitutes for first time
12   T   28 May   USA   Los Angeles   W 8–1   ***
Billy Wright's swansong: 105th cap, 70th in succession, captain for 90th
time

1959–60

13   HC   17 October   Wales   Ninian Park   D 1–1
Five new caps including Brian Clough; youngest England line-up for
75 years
14   F   28 October   Sweden   Wembley   L 2–3   *
World Cup runners-up (1958) deserve victory
15   HC   9 April   Scotland   Hampden Park D 1–1   *
Bobby scores one penalty, hits the goalkeeper with another but shoots
retake wide!
16   F   11 May   Yugoslavia   Wembley   D 3–3
Debut at centre back for Peter Swan; Johnny Haynes levels in 89th
minute
17   T   15 May   Spain   Madrid   L 0–3
Spain slightly flattered by final scoreline; Johnny Haynes captains England
18   T   22 May   Hungary   Budapest   L 0–2
International debut for Dennis Viollet at inside forward; England on
defensive

1960–61

19   HC   8 October   N Ireland   Windsor Park   W 5–2   *
Bobby heads goal (50 minutes); Ireland hit woodwork three times
20   WCQ 19 October   Luxembourg   Luxembourg   W 9–0   ***
Hat-tricks for Jimmy Greaves and Bobby in away-day goal avalanche

21   F   26 October   Spain   Wembley   W 4–2
Played in torrential rain; Spain equalise twice
22   HC   23 November   Wales   Wembley   W 5–1   *
Jimmy Greaves opener (2 minutes) is England's 1,000th international goal
23   HC   15 April   Scotland   Wembley   W 9–3
England's highest score in the series; Johnny Haynes' last-minute goal
disallowed!
24   F   10 May   Mexico   Wembley   W 8–0   ***
Debut goal for Gerry Hitchens (90 seconds); Bobby scores hat-trick
25   WCQ   21 May   Portugal   Lisbon   D 1–1
Ron Flowers salvages draw in 81st minute
26   T   24 May   Italy   Rome   W 3–2
Two for Gerry Hitchens; Jimmy Greaves scores 85th-minute winner
27   T   27 May   Austria   Vienna   L 1–3
Jimmy Greaves' 13th of season beats George Hilsdon's and Dixie Dean's
record

1961–62

28   WCQ   28 September Luxembourg   Highbury   W 4–1   **
England field new inside-forward trio; Jimmy Armfield captains team
29   HC   14 October   Wales   Ninian Park D 1–1
Ray Wilson returns at left back after ten-match absence
30   WCQ   25 October   Portugal   Wembley   W 2–0
England need draw to qualify; Portugal hit the bar three times
31   HC   22 November   N Ireland   Wembley   D 1–1   *
Ray Crawford, first Ipswich Town player fully capped, hits crossbar
32   F   4 April   Austria   Wembley   W 3–1
Rain-affected match; first caps for Stan Anderson and scorer Roger Hunt
33   HC   14 April   Scotland   Hampden Park L 0–2
First Scottish win over England at Hampden Park for quarter of a century
34   F   9 May   Switzerland   Wembley   W 3–1
Scoreline flatters England as Switzerland extremely unlucky to lose
35   F   20 May   Peru   Lima   W 4–0
First caps for Bobby Moore and Maurice Norman; Ron Springett saves a
penalty
36   WCF   31 May   Hungary   Rancagua   L 1–2
Rain-affected match; Ron Flowers equalises from penalty spot

37   WCF   2 June   Argentina   Rancagua   W 3–1   *
Alan Peacock robbed of 17th-minute debut goal by penalty chance for
Ron Flowers
38   WCF   7 June   Bulgaria   Rancagua   D 0–0
Dour game influenced by England's need to draw
39   WCF   10 June   Brazil   Santiago   L 1–3
Garrincha shines for Brazil in fine match; invading dog retrieved by
Jimmy Greaves

1962–63

40   ENCQ 27 February   France   Paris   L 2–5
Baptism of fire for Alf Ramsey, England's first manager to be solely in
charge
41   HC   6 April   Scotland   Wembley   L 1–2
Scotland's Eric Caldow breaks leg in sixth minute
42   F   8 May   Brazil   Wembley   D 1–1
George Eastham Jnr is the first son of an international to play for
England
43   T   29 May   Czechoslovakia Bratislava   W 4–2   *
Bobby Moore becomes England's youngest captain at 22 years 47 days
44   T   2 June   East Germany   Leipzig   W 2–1   *
Bobby hits 70th-minute winner; England concede 500th goal
45   T   5 June   Switzerland   Basle   W 8–1   ***
Bobby scores first and last to equal Tom Finney and Nat Lofthouse on
30 goals

1963–64

46   HC   12 October   Wales   Ninian Park W 4–0   *
New England scoring record as Bobby registers his 31st in 85th minute
47   F   23 October   FIFA XI   Wembley   W 2–1
FA Centenary match; Jimmy Greaves scores 87th-minute winner after
Bobby's shot blocked
48   HC   20 November   N Ireland   Wembley   W 8–3
Wembley's first evening international under floodlights; Jimmy Greaves
scores four

49   HC   11 April   Scotland   Hampden Park   L 0–1
Scotland's third win in a row over England; HC shared
50   F   6 May   Uruguay   Wembley   W 2–1
First full cap for George Cohen at right back (Jimmy Armfield injured)
51   T   17 May   Portugal   Lisbon   W 4–3   *
Personal triumph for Johnny Byrne with hat-trick, including 88th-minute winner
52   F   24 May   Rep of Ireland Dublin   W 3–1
Tony Waiters, Blackpool goalkeeper, awarded first full cap for England
53   T   27 May   USA   New York   W 10–0   *
Fred Pickering treble on first appearance; Roger Hunt scores four; Bobby, on as sub, scores one
54   T   30 May   Brazil   Maracana (Rio) L 1–5
Brazil's 50th anniversary tournament; England's worst defeat since 11 May 1958 (Yugoslavia)
55   T   6 June   Argentina   Maracana (Rio) L 0–1
Argentina take Brazil's Jubilee trophy with third win and no goals conceded

1964–65

56   HC   3 October   N Ireland   Windsor Park   W 4–3
Jimmy Greaves (hat-trick) overtakes Bobby's record with 34th England goal
57   F   9 December   Holland   Amsterdam   D 1–1
75th anniversary of Netherlands FA; crowd 60,000
58   HC   10 April   Scotland   Wembley   D 2–2   *
England finish with nine fit players: Ray Wilson off, Johnny Byrne limping

1965–66

59   HC   2 October   Wales   Ninian Park   D 0–0
Jimmy Greaves heads against the bar (80 minutes)
60   F   20 October   Austria   Wembley   L 2–3   *
Bobby scores after four minutes; Austria register first win in England
61   HC   10 November N Ireland   Wembley   W 2–1
Joe Baker, recalled after five years, scores in heavy rain
62   F   8 December   Spain   Madrid   W 2–0
England in 4–3–3 mode gain first win in Spain; Norman Hunter first cap (sub)

63   F   23 February   West Germany   Wembley   W 1–0
Nobby Stiles (wearing No.9) scores; first caps for Geoff Hurst and Keith
Newton
64   HC   2 April   Scotland   Hampden Park W 4–3   *
25th championship for England; Bobby scores winner with vintage
25-yard effort
65   F   4 May   Yugoslavia   Wembley   W 2–0   *
Martin Peters makes his debut; Jimmy Armfield returns as captain
66   T   26 June   Finland   Helsinki   W 3–0
Alan Ball's 14th-minute penalty saved by Matti Halme; Jack Charlton scores
67   T   29 June   Norway   Oslo   W 6–1
Personal triumph for Jimmy Greaves with four; Bobby Moore scores!
68   T   5 July   Poland   Chorzow   W 1–0
Another milestone in England's international history – first visit to Poland
69   WCF   11 July   Uruguay   Wembley   D 0–0
Gordon Banks' tenth clean sheet equals Harry Hibbs' achievement in goal
70   WCF   16 July   Mexico   Wembley   W 2–0   *
Banks keeps record 11th clean sheet; vintage goal from Bobby
71   WCF   20 July   France   Wembley   W 2–0
Two goals from Roger Hunt, celebrating his 28th birthday
72   WCF   23 July   Argentina   Wembley   W 1–0
Antonio Rattin dismissed in 35th minute; England make it six
consecutive clean sheets
73   WCF   26 July   Portugal   Wembley   W 2–1   **
Eusebio penalty ends England's sequence of 708 minutes without
conceding a goal
74   WCF   30 July   West Germany   Wembley   W 4–2
England's finest footballing occasion, achieved after extra time, having
conceded first goal

1966–67

75   HC/   22 October   N Ireland   Windsor Park W 2–0
     ECQ
England field World Cup-winning team; Ireland finish with ten players
76   F   2 November   Czechoslovakia Wembley   D 0–0
First visit for Czechoslovakia since 1929 when they lost 5–4 at White
Hart Lane

77 HC/ 16 November Wales   Wembley   W 5–1   *
    ECQ
Bobby Moore wins 50th cap; England unchanged for a record sixth
occasion
78 HC/ 15 April   Scotland   Wembley   L 2–3
    ECQ
Jack Charlton scores England's 150th v. Scotland after breaking his toe in
the 12th minute

1967–68

79 HC/ 21 October   Wales   Ninian Park   W 3–0   *
    ECQ
One unstoppable shot from Bobby, one outstanding save by Gordon
Banks
80 HC/ 22 November   N Ireland   Wembley   W 2–0   *
    ECQ
Dave Sadler's first full international at centre back (Jack Charlton
injured)
81 F   6 December   USSR   Wembley   D 2–2
Cyril Knowles makes debut at right back; Soviets bring the snow!
82 HC/ 24 February   Scotland   Hampden Park   D 1–1
    ECQ
Mike Summerbee makes his bow at centre forward
83 ECQ 3 April   Spain   Wembley   W 1–0   *
Martin Peters' goal (two minutes) ruled out for hands; clever goal from
Bobby from free kick
84 ECQ 8 May   Spain   Madrid   W 2–1
Norman Hunter scores spectacular winner with his 'wrong' right foot
(80 minutes)
85 F   22 May   Sweden   Wembley   W 3–1   *
Bobby's 45th and record England goal; first caps for Alex Stepney and
Colin Bell
86 ECF 5 June   Yugoslavia   Florence   L 0–1
England's 424th full international; Alan Mullery first England player to
be sent off
87 ECF 8 June   USSR   Rome   W 2–0   *
Tommy Wright makes debut at right back; England third

1968–69

88 F 6 November Romania Bucharest D 0–0
Out-of-sorts England in first visit to Romania since 1939 pre-war summer tour

89 F 11 December Bulgaria Wembley D 1–1
First caps for Gordon West, Francis Lee and Paul Reaney (sub) on raw night

90 F 15 January Romania Wembley D 1–1
Jack Charlton heads in Bobby's corner then concedes penalty for hands (76 minutes)

91 HC 3 May N Ireland Windsor Park W 3–1
England win against run of play as Ireland pay dearly for defensive lapses

92 HC 7 May Wales Wembley W 2–1 *
Francis Lee hits penalty kick against crossbar; Jeff Astle makes debut

93 HC 10 May Scotland Wembley W 4–1
Match of flowing football; result does nothing to diminish Scotland's endeavour

94 T 1 June Mexico Mexico City D 0–0
Heat and altitude provide ideal practice for upcoming World Cup finals

95 T 12 June Brazil Maracana (Rio) L 1–2
Gordon Banks saves Carlos Alberto penalty; Brazil score twice in last 11 minutes

1969–70

96 F 5 November Holland Amsterdam W 1–0
Fortunate victory against the Dutch; first cap for Emlyn Hughes at left back

97 F 10 December Portugal Wembley W 1–0
Portugal weakened compared with 1966; Francis Lee puts penalty wide

98 F 14 January Holland Wembley D 0–0
Bobby scores after final whistle! Ian Storey-Moore makes debut

99 HC 18 April Wales Ninian Park D 1–1
Wales field just five First Division players; Francis Lee scores ferocious equaliser!

100   HC   21 April   N Ireland   Wembley   W 3–1   *
Bobby made captain for 100th cap; scores his 48th England goal
101   T   20 May   Colombia   Bogota   W 4–0   *
England's 39th international opponents, 37th for Bobby
102   T   24 May   Ecuador   Quito   W 2–0
First non-Latin opponents for Ecuador at this level
103   WCF   2 June   Romania   Guadalajara   W 1–0
Francis Lee hits the bar in first half; Geoff Hurst scores in
65th minute
104   WCF   7 June   Brazil   Guadalajara   L 0–1
Gordon Banks' finest ever save: point-blank from Pelé; Alan Ball hits
crossbar
105   WCF   11 June   Czechoslovakia Guadalajara   W 1–0
Bobby equals Billy Wright's 105 caps; Allan Clarke scores penalty on
debut
106   WCF   14 June   West Germany   Leon   L 2–3
England's first loss after two-goal lead for 41 years; Bobby subbed by
Colin Bell

UNDER-23   6 caps, 5 goals

1958–59

1	24 September	Poland	Hillsborough	W 4–1	***
2	15 October	Czechoslovakia	Norwich	W 3–0	**
3	18 March	France	Lyon	D 1–1	

1959–60

| 4 | 23 September | Hungary | Everton | L 0–1 |
| 5 | 2 March | Scotland | Ibrox | D 4–4 |

1960–61

| 6 | 2 November | Italy | Newcastle | D 1–1 |

YOUTH 1 cap, 1 goal

1953–54

1	8 May	N Ireland	Belfast	D 2–2	*

SCHOOLBOY 4 caps, 5 goals

1952–53

1	28 March	Wales	Wembley	D 3–3	**
2	18 April	Wales	Cardiff	W 4–2	*
3	25 April	Rep of Ireland	Portsmouth	W 8–0	**
4	9 May	Scotland	Leicester	D 0–0	

FOOTBALL LEAGUE 8 appearances

1960–61

1	22 March	Scottish League	Ibrox	L 2–3

1961–62

2	11 October	League of Ireland	Eastville	W 5–2
3	8 November	Italian League	Old Trafford	L 0–2
4	21 March	Scottish League	Villa Park	L 3–4

1963–64

5	9 May	Italian League	Milan	L 0–1

1964–65

6	17 March	Scottish League	Hampden Park	D 2–2

1965–66

| 7 | 16 March | Scottish League | Newcastle | L 1–3 |

1967–68

| 8 | 20 March | Scottish League | Middlesbrough | W 2–0 |

HC	Home International Championship
F	Friendlies
T	Tour matches
WCQ	World Cup Qualifier
WCF	World Cup finals
ENCQ	European Nations Cup Qualifier
ECQ	European Championship Qualifier
ECF	European Championship finals

INDEX

Note: 'BC' denotes Bobby Charlton. All references are to BC's England career unless otherwise stated. References to countries, cities and towns are to teams unless otherwise indicated.

PICTURE CREDITS

Credits are listed according to the order the pictures appear on each page, left to right, top to bottom.

'BC' denotes photographs that are courtesy of Sir Bobby Charlton.

Section 1
Page 1: Popperfoto/Getty Images; page 2: PA Photos, PA Photos, BC, Getty Images; page 3: Topfoto, Mirrorpix, Popperfoto/Getty Images, Colorsport; page 4: PA Photos, PA Photos; page 5: PA Photos, Popperfoto/Getty Images, Popperfoto/Getty Images, Popperfoto/Getty Images, Popperfoto/Getty Images; page 6: PA Photos, BC; page 7: PA Photos, PA Photos, PA Photos; page 8: PA Photos, BC.

Section 2
Page 1: PA Photos, Popperfoto/Getty Images, Offside/L'Equipe, PA Photos; page 2: Offside/L'Equipe, Mirrorpix, PA Photos, PA Photos, Getty Images; page 3: PA Photos, PA Photos, Topfoto, PA Photos, Mirrorpix; page 4: *Daily Mirror*, *Daily Mail*, PA Photos, PA Photos; page 5: Topfoto, Offside/Gerry Cranham, PA Photos, PA Photos, PA Photos, PA Photos, PA Photos; page 6: *Daily Mirror*, Getty Images, PA Photos, PA Photos, PA Photos; page 7: PA Photos, PA Photos, *Daily Mirror*, *Daily Mirror*; page 8: Popperfoto/Getty Images, Getty Images, PA Photos.

Section 3
Page 1: Getty Images, Offside/L'Equipe, Popperfoto/Getty Images; page 2: Harry Goodwin, Mirrorpix, Getty Images, Getty Images; page 3: Popperfoto/Getty Images, Popperfoto/Getty Images, Mirrorpix; page 4: Mirrorpix, Popperfoto/Getty Images; page 5: PA Photos, Popperfoto/Getty Images, Popperfoto/Getty Images; page 6: Action Images/Sporting Pictures, Popperfoto/Getty Images; page 7: PA Photos, Popperfoto/Getty Images, Mirrorpix; page 8: Getty Images.

Sweden 1958 World Cup squad photo
Back row, l–r: Edward Hopkinson, Don Howe, Ronnie Clayton, Eddie Clamp, Tom Finney, Bobby Robson, Bryan Douglas, Colin McDonald, Derek Kevan, Peter Brabrook, Bobby Smith, Johnny Haynes
Front row, l–r: Alan A'Court, Maurice Norman, Bill Slater, Billy Wright, Bobby Charlton, Peter Sillett, Peter Broadbent, Tom Banks

Chile 1962 World Cup squad photo

Back row, l–r: Bobby Moore, Ray Wilson, Stan Anderson, Ron Flowers, Don Howe, Ron Springett, Alan Hodgkinson, Peter Swan, Bobby Robson, Maurice Norman, Jimmy Armfield
Front row, l–r: Brian Douglas, Bobby Charlton, Johnny Haynes, Gerry Hitchins, Jimmy Greaves, John Connolly, George Eastham, Roger Hunt, Alan Peacock

England 1966 World Cup squad of 27 photo

Standing, l–r: John Connolly, Gordon Milne, Bobby Moore, Ian Callaghan, Jack Charlton, Peter Bonetti, Gordon Banks, Ron Flowers, Bobby Charlton, Jimmy Armfield, Nobby Stiles, trainer Les Coker, coach Wilf McGuinness, Norman Hunter, trainer Harold Shepherdson, Gerry Byrne, George Cohen, Ron Springett
Sitting, l–r: Peter Thomson, John 'Budgie' Byrne, George Eastham, Geoff Hurst, Martin Peters, Keith Newton, Alan Ball, Terry Paine, Jimmy Greaves, Roger Hunt (Ray Wilson and Bobby Tambling are missing.)

England 1966 World Cup squad of 22 photo

Back row, l–r: trainer Harold Shepherdson, assistant trainer Les Cocker, Roger Hunt, Ron Flowers, Peter Bonetti, Ron Springett, Gordon Banks, Bobby Moore, Jimmy Greaves, manager Alf Ramsey
Middle row, l–r: Jimmy Armfield, Ian Callaghan, Gerry Byrne, George Eastham, Geoff Hurst, Jack Charlton, Alan Ball, Nobby Stiles
Front row, l–r: Norman Hunter, George Cohen, Terry Payne, Ray Wilson, Bobby Charlton, Martin Peters, John Connolly

Mexico 1970 World Cup song photo

Back row, l–r: Peter Osgood, Brian Kidd, Emlyn Hughes, Bobby Charlton, Peter Bonetti, Colin Bell, Allan Clarke, team doctor Neil Phillips
Middle row, l–r: Peter Shilton, trainer Harold Shepherdson, David Sadler, Nobby Stiles, Francis Lee, Keith Newton, Ralph Coates, Peter Thompson, assistant trainer Les Cocker, Terry Cooper, Tommy Wright, Alan Ball, Norman Hunter
Front row, l–r: Brian Labone, Geoff Hurst, Alex Stepney, Gordon Banks, Bobby Moore, Jack Charlton, Jeff Astle, Alan Mullery, Martin Peters

Mexico 1970 World Cup squad photo

Back row, l–r: manager Alf Ramsey, team doctor Neil Phillips, Jack Charlton, Peter Bonetti, Jeff Astle, Martin Peters, Terry Cooper, Alex Stepney, Brian Labone, Brian Kidd, Peter Shilton, Allan Clarke, Bobby Charlton, trainer Harold Shepherdson, Gordon Banks, Keith Newton, Colin Bell, Norman Hunter, Geoff Hurst
Front row, l–r: Alan Ball, assistant trainer Les Cocker, Tommy Wright, Peter Thompson, Peter Osgood, Emlyn Hughes, Bob McNab, David Sadler, Alan Mullery, Ralph Coates, Nobby Stiles, Bobby Moore